EIGHTEENTH CENTURY EMIGRANTS FROM LANGENSELBOLD IN HESSE TO AMERICA

by

**Annette Kunselman Burgert,
F.A.S.G., F.G.S.P.**

Wappen von Langenselbold

AKB Publications
Myerstown, Pennsylvania
1997

Library of Congress Catalog Card Number 97-94347
International Standard Book Number 1-882442-15-6

Available from:
AKB PUBLICATIONS
691 Weavertown Road
Myerstown, PA 17067-2642

Manufactured in the United States of America
using acid-free paper

CONTENTS

Preface and Acknowledgments   iii

Abbreviations and Short Citations   vi

Annotations   vii

Bibliography   viii

Glossary   ix

Introduction   xi

The Emigrants   1-126

Appendices:
  A. 1709/1710 emigrants from the area to New York   127
  B. Other possible, but unproven, emigrants   139
  C. Related emigrant families from nearby villages   147

Indices:
  1. Index to ships   153
  2. Index to place names   155-160
  3. Full name index   161-192

LIST OF ILLUSTRATIONS AND MAPS

The Protestant Church in Langenselbold   ii
Modern map of area, showing location of Langenselbold   v
Map showing Marienborn and Herrnhaag   xi
Archival emigration document dated 1742   xiv
1797 map showing the Wetterau   xvi
Half-timbered house in Langenselbold   31
Half-timbered structure near the church in Langenselbold   105
Detailed map of Langenselbold   126
St. John's (Hain's) Reformed Church, established 1735   154

The Protestant Church in Langenselbold.
In the marriage records, the new church
is first mentioned on 7 September 1735.

PREFACE AND ACKNOWLEDGMENTS

This work would not have been possible without the help of several dedicated researchers. Several of the immigrants in the following pages have long been known to have emigrated from Langenselbold, and research on those families has been done and published. This study attempts to bring together the known information on those families and to supplement that knowledge with further research, locating families who were previously unknown as Langenselbold emigrants. There are quite likely other emigrant families yet to be located in the Langenselbold records; all data located has been presented here with the hope that other researchers might locate a family of interest in the many names affiliated with these emigrant families. There are likely errors in identification in some cases; a few potential emigrants who could not be proven have been included in an appendix. Most of the emigrant families traveled in a group, arriving on a ship together, and locating near each other in the New World. An exceptionally large group settled together in Lower Heidelberg Township, Berks County, Pennsylvania, where they obtained land warrants adjacent to each other, and attended St. John's (Hain's) Reformed Church. There they sponsored each other's children, and their children continued to marry into other Langenselbold families. In the following pages, each family sketch contains the translated German data found in the Langenselbold records, plus a few entries from nearby village records, limited of course by their availability. Also included is their ship arrival data, when found. An attempt to locate each family in Pennsylvania or other American records is made to provide confirmation that the family documented in European records is the same family located in American records. Of course, there can be no guarantee that the family located in Europe is the same family identified in the American records; these findings are presented as possible research clues for others who wish to study the family further. Also for some families there is much more information available than that presented here, since some of the persons became quite prominent.

Kenneth Smith of Columbus, Ohio, deserves my greatest appreciation for sharing so many of the Langenselbold records. This book would not have been possible without his input. He has made several trips to Langenselbold, and each time returned with copies of records that made this study possible.

Carla Mittelstaedt-Kubaseck, now deceased, made many trips to Langenselbold, documenting several of the families there for Hank Jones, and at the same time, verifying for my research project that records existed there on later emigrant families to Pennsylvania. She spent many hours in the *Kirchengemeindeamt* in Langenselbold in 1981 and 1982, assembling records on my Gerhard ancestors.

iii

Also, thanks to C. Siebert, Pastor of the *Evangelisches Pfarramt Langenselbold* for sending extracts from the baptismal, marriage, and death records for the immigrant generation of the Gerhards in 1974. These documents confirmed that the family data presented in Morton L. Montgomery's 1909 volumes *Historical and Biographical Annals of Berks County, Pennsylvania* was incorrect. The desire to correct that data was a motivating force behind this study.

Henry Z (Hank) Jones, Jr., F.A.S.G., has kindly given his permission to use his previously published work on the Langenselbold/Hüttengesäss emigrants in Appendix A, documenting the earliest emigrants from the area and their settlement in New York.

Patricia Gunderson provided a typed copy of her translation of the Hüttengesäss Protestant Church Record, dated 1700 to 1875, in which additional data on some of the 1710 New York emigrants was located.

David Green, F.A.S.G., shared his theory that Gertrude Nowlane was a member of the Lerch family of Langenselbold; he later published his study, demonstrating the use of circumstantial evidence in documenting these immigrant families.

William Kershner of North Carolina, Editor of *Kershner Kinfolk,* generously provided a list of ten emigrants from Langenselbold, dated 28 Apr. 1742. This document was located by Rolf Kirschner of Langenselbold, Hesse, and was first published in Vol. 7 of *Kershner Kinfolk;* it is republished here with William Kershner's kind permission.

Linda Gail Komar has long been interested in the Grauel family of Langenselbold, and publishes the newsletter *Crowl Connections.* She continues to share the informative issues of this newsletter.

Grace and A.G. Thompson of Burlington, NC, are descendants of the Faust family. We shared a wonderful day in Langenselbold visiting with the *Family Faust* in 1989. Grace has also provided photographs of her ancestral Faust gravestones in North Carolina.

Alice Spayd has once again provided the much needed typing service in preparing the manuscript for publication.

Last, but certainly not least, my husband Richard A. Burgert, Sr. has once again been most tolerant and understanding about the time needed for this research.

Annette K. Burgert, F.G.S.P., F.A.S.G.

Myerstown, PA
1997

iv

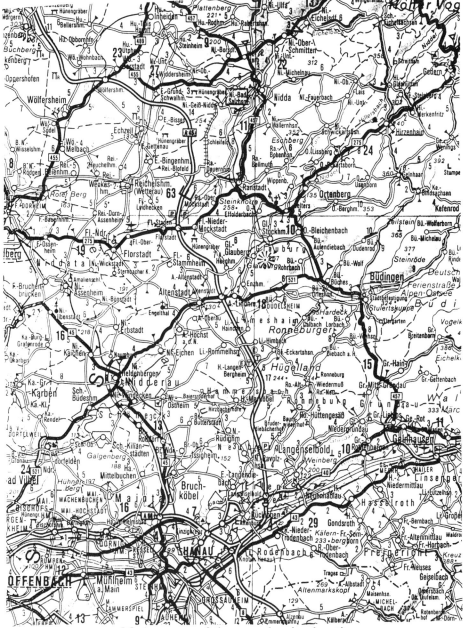

Modern map of the area showing location
of Langenselbold and other nearby villages.

ABBREVIATIONS AND SHORT CITATIONS

A. or a. = acres
Adm. = Administration
Admr.(s) = Administrator(s)
b. = born
bp. = baptized
Co. = County
Conf. = confirmed
d. = died
dau. = daughter
dec'd. = deceased
Em. = emigrated
Ex, Exr. = Executor
Exrs. = Executors
H. = Herr
KB = Kirchenbuch (church book)
m. = married

MD = Maryland
mo. = month(s)
Mstr. = Meister, Master
Nat. = Naturalized
NY = New York
PA = Pennsylvania
q.v. = which see
Rev. = Reverend, Pastor
Sh. = shillings
Sp. = Sponsor (at baptism)
trans. = translation
Twp. = Township
VA. = Virginia
Wit. = witness(es)
y. = year(s)

SHORT CITATIONS

Chalkley's Chronicles

Lyman Chalkley, *Chronicles of the Scotch-Irish Settlement in Virginia; Extracted from the Original Court Records of Augusta County,* 1745-1800. 3 vols. (1912;reprinted Baltimore, 1974).

Montgomery, History of Berks County

Morton L. Montgomery, *Historical and Biographical Annals of Berks County, Pennsylvania.* 2 Volumes. J.H. Beers & Co., (Chicago, 1909.)

S-H, I:	Ralph Beaver Strassburger and William John Hinke, *Pennsylvania German Pioneers.* 3 vols. (Norristown, 1934). This citation refers to Vol. 1.
Rev. John Waldschmidt's records:	"Baptismal and Marriage Records. Rev. John Wald-schmidt, 1752-1786, in *Pennsylvania Archives,* Sixth Series, Vol. 6, pages 147-282.(Harrisburg, 1907).

ANNOTATIONS

The Pennsylvania Church records have been studied from existing translations and/or microfilms of the originals in various libraries and archives. The researcher studying a specific family is urged to try to locate and consult the original records where ever possible. There are mistakes in most translations. For additional information on the location of the churches and their records, consult Charles H. Glatfelter, *Pastors and People: German Lutheran and Reformed Churches in the Pennsylvania Field,* 1717-1793. Volume 1. (Breinigsville, 1979.)

Naturalizations: 1) Pennsylvania: Acts of the colonial legislature in *Statutes at Large,* M. S. Giuseppi, *Naturalizations of Foreign Protestants in the Amrican and West Indian Colonies* (London, 1921; reprinted Baltimore 1964, 1969, 1979). See also Pennsylvania Archives, Second Series, 2:347-486; 2) Maryland: Jeffrey A. Wyand and Florence L. Wyand, *Colonial Maryland Naturalizations* (Baltimore, 1975).

As an accommodation to American readers, the entries have been arranged and indexed without reference to umlauts. These two marks above an a, o or u amount to adding an e behind them. In German alphabetizing these letters are treated as ae, oe and ue.

Abstracts of wills, administrations, and orphans' court records have been used, and as is the case with the church record translations, the researcher is advised to obtain a copy of the original documents for their family of interest. References to wills are abstracted as follows:
Decedent's name, location, occupation if given, date of will-date of probate. Wife; children (or other heirs). Executors; Witnesses.

BIBLIOGRAPHY

There are various published sources that are cited throughout the text. In addition to those volumes, there have been published several volumes concerning specific families; a short and probably incomplete bibliography of those sources is presented here for further reading on individual family research.

Rev. W.J. Kershner and Adam G. Lerch, *History of St. John's (Hain's) Reformed Church, Lower Heidelberg Township, Berks County, Pennsylvania.* Reading, PA (1916). Also,
History of St. John's (Hain's) Reformed Church, Lower Heidelberg Township, Berks County, Pennsylvania. Bicentennial Supplement (1935). [This issue contains family histories of many of the early settlers, including several Langenselbold families. A third supplement was issued in 1970.]

Dr. Howard M. Faust, *Faust-Foust Family in Germany and America.* Gateway Press, Baltimore (1984).

The Kershner Families of Maryland, 1731-1977:
Vol. 1 by Mary Kershner Maxwell (1978); Vol. 2 by Ruth Bownds Kershner (1978); Vol. 3 by Mary Maxwell and Ruth Kershner (1981).
Also a quarterly *Kershner Kinfolk* edited by William E. Kershner, published since 1982.

John R. Spannuth, *Gerhart - Gerhardt - Gehrhart Family of Berks and Lebanon Counties, Pennsylvania.* (1966).

Elmer Denniston, *Genealogy of the Stukey, Ream, Grove, Clem and Denniston Families.* Harrisburg, PA (1939). [Contains a chapter on the Leinbach family.]

Martha L. Hetrick, *The Hetrick Family, 1651-1955.* Harrisburg, PA (1955)

Kathy M. Scogna, *Lower Heidelberg Twp., Penna. 150th Anniversary. Now and Then.* Lower Heidelberg Township (Berks County, PA) (1992). [Contains a section on early land grants, including a connected warrantee map showing the location of land of Frederick Gerhart, Martin Armolt, Casper Lersh (Lerch), Joost Hetrig, Michael Keiser, Adam Shawde, Peter Dressler, John Rebart (Reber), Adam Hedrick, Christian Kallgleaser, John Fischer, John Heterich, John Hermantrout (Ermantraut), Hans Rever (Reber), several other Ermantrouts, John Lerch, William Hetrig, Peter Foust, Philip Philsmoyer and Fitzmeyer (Filtzmeyer).]

GLOSSARY

Certain words have been left untranslated in the text, and appear in italics. These words usually refer to an occupation or an official status, and often have no equivalent English translation. Other words appear in the eighteenth century records that are now obsolete. An approximate meaning is offered for some of these phrases. The spellings are given as they appear in the eighteenth century records and may differ slightly from the currently accepted spelling.

Almosenpfleger = Almoner (of church congregation)
Ambt (Amt, Ampt) = district
Baumeister = building contractor
Bestandmüller = tenant at the mill
Beysass = (rental) inhabitant without citizenship
Bierbrauer = beer-brewer
Binder, Bender = cooper
Bürckmüller = miller at the Bürckmühl in Langenselbold
Burgmüller = ? miller at the mill at the castle
Christr. Mitbruder = fellow Christian (? Brethren)
Churpfälz = Electoral Palatinate
Cintgraff = Centgraff = tax collector
Einwohner = inhabitant
Fasbinder, Fassbinder, Fassbinds = cooper
Frembdmann = foreigner
Fruchtschreiber = business manager of vineyard or orchard
Gemeinenhirt = community herdsman
Gemeinhaus = town hall
Gemeinsmann = citizen of a community with full rights
Gemeinsschmid, - schmied = community smith
Gerichts = member of the community court
Gerichts, Freyenstein, des = member of the Freyenstein court
Gerichtsdiener = court bailiff
Gerichtsschöff, Gerichtsschöffen = lay member of the court, juryman
Gerichtsschultheis = court magistrate
Grissmüller = possibly Grützmüller = grain miller
Herr = a title of respect: schoolmaster, pastor, official.
Herrschaftl. Fruchtschreiber = business manager of the vineyards or orchards of the nobility of the territory.
Herrschaftl. Hoffmann = administrator of the nobility's farm
Hirt = herdsman

Hoffmann = farmer
Inwohner = see Einwohner = inhabitant
Jäger = hunter
Klosterwirth = steward at the cloister; innkeeper
Knecht = servant
Landreuther = regional calvary
Marckt = border
Meister = Mstr. = master (craftsman)
Mitnachbar = fellow resident
Nachbar = neighbor
Ochsenhirt = oxen herdsman
Pfarrknecht = servant of the parish
Reuter = calvary
Rosshirt = horse herdsman
Schäffer, Schäfer = shepherd
Schäfferknecht = apprentice shepherd
Schlosser = locksmith
Schmid = smith
Schneider = tailor
Schreiner = woodworker, joiner
Schuknecht = apprentice shoemaker
Schuldiener = school teacher
Schultheiss, -en = head of the village governing body
Schwager = brother-in-law
Schweinhirt = pig herdsman
Seiler = rope maker
Senioris = ?Seniores = (elected) leader of (free) farmers
Siebmacher = sieve maker
Unterthanens = subject, serf
Vorst(eher) = lay leader of congregation
Wagner = wagon builder, cartwright
Ziegler = tile or brick maker

INTRODUCTION

Langenselbold was a part of the Isenburg territory, and head of state in the late seventeenth century was Count Charles August of Ÿsenburg-Büdingen-Marienborn (1667-1705). This German region suffered much damage in the Thirty Years' War. To help repopulate, Ernest Casimir of Ÿsenburg-Büdingen (1687-1749) issued an Edict on Mar. 22,1712 promising religious freedom to artisans and others who would settle in his lands. From 1707 to 1714 expelled pietists from the Palatinate found an asylum in Ÿsenburg-Büdingen. Most of them settled in that part of the territory known as Marienborn. Marienborn was located north of Langenselbold and just a short distance south of Eckartshausen. Both Marienborn and Herrnhaag, located north east of Langenselbold, were Moravian strongholds in the eighteenth century. The map below shows their locations.

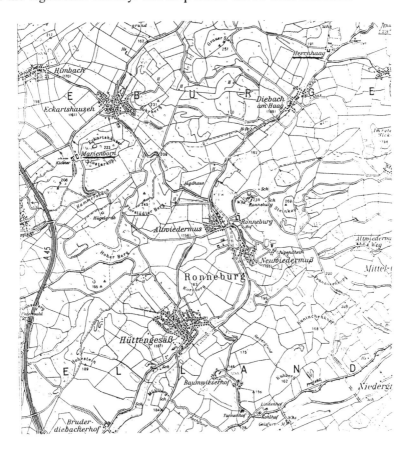

Several of the Langenselbold emigrant families were to become members of the Moravian Church after their arrival in Pennsylvania. It is quite likely that the immigrants had been exposed to the Moravian teachings prior to their emigration.

Other Brethren were also active in this area. Alexander Mack publically baptized a daughter of Eva Elizabeth Hoffmann, who resided in the distrct of Eckartshausen. On 15 Oct. 1711 at Marienborn the Ÿsenburg councilors ordered her expulsion from the territory, but she did not leave. Expulsion was reordered 10 Nov. 1711.

There was a monastery or cloister which was dissolved in 1543, but the buildings remained into the eighteenth century when Count Wolfgang Ernst had them removed to build his baroque castle. The stones of the old monastery were used to build the "new" church on the Klosterberg from 1727 until 1735. This church is still in use today.

Since the church records were the primary source of information about these families, a few words about the books are in order. The Langenselbold records start in 1563 and the first church book contains entries from that date until 1726. There are a few gaps in the records, primarily during the Thirty Years' War. The original name of the town was Selbold; this name first appeared in a document in 1108, and the name continued to be used through the seventeenth and into the eighteenth century church records. By the eighteenth century Langenselbold appears on official documents, such as the emigration permits brought to America. A second book starts in 1726 and continues through the period of emigration.

In addition to the Selbold entries, the church books also contain entries for Bruderdiebach, Baumwiesen, and Hüttengesäss, until September 1700. Also, entries for Ronneburg Hoff and Langendibach are found in the 1670s.

Langenselbold is one of those German villages where the same given names are conferred on two children, both of whom lived. Example: Johannes Keyser, master cartwright, had several children, [see family in text] including two daughters named Anna Elisabeth. The first one, born in 1677, married in 1709 Henrich Scherer. The second one, born in 1680, married in 1707 Wilhelm Gerhard. She died in Langenselbold; he emigrated with their son Friedrich Gerhard in 1739. One more example should suffice: Joh. Caspar Koch married in 1722 Anna Maria, daughter of Conrad Fischer. They had several children including two daughters named Anna Catharina. The first Anna Catharina, born in 1722, came to America with her widowed mother, probably in 1746. This Catharine married Joseph Moeller. The second Anna Catharine, born in 1731, married Joh. Friedrich Ziegler. Both are buried in the Bethlehem Moravian Cemetery. [See the family records in the text for more data.]

Another feature of the records for this town is the use of dialect forms for both given and surnames. Thus, Gerhard appears in the records as Geret, Geerdt, and other variant spellings. This is also true of given names; two of the more unusual are Lips for Philipps and Giel for Juliana. Tönges is a shortened version of Antonius. Researchers should be aware that usually two names are given to each child at baptism, and the call name by which that child is generally known is the second given name. Example: Johann Adam is usually known simply as Adam. There are, of course, a few exceptions to this statement.

There are two clues in the Langenselbold church book entries about the emigration. the first of these is found in the baptismal records in 1742, at the birth of the illegitimate child of Philippina Dippel, where the supposed father of the child, Joh. Henrich Dressler "went secretly to the Island". In another place in the church book, at the baptismal record of Joh. Conrad Hix, a marginal notation mentions that an abstract of his baptismal record was sent to America 21 May 1789. Some of the immigrants brought an emigration permit with them, and at least two of these have survived. One was given to Wilhelm Fischer and it is pictured in the published *History of Hain's Church,* 1916 edition compiled by Rev. Kershner; the other was given to Johannes Reber and is pictured in Lower Heidelberg Twp., (Berks County) 150th Anniversary History titled *Now and Then,* by Kathy Scogna (1992).

The archival emigration document shown on the following page was located by Rolf Kirschner of Langenselbold in the *Hess. Staatsarchiv in Marburg* and sent by William Kerschner of North Carolina, editor of the quarterly *Kershner Kinfolk.* It is reproduced here with his kind permission. The document is dated 28 Apr. 1742 and concerns the payment of the 10% emigration tax by ten married and single persons who wished to emigrate that year. Almost all of the names on this document appear on the ship list of the *Francis and Elizabeth* in 1742. The names on the document are:

1. Johann Martin Kirschner
2. Johannes Räber [see Reber in text].
3. Johann Conrad Bloss
4. Adam Hedderich
5. Joh. Georg Faust
6. Jost Fuchs
7. Johannes Eccard [see Eckert in text].
8. Joh. Adam Stamm
9. Niclaus Röhrig
10. Georg Röhrig's daughter Eva Catharina.

Data on all of these individuals appear in the text, with the exception of the last named Eva Catharina Röhrig.

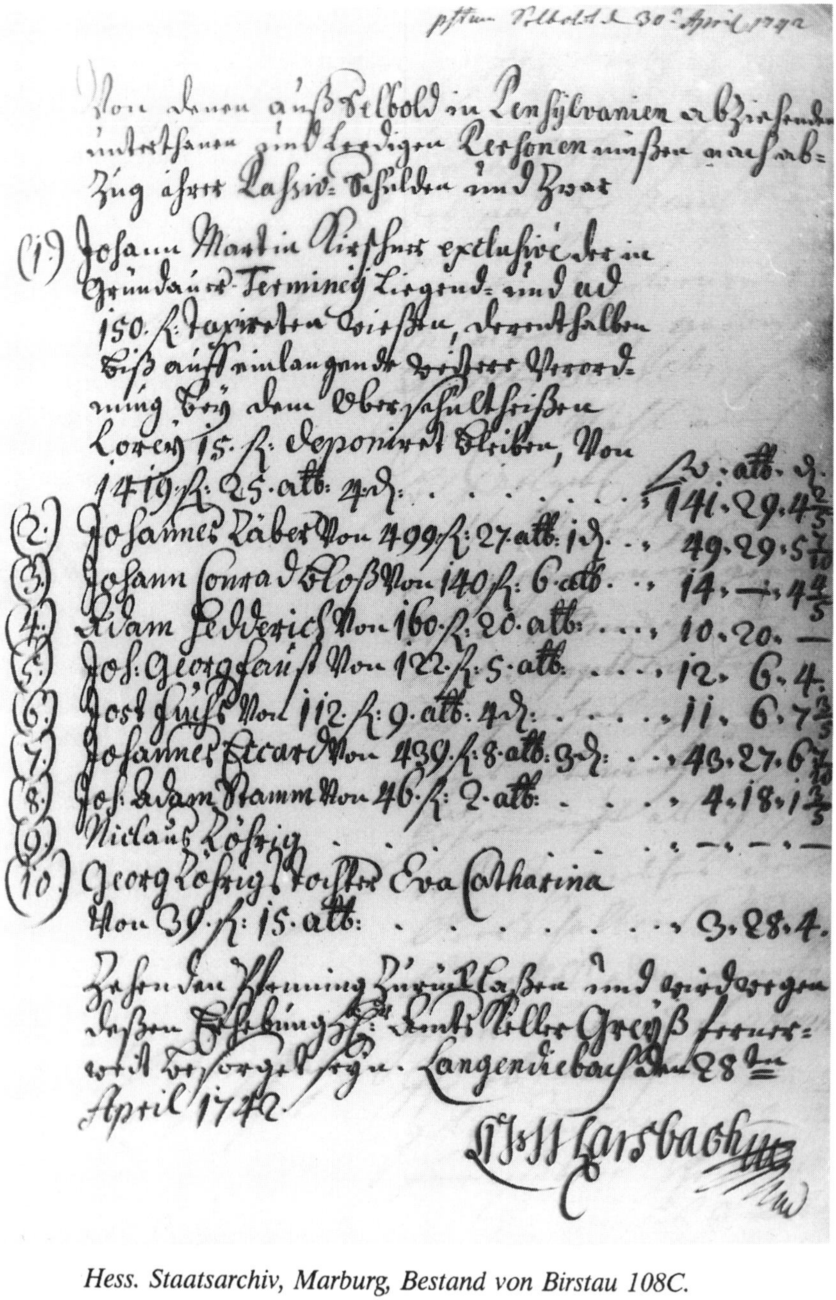

p1tum Velbold d 30.ten April 1742

Von denen auß Velbold in Pensylvanien abziehenden unterthanen sind derselben Personen müßen nach ab=
Zug ihrer Paßiv: Schulden und Prat

(1) Johann Martin Riethnot exclusivè die in
Grundzinß Termineg Liegend= und ad
150. f. tarxeten Wiesen, deromthalben
diß auß einlangender hochster Verord=
nung bey dem Oberschultheißen
Lorenz 15. f. deponiret bleiben, Von
1419.f. 25. alb. 4d: 141.29.4⅗

(2) Johannes Räber Von 499.f: 27.alb: 1d . . 49.29.5⁷⁄₁₀

(3) Johann Contrad Cloß Von 140.f. 6.alb . . 14. —. 4⅘

(4) Adam Federich Von 160.f. 20.alb: . . . . . 10.20. —

(5) Joh: Georg Feuß Von 122.f. 5.alb . . . . . 12. 6. 4.

(6) Jost Guß Von 112.f. 9.alb. 4d: 11. 6.7⅗

(7) Johannes Ricard Von 439.f.8.alb. 3d: . . 43.27.6⅔

(8) Joh: Adam Stamm Von 46.f. 2.alb 4.18.1⅘

(9) Niclauß Röstig . . . . —. —. —

(10) Georg Röstig? Tochter Eva Catharina
Von 39.f. 15.alb: . . . . 3.28.4.

Behn den Henning Zu einer Plaßen und agio dergen
dohren Verehnungen Sind Silber Greyß freuer=
wird versorget geven. Langendiebach den 28.ten
April 1742.

J. H. Carsbach

Hess. Staatsarchiv, Marburg, Bestand von Birstau 108C.

All names, both given and surname, are given as they appear in the various records (both European and American) with no corrections made even when the spelling error is obvious. This is also true of the place name spellings; an index to places is included and the current spelling of the place name, along with the D- five digit zip code for specific identification, is presented in this index.

The interrelationships of these Langenselbold families could not all be pointed out in the text; the researcher is advised to study all references to each family of interest. For example, Peter Lamm who emigrated in 1742 appears to be a first cousin of Friedrich Gerhart who emigrated in 1739 and also the emigrant Martin Kirschner. Their mothers were all daughters of the cartwright Johannes Keÿser. The Keÿser family is included in the following study because of their relationship to many of the immigrant families.

There are some uncommon surnames in the Pennsylvania passenger lists that also appear in the Langenselbold records, but attempts to locate the individuals in Langenselbold church books failed. An immigrant named Wagenhorst appears in S-H. I: page 741. Another immigrant with the surname Lofinch appears in S-H, I: page 699; see Appendix B for other possible emigrant families. These surnames all appear in the Langenselbold records, but there are problems with the specific identification of the individuals in question.

It should be noted that Johannes Fischer Sr. and Johannes Fischer Jr. both appear in the same church records in Pennsylvania, and are given the Sr. and Jr. designations to simply distinguish between them, according to their age. They are not father and son; one came from Langenselbold [see text] and the other from Eckartshausen [see Appendix C].

Several *Hessische soldaten*, soldiers, are mentioned in 1690-1695 period in the Langenselbold record, including a Hans Jörg Schwalm, who, with wife Anna Catharina (both born in Gerstorff by Hirschfeld) had a daughter Anna Margretha bp. 16 Nov. 1695, Sp.: Anna Margretha, wife of Adam Zinck, another soldier in the same company. There were other transients through the area who appear briefly in the records, and then disappear.

The area where many of the villages and towns mentioned in the following study were located was known as *Die Wetterau* and was also called the Wetterau in American records of the period. The map reproduced on the next page, dated 1797, shows the location of a few of the places in this region, including Langenselbold, located north east of Hanau.

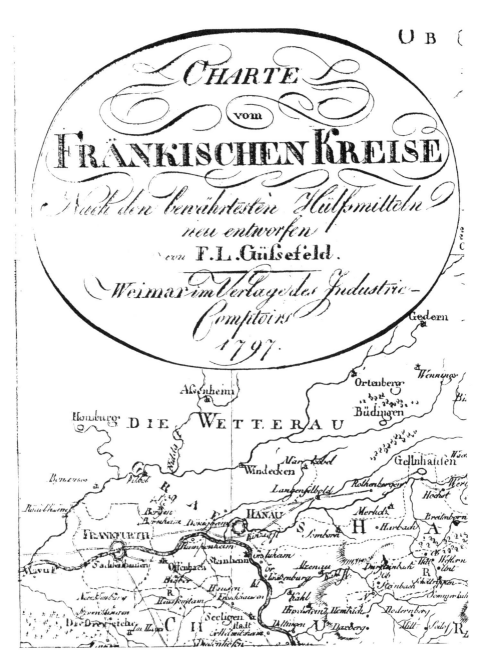

1797 map of the area called the Wetterau
showing location of Langenselbold near Hanau.

THE EMIGRANTS

1. ADAM, JOH. HENRICH   age 28
Samuel, 1733
S-H, I: 107, 111, 112
with Catharina Adam, age 26 and Catharina Adam, age 2

EUROPEAN RECORDS

Langenselbold Reformed KB:
Philips Adam, son of Conrad Adam, m. 12 Feb. 1690 Anna Catharina, daughter of Friederich Hix from Wittgenborn. They had children:
1. Johannes, bp. 4 June 1690.
   Sp. was the father's brother, a son of Conrad Adam.
2. Magdalena, bp. 24 Mar. 1692.
   Sp.: the child's grandmother, wife of Conrad Adam.
   She m. 5 Jan. 1713 Joh. Peter Faust [q.v., 1733 immigrant], son of the late Johann Faust.
3. Magdalena Elisabeth, bp. 15 Sept. 1695.
   Sp.: a daughter of Hans Wetzel.
4. Johannes, bp. 6 June 1697.
   Sp.: Johannes, single son of Hans Faust.
5. Johann Conrad, bp. 15 Oct. 1699.
   Sp.: Joh. Conrad Adam, the father's brother.
6. Johann Wilhelm, bp. 28 Aug. 1701.
   Sp.: a son of *Meister* Philips Wagner, *Fasbinder and Bierbrauer* in Marienborn. Johann Wilhelm d. 6 July 1783.
7. **Johann Henrich,** bp. 17 Nov. 1703.
   Sp.: a single son of Johan Conrad Fischer.

Johann Henrich Adam, son of the late Philips Adam, m. 16 Jan. 1726 Catharina, daughter of Anton Haeffner (or Hoeffner). They had children:
1. Anton, bp. 17 Mar. 1728.
   Sp.: Anton Haeffner, the child's grandfather.
2. Anna Catharina, bp. 3 Sept. 1730.
   Sp.: the paternal grandmother.

AMERICAN RECORDS

Christ "Little" Tulpehocken Lutheran KB, Berks Co., PA:
Joh. Heinrich Adam was the sponsor for Joh. Heinrich Fischer, b. 5 Oct. 1734, bp. 8 Jan. 1735, son of Johannes Fischer [q.v.].

A single man named "Lips" Adam appears on the Windsor Twp., Berks Co. tax list in 1754. The shortened name "Lips" is frequently used in the Langenselbold area for Philips.

Another possible immigrant from the area is Michael Adam, age 36, who arrived on the ship *Samuel*, 1739. He is mentioned in Rev. John Caspar Stoever's records as residing in Moselem and had a son John George who was sponsored by John George Faust in 1741. Michael Adam appears on the Richmond Twp., Berks Co. tax list in 1754. He was not located in the Langenselbold record, but may be from a nearby village.

2. ALT, JOHANNES   age 40
Queen Elizabeth, 1738
S-H, I: 217, 219, 220

EUROPEAN RECORDS

Langenselbold Reformed KB:
Caspar Kniss, son of Caspar Kniss, m. 1 Feb. 1683 Anna Barbara, daughter of Georg Nirer, from ?*Raedgen in Busecker Thal*?. They had a daughter:
    Elisabeth, bp. 12 Dec. 1700.
    Sp.: the single daughter of Melchior Drechsler, master tailor.

Johannes Alt, widower and *Gemeinsmann* from Offenbach, m. 16 Oct. 1720 Anna Elisabetha Kniess, daughter of Caspar Kniess. They had children:
    1. Anna Maria, bp. 11 Mar. 1725. She d. 19 July 1733.
        Sp.: daughter of the late master miller, Bartel Wacker.
    2. Joh. Adam, bp. 18 May 1727.
        Sp.: Joh. Adam Gerlach, master stone cutter at Meerholtz.
    3. Johann Martin, bp. 4 June 1730. He d. 4 May 1736.
        Sp.: Martin Weiss, master mason here.
    4. Elisabeth Catharine, bp. 9 Jan. 1735. She d. 26 Apr. 1736.
        Sp.: the daughter of Joh. Peter Dreut.
    5. Anna Margretha, bp. 27 Apr. 1738. She d. 14 Feb. 1740.
        Sp.: the child's mother's sister from Langendiebach, wife of Johannes Dein, carpenter.

AMERICAN RECORDS

John Alt, Marlborough twp., Philadelphia co., nat. 11 Apr. 1763.

3. BECK, MATTHIAS, age 39
Richard and Elizabeth, 1733
S-H, I: 127, 129, 130
with Engelina Beck, age 37; Antony, age 12; Joh. Henrich, age 7 and Anna
Catharina, age 10. S-H, I: 128.

EUROPEAN RECORDS

Langenselbold Reformed KB:
Herman Beck, *Gerichts Schultheis*, and wife Magdalena had a son:
Herman Christoph bp. 19 May 1667

Herman Christoph Beck, son of Herman Beck, *Gerichts-schuldeisen* in
Selbold, m. 12 Jan. 1693 Elisabetha, daughter of Wörner Schieser,
Gerichtsschäffen und Senioris.

Died 6 Dec. 1726- Herman Christoph Beck, age 59 y., 7 mo., less days.
Died 21 Nov. 1737- Anna Elisabetha, widow of Herman Beck, age 64 y., 9
mo., and some days.

Christoff Herman Beck and wife Elisabetha nee Schieser had children:
    1. Matthias, bp. 21 Jan. 1694 at Selbold
      Sp.: the Pastor's son, Matthias Ruth.
    2. Anna Catharina, bp. 21 July 1695
      Sp.: the daughter of Jörg Fried. Lammersdorff
    3. Johan Peter, bp. 15 Oct. 1697
      Sp.: Johan Peter Schieser, son of Wörner Schieser
    4. Anna Maria, bp. 1 Jan. 1700
      Sp.: the wife of Wörner Schieser, Jr.

Matthias Beck, son of Hermann Beck, *Mitnachbar* here, m. 26 Jan. 1719
Anna Engel, daughter of Tönges Hübener, also *Mitnachbar* here. Engel,
daughter of Tönges Hübener and his wife Rosina, was bp. 6 Oct. 1695.
Matthias and Engel Beck had children:
    1. Joh. Peter, b. 10 Dec. 1719
      Sp.: Tönges Schieser's eldest single son.
    2. Antony, bp. 24 Sept. 1721
      Sp.: the child's maternal grandfather.
    3. Anna Catharina, bp. 9 Feb. 1724
      Sp.: single daughter of Johannes Fuchs.
    4. Joh. Henrich, bp. 23 June 1726
      Sp.: Johann Henrich Lohfinck.
    5. Joh. Conrad, bp. 8 Aug. 1728; sp.: Conrad Lehr.

AMERICAN RECORDS

1754 Berks County tax list, Ruscombmanor Township: Anthony Peck.

Moselem Lutheran KB, Berks Co., PA:
Johan Conrad Kirschner [q.v.] and wife Catharina nee Beck had:
1. Johan Conrad, b. 1 Aug. 1744, bp. 12 Aug. 1744
    Sp.: Martin Kirschner and Anna Margaretha
2. Johan Peter, b. 7 May 1749, bp. Trin. 1749
    Sp.: Johannes Rothermel and Sybilla.

Anna Catharina Beck was a sp. in 1746 for a child of Joh. Nicolaus Gottschalk.

Berks County, PA, will abstracts:
Anthony Beck, Oley; 6 Jan. 1755; 22 Mar. 1755.
"Anthony Beck's wife shall have for her portion" £25 and a cow, but as to what belongs to the father's estate the children shall have it after the death of Matheas Beck. Letters of administration to Elizabeth Beck, the widow. Wit.: George Swartz and Mathias Beck, the father of the testator. Translation.

Mathias Beck, Maidencreek; 28 Aug. 1765; 30 May 1769.
Provides for wife, Ingel. To Elisabeth Peck, the eldest daughter of son Anthony, dec'd, £50; to Susanna, the other daughter of said son, £50; to my two daughters, viz: Catharine, wife of Conrad Kersner and Elizabeth, wife of Michael Dunkel, 5 sh. each. sons-in-law Conrad Kersner and Michael Dunkel, exrs. Wit.: John Starr, Francis Parvin, Jr. and William Parvin.

Engel Beck, Maidencreek; 6 Sept. 1786; 2 June 1787.
To daughter Catharina, wife of Conrad Kerstner [Kirschner, q.v.] of Windsor Twp., 5 sh. To the heirs of son Anthony, dec'd, 5 sh. To son-in-law Michael Dunkel remainder of estate, real and personal. Michael Dunkel, ex. Wit.: John Reeser, George Fegely.

Matthias Beck, Philadelphia Co., nat. without oath, 1743.

4. BLOSS, CONRAD
Francis and Elizabeth, 1742
S-H, I: 327, 329

EUROPEAN RECORDS

Langenselbold Reformed KB:
Johannes Bloss, linenweaver, son of Henrich Bloss, *Gemeinsmann* at Vilbel, m. 16 July 1716 Anna Margretha, daughter of the late Hans Wolff, here. Hans Wolff, *Jäger,* and wife Engel had a daughter Anna Margretha, bp. 3 Nov. 1693. Johannes Bloss and Anna Margretha had children:
1. **Johann Conrad**, bp. 5 Jan. 1718
   Sp.: the elder single son of Philips Treud, master miller.
2. Maria Barbara, bp. 24 Mar. 1720
   Sp.: the late Caspar Eygelbörner's single daughter.
3. Johan Daniel, bp. 27 Sept. 1722
4. Johann Peter, bp. 17 Apr. 1726 [q.v.]
   Sp.: Johann Peter Stein from Langendiebach.
5. Maria Barbara, bp. 30 Mar. 1729
   Sp.: The wife of Johannes Petz, here.

Died 4 Sept. 1744: Master Johannes Bloss, linenweaver, age 53 years.

Johann Conrad Bloss, son of Johannes Bloss, linenweaver and inhabitant here, m. 30 Nov. 1740 Anna Magdalena, daughter of Bernhard Reber, also inhabitant here.[For Reber family, see Conrad Reber, 1746 immigrant]. Johann Conrad Bloss and wife Anna Magdalena had:
1. Anna Margretha, bp. 12 Nov. 1741
   Sp.: the daughter of the late master tailor Jost Caspar Wolff.

AMERICAN RECORDS

Tohickon Reformed KB, Bucks Co., PA:
Confirmed in Heidelberg Twp. (today Lehigh Co.), Easter 1757:
   Anna Elizabeth Blos
   Anna Margaret Blos
(Conrad Bloss was the first constable in Heidelberg Twp. in 1752.)

Tombstone, Heidelberg Church, Saegersville, Lehigh Co., PA:
   Johann Georg Bloss
   b. 15 Oct. 1744
   d. 19 Apr. 1815, age 71 years, 7 months, 4 days.

Egypt Reformed KB, Lehigh Co., PA:
Conrad Blose and wife Magdalena were sp. in 1753 for a child of Jacob

Daubenspeck and his wife Juliana.

PA Archives, Fifth Series, **Vol. 8**: 226, 233, 459, 471, 510, 527:
George Bloss was enrolled as a private in the 7th class, 5th company, 3rd
battalion (later 6th battalion), Northampton Co. Militia.

Conrad Blotz, Heidelberg Twp., Northampton Co., nat. autumn, 1765.

5. BLOSS, PETER
Chance, 1766
S-H, I: 709

EUROPEAN RECORDS

Langenselbold Reformed KB:
Herman Schlemmer, joiner, m. 19 Apr. 1714 Anna Margretha, daughter of
the late H. Johann Jacob Neuman, former *Schuldiener* here. Their daughter:
        Maria Dorothea, bp. 16 Feb. 1716
        Sp.: the child's mother's sister

Johannes Bloss, linenweaver, son of Henrich Bloss, *Gemeinsmann* at Vilbel,
m. 16 July 1716 Anna Margretha, daughter of the late Hans Wolff, here.
They had children:
        1. Johann Conrad, bp. 5 Jan. 1718 [q.v.]
            Sp.: the elder single son of Philips Treud, master miller.
        2. Maria Barbara, bp. 24 Mar. 1720
            Sp.: the late Caspar Eygelbörner's single daughter.
        3. Johan Daniel, bp. 27 Sept. 1722
        4. **Johann Peter**, bp. 17 Apr. 1726
        5. Maria Barbara, bp. 30 Mar. 1729

Died 4 Sept. 1744: Master Johannes Bloss, linenweaver, age 53 years.

Johann Peter Bloss, son of the late Johannes Bloss, master linenweaver, m.
9 Feb. 1752 Maria Dorothea, daughter of Hermann Schlemmer, master
joiner and inhabitant here. They had children:
        1. Maria Margretha, bp. 8 Oct. 1752
            Sp.: daughter of the late master tailor Johann Christian Neuman.
        2. Conrad, bp. 11 May 1755
            Sp.: Conrad Schlemmer, master joiner, the child's uncle.
        3. Johann Henrich, bp. 12 Feb. 1758
            Sp.: Johann Henrich Schlemmer, *Schuknecht*, the mother's brother
                son of Hermann Schlemmer, joiner.

6. BRAUMÜLLER, JOHANNES, age 26
Samuel, 1739
S-H, I: 256, 259, 260

EUROPEAN RECORDS

Langenselbold Reformed KB:
Johann Henrich Braumüller, linenweaver, son of Master Johan Nicklas Braumüller from Ziegenhain in Hessen, m. 15 Nov. 1703 Anna Maria, daughter of the late Johann Faust. (Anna Maria Faust was bp. 13 May 1683, daughter of Johann Faust and wife Kunigunda). They had children:
1. Magdalena, bp. 17 Aug. 1704
   Sp.: The child's mother's sister, dau. of the late Johann Faust.
2. Anna Maria, bp. 11 Nov. 1706
   Sp.: the wife of Johann Faust
3. **Johannes**, bp. 22 Nov. 1711 at Selbold.
   Sp.: Johannes Wolff, inhabitant at this place.

Died 4 May 1752: Johann Henrich Braumüller, linenweaver, aged 76 years.

Died 15 Sept. 1757: Anna Maria, widow of Johann Henrich Braumüller, master linenweaver, aged 74 years, 4 months.

AMERICAN RECORDS

Montgomery, *History of Berks County, Pennsylvania*, p. 1704:
The Brownmiller family in America had its origin in Johannes Braunmiller, born about 1712, who emigrated to this country on the ship *Samuel* in 1739. Tradition says that Johannes settled in New Jersey, where he reared a large family. Luttwick Braunmiller (Ludwig Brownmiller), son of the immigrant Johannes, crossed the upper Delaware river into Pennsylvania, and located in Northampton County before the Revolutionary war. From that place members of the family moved to Hokendauqua, Lehigh County, and later to the vicinity of Lenhartsville, Berks County, and still later to Delaware County, Ohio where many of the family now reside. Luttwick Brownmiller served as a soldier in the Revolutionary war. In 1781 he was a member of Capt. Frederick Kern's company. (This biographical sketch continues with later descendants.)

Berks County, Adm. Book B, page 466:
Nicholas Brownmiller of Greenwich Twp. Letters of Adm. granted 31 Aug. 1822 to Samuel Keller, a brother-in-law, and Philip Fischer, a friend, the widow having renounced.

7. CASSELER, JOH. LUDWIG
Edinburgh, 1750
S-H, I: 430

EUROPEAN RECORDS

Langenselbold Reformed KB:
Johannes Casseler from Okriftel m. 26 Oct. 1712 Maria Elisabeth Bender
from Hoingen (Hungen). It is mentioned in the record that they were both
servants here of the Herrn von Eysenberg and they were ordered to be
married since they had been sleeping together, unmarried; after atonement,
they were married. They had children, surname Kasseler in some records,
residing at the *Eysenbergische Hoff*:
> 1. Henrich Wilhelm, bp. 22 Dec. 1715
>   Sp.: Herr Hauptmann von Horn
> 2. **Johann Ludwig**, bp. 3 Apr. 1718
>   Sp.: the single son of Herr Joh. Peter Höyn, schoolteacher
> 3. Philip Henrich, bp. 20 Oct. 1720
>   Sp.: the child's uncle from Hungen, an apprentice tanner.
> 4. Wilhelm Christian, bp. 17 Feb. 1723 [q.v.- 1753 immigrant.]

AMERICAN RECORDS

First Moravian KB, Philadelphia, PA:
Ludwig Kassler and wife Ann Elisabeth had twins:
> Ludwig, b. 13 Oct. 1751, d. 16 July 1752
> Peter, b. 13 Oct. 1751, d. 3 Aug. 1752

Burials: Ann Elisabeth, wife of Brother Ludwig Kassler, departed this life in
a very happy manner in her thirty third year of age, in Philadelphia on the
26 Dec. 1752, and her corpse was buried the next day in Potter Field by Br.
Abr. Reincke, close to the graves of her little twins.

Ludwig Kassler and wife Christina had:
> Wilhelm b. 12 July 1754, bp. 14 July 1754
> Ludwig b. 14 Oct. 1756, bp. same day.

Taxables in the City of Philadelphia 1756:

Mulberry Ward:	Ludwig Kasler, shoemaker	£18
	William Kasler	£14

Manheim Lutheran KB, Lancaster Co.:
13 Sept. 1781, after 3 proclamations: Ludwig Cassler and Catharina
Maser(in) were married, both single people in Libanon (sic) Twp., Lancaster
Co. (This appears to be the Ludwig Kassler b. 1756, son of the immigrant.)

Old Moravian Cemetery records, Bethlehem, PA:
page 38: Louis Cassler, 1718-1805, from Langenselbold, Principality of Birstein, Hessen, Germany; a shoemaker. After the death of his first wife whose maiden name was Ruth, he married Anna C. Goettling; moved to Lititz and built himself a house there, the first private house in that place. In 1800 he visited his children in Bethlehem and moved to this town. He had 13 children. [Tombstone dates: b. 12 Apr. 1718; d. 10 Sept. 1805].

Lititz (Warwick) Moravian burials, Lancaster Co., PA:
Buried 19 Apr. 1760 - Elisabetha Cassler, infant daughter of Lewis Cassler.
Buried 18 Apr. 1769 - Christina Cassler, third daughter of Lewis and Christina Cassler, b. 1765, died of small pox.
Buried 27 Apr. 1769 - Anna Elisabetha, daughter of Lewis and Christina Cassler, b. 3 July 1767, died of small pox.
Buried 17 Sept. 1781 - Anna Maria Cassler, unmarried sister, b. in Lititz 1 Apr. 1761, dau. of Lewis and Christina Cassler.
Buried 6 May 1829 - William Cassler b. in Philadelphia 15 July 1754; married Rosina, daughter of David Tannenberg. Four sons survive.
Buried 12 Nov. 1817 - Anna Christina Cassler, maiden name Goettel, b. 14 Nov. 1726 in Seligen, Rhenish Bavaria, wife of *William* Cassler. (Note: possible error here; it appears from other records that she was the wife of *Ludwig* or Lewis Cassler and the mother of William Cassler.) They had 10 children.

Lititz Moravian catalog of members, 1765;
Ludwig Cassler, b. 12 Apr. 1718
Christina, his wife, b. 14 Nov. 1728.

Dauphin County Mortgage Book D: 426:
Ludwick Cassler and Yost Miller, Adms. of Philip Enders, the younger of Middle Paxton Twp., present settlement, 19 Apr. 1796.

Dauphin County Deed Book H-1: 361, 363, 365:
Deeds dated 1795, Philip Enders, Sr. estate, Upper Paxton Twp., 220 A; admrs. sell to Jacob Feather, innkeeper at Herrisburg. Same date, Jacob Fetter and wife Barbara sell the same 220 A to Ludwick Casler, Upper Paxton Twp.

Lewis Caslar, nat. by affirmation, Philadelphia, 24 Sept. 1757.

8. CASSELER, WILHELM CHRISTIAN age 30
Edinburgh, 1753
S-H, I: 576, 578, 580

EUROPEAN RECORDS

Langenselbold Reformed KB:
Johannes Casseler from Okriftel m. 26 Oct. 1712 Maria Elisabeth Bender from Hoingen (Hungen). It is mentioned in the record that they were both servants here of the Herrn von Eysenberg and they were ordered to be married since they had been sleeping together, unmarried; after atonement, they were married. They had children, surname Kasseler in some records, residing at the *Eysenbergische Hoff*:

    1. Henrich Wilhelm, bp. 22 Dec. 1715
       Sp.: Herr Hauptmann von Horn
    2. Johann Ludwig, bp. 3 Apr. 1718 [q.v., 1750 immigrant].
       Sp.: the single son of Herr Joh. Peter Höyn, schoolteacher
    3. Philip Henrich, bp. 20 Oct. 1720
       Sp.: the child's uncle from Hungen, an apprentice tanner.
    4. **Wilhelm Christian,** bp. 17 Feb. 1723

AMERICAN RECORDS

Taxables in the City of Philadelphia 1756:

Mulberry Ward:	Ludwig Kasler, shoemaker	£18
	William Kasler	£14

Philadelphia Wills and Administrations, Adm. Book G: 209:
William Christian Cassler, dated 18 Nov. 1761: about to embark from this place to Germany, on board the ship *King George*, owned by McMichael & Morris, merchants, and commanded by Captain Dingee, from Philadelphia to London; mentioned Mr. Plumsted, merchant, and his son-in-law, His Majesty's paymaster; Rees Meredith, merchant; mentioned his mother, name not given; brother's children in Germany; "brother's children in Pennsylvania, Ludiwig Cassler.." if they continue with the Brethren, if not, part shall be for the poor children of said congregation; And. Schlosser in Philadelphia, exr., and Jacob Franck in Lancaster. Wit.: Jacob Franck and George Schlosser. Adm. to Ludwig Cassler, brother of the deceased, 22 May 1762. (named exrs. renounced).

9. DÄNIG, JOHAN HENRICH age 33
Elizabeth, 1733
S-H, I: 113, 114, 115, 765-767
  The list on pg. 765 gives his occupation as joiner, and also lists the
following family members: Anna Margret age 36; Anna Barbara age 8;
Michael (dead) age 5; Anna Margaret (dead) age 1½.

EUROPEAN RECORDS

Langenselbold Reformed KB:
Balthasar Denig, a joiner, son of Johannes Denich, citizen and inhabitant at
Brixen in Tyrol [today Bressanone, Italy], m. 11 Jan. 1700 Anna Elisabetha,
daughter of the late Caspar Böhl from Niederlisingen, Fürst. Unterhessen
Ampts Zierenberg [Niederlistingen]. Their son:
  Johan Henrich, bp. 28 Oct. 1700 in Selbold.
  Sp.: Joh. Henrich Schad, son of Johan Schad.

Died 22 May 1731 - Anna Elisabetha, wife of Balthasar Dönig, aged ?52
years.

Died 18 Apr. 1734 - the master joiner Balthasar Dönig, aged about 75 years.

Johann Heinrich Dönig, son of Balthasar Dönig, master joiner here, m. 28
Jan. 1722 Anna Margaretha, daughter of Philip Gosche, master gardener
here. They had children:
  1. Johann Jörg, bp. 6 May 1723; died 24 Aug. 1724.
    Sp.: the child's grandfather on the father's side
  2. Maria Barbara, bp. 21 May 1725
    Sp.: the child's mother's sister, single
  3. Michael, bp. 15 Oct. 1727; died on voyage, 1733
    Sp.: Master Michael Spindler
  4. Anna Philippina, bp. 24 July 1729; died 22 Apr. 1733
    Sp.: single daughter of Joh. Henrich Dippel
  5. Anna Margretha, bp. 18 Nov. 1731; [died on voyage, 1733]
    Sp.: single daughter of Joh. Peter Koch.

Died 22 Feb. 1728 - Anna Catharina, wife of the master gardener Philips
Gasche, aged 65 years, 5 months.

AMERICAN RECORDS

Philadelphia Wills & Adm. Index:
Henry Domig [?Danig?]   1760 #281   Will Book L: 439
Jacob Denig   1776 #287   Will Book Q: 344

Henry Denig was a witness to the will of Mathias Nasse, blacksmith, in Philadelphia in 1741.

German Reformed KB, Germantown, Philadelphia Co., PA:
Jacob Daenig and wife Anna Maria had a daughter:
>   Anna Margaret, b. 26 May 1759, bp. 31 May 1759
>   Sp.: Anna Margaret Daenig

Conf. 12 May 1769: Henry Tenig, age 16.

Conf. 12 May 1769: Barbara Tenig, age 15.

Buried 17 Sept. 1759: Jacob Doenig, age 2 years, 4 months.

10. DIPPEL, JOHANN HERMANN
Edinburgh, 1750
S-H, I: 430

EUROPEAN RECORDS

Langenselbold Reformed KB:
Joh. Henrich Dippel, son of the late Martin Dippel, formerly from ?Bergheim, m. 31 Mar. 1712 Christina Philippina, daughter of the master gardener Johan Philipps Gage [elsewhere in the records this name is given as Gosche, Gasche, Goshe]. They had children:
>   1. Anna Philippina, bp. 5 Mar. 1713; died 25 Apr. 1756.
>   [see immigrant Joh. Henrich Dressler for further information].
>   2. Maria ?Loysa, bp. 6 Feb. 1715
>   3. Johann Philips, bp. 12 July 1716
>   4. Johann Peter, [q.v.] bp. 5 Feb. 1719
>   5. Joh. Matthias, bp. 6 Apr. 1721
>   6. **Johann Hermann,** bp. 14 Apr. 1723
>   Sp.: Master Joh. Hermann Hildebrand.

Died 26 Mar. 1747 - Philippina, wife of Joh. Henrich Dippel, aged 57 years.

Died 30 Dec. 1762 at Selbold - Johann Henrich Dippel, aged 79 years, 4 months, 2 weeks and 4 days.

Herman Dippel, son of Johann Henrich Dippel, m. 15 Apr. 1750 Catharina, daughter of Jacob Knaus from Frohnhausen.

AMERICAN RECORDS

Germantown Reformed KB, Philadelphia Co., PA:
(?Herman) Henry Dippel and wife Catharina had:
    Anna Maria, bp. 20 May 1753
    Sp.: Henry Scherflex? and Anna Maria

John Peter Dippel and wife Magdalena had:
    John Herman, bp. 22 Sept. 1754
    Sp.: John Herman Dippel and Catharina

Herman Dippel and wife (N.N.) had:
    Anna Elisabeth, bp. 16 Nov. 1755
    Sp.: Anna Elisabeth Franck

Herman Düppell and wife Catharina had:
    Susan Louisa, b. 24 Sept. 1758

Confirmed 9 June 1764 - Catharine Dueppel, age 15
Confirmed Easter 1766 - Margaret Dippel, age 15.

Joh. Herman Dippel and wife Catharina were sp. in 1753 for a son of Joh. Philip Sulzbach and his wife.

11. DIPPEL, JOHANN PETER
Snow *Good Hope*, 1753
S-H, I: 573, 574, 575

EUROPEAN RECORDS

Langenselbold Reformed KB:
Joh. Henrich Dippel, son of the late Martin Dippel, formerly from ?Bergheim, m. 31 Mar. 1712 Christina Philippina, daughter of the master gardener Johan Philipps Gage [elsewhere in the records this name is given as Gosche, Gasche, Goshe]. They had children:
    1. Anna Philippina, bp. 5 Mar. 1713; died 25 Apr. 1756.
       [see immigrant Joh. Henrich Dressler for further information].
    2. Maria ?Loysa, bp. 6 Feb. 1715
    3. Johann Philips, bp. 12 July 1716
    4. **Johann Peter**, bp. 5 Feb. 1719
       Sp.: the single son of Bartel Wacker, the *Obermüller*.

   5. Joh. Matthias, bp. 6 Apr. 1721
   6. Johann Hermann, [q.v.] bp. 14 Apr. 1723
      Sp.: Master Joh. Hermann Hildebrand.

Died 26 Mar. 1747 - Philippina, wife of Joh. Henrich Dippel, aged 57 years.

Died 30 Dec. 1762 at Selbold - Johann Henrich Dippel, aged 79 years, 4 months, 2 weeks and 4 days.

AMERICAN RECORDS

Germantown Reformed KB, Philadelphia Co., PA:
John Peter Dippel and wife Magdalena had a son:
      John Herman, bp. 22 Sept. 1754
      Sp.: Johan Herman Dippel and Catharina.

Peter Dippel and wife Magdalena were sp. in 1758 for a daughter of Henry Koch and wife Margaret; and also sp. in 1758 a son of Henry Blecker and wife Barbara Christina.

Berks Co. Will Book B: 66 and Adm. Book 3: 36, 347, 428:
Peter Dippel, Reading. Dated 23 June 1778; probated 26 Aug. 1783.
To wife Mary Magdalena all estate real and personal during life, and what remains at her death to daughter Anna Mary Daubert. Wife Mary Magdalena , exr. Wit: Andreas Engel, William Reeser.
Letters to Peter Daubert and his wife Catharine, the exr. named being deceased.

Reading Lutheran KB, Berks County, PA:
Died 22 Aug. 1783- Peter Dippel, aged 64 years, 6 months, 3 weeks.
Died the same day- Maria Magdalena, wife of Peter Dippel, aged 63 years, 2 months. They had 1 daughter and 8 grandchildren; buried at the same time on the Reformed Cemetery.

Hain's (St. John's) Reformed KB, Berks Co., PA:
Peter Daubert (and wife) had children:
      1. Maria Magdalena, bp. 18 July 1773
         Sp.: Peter *Tippel* and Maria Magdalena
      2. John, bp. 18 Feb. 1776
         Sp.: John Hain and Magdalena.

12. DRESSLER, JOH. HENRICH
Francis and Elizabeth, 1742
S-H, I: 329

EUROPEAN RECORDS

Langenselbold Reformed KB:
Melchior Trechssler, born in *Brieg in Schlesien*, a soldier and tailor, m. 21 Oct. 1680 Susanna Elisabetha, daughter of Jörg Barthel, former shoemaker at Franckfurt. They had children:
1. Johannes, bp. 28 Aug. 1681
   Sp.: Johannes Herger
2. a daughter, bp. 14 Oct. 1683, died 1686
   Sp.: Anna Margreth, the mother's sister from Franckfurth
3. Elisabeth, bp. 15 Sept. 1686
   Sp.: Johann Wörner's daughter here
   [Elisabeth m. 7 Dec. 1713 Jost Henrich Fischer, son of Conrad
   Fischer, and they were the parents of Elisabetha bp. 5 Sept. 1714,
   first wife of Friederich Gerhard, q.v., 1739 immigrant.]
4. Henrich, bp. 27 Oct. 1689, died 1698.
   Sp.: Henrich Ruth, Pastor at Selbold.

Died 13 May 1718: Susanna, wife of Melchior Drechssler, master tailor and *Herrschaftl. Fruchtschreiber* here; her age 60 years and several months.
Died 29 July 1731: Meister Melchior Dressler, *d. alte Fruchtschreiber*, aged 80 years.

Meister Johannes Dressler, tailor, son of Melchior Dressler, *Herrschafftl. Fruchtschreiber*, m. 24 Jan. 1709 Charlotta Eleonora, daughter of *Meister* Georg ?Pflässer, *Seiler* here. They had children:
1. **Johan Henrich,** bp. 12 Apr. 1711
   Sp.: Henrich Fischer, single son of Joh. Conrad Fischer,
        Gerichtschöffen here.
2. Johann Peter, bp. 11 Nov. 1714 [q.v., emigrated 1739]
   Sp.: Henrich Lofinck, the child's father's *Schwager, Mitnachbar*
        here.
3. Anna Elisabeth, bp. 10 Nov. 1717
   Sp.: the child's father's sister, Jost Fischer's wife.
4. Johannes, bp. 4 Mar. 1722
   Sp.: Henrich Ruth's single son.

Died 19 Sept. 1751: Mstr. Johannes Dressler, tailor, aged 70 years, 1 month, less several days.

Died 21 Apr. 1752: Charlotta Eleonora, widow of the late Mstr. Johannes
Dressler, aged 70 years.

On 11 May 1742, an illegitimate daughter named Elisabetha Catharina
Judith was baptized. The mother was Philippina Dippel, Johann Henrich
Dippel's eldest daughter. [See immigrant Joh. Herman Dippel for family
record]. The father was named as Johann Henrich Dressler, son of Mstr.
Johannes Dressler, the tailor. Sp.: Magdalena Elisab. Faust, daughter of
Philips Faust, and Judith, daughter of Johannes Winck.
[An added notation to the baptismal record indicates that Joh. Henrich
Dressler had been called before the Presbyterium and he promised to marry
her, but then secretly went away, "*in the Insul gezogen*". The mother of this
child never married. She died in Langenselbold 25 Apr. 1756, age 43 years,
one month and several days.]

13. DRESSLER, PETER
Samuel, 1739
S-H, I: 256, 259, 261

EUROPEAN RECORDS

Langenselbold Reformed KB:
Melchior Trechssler, born in *Brieg in Schlesien*, a soldier and tailor, m. 21
Oct. 1680 Susanna Elisabetha, daughter of Jörg Barthel, former shoemaker
at Franckfurt. They had children:
     1. Johannes, bp. 28 Aug. 1681; Sp.: Johannes Herger
     2. A daughter, bp. 14 Oct. 1683, died 1686
       Sp.: Anna Margreth, the mother's sister from Franckfurth
     3. Elisabeth, bp. 15 Sept. 1686
       Sp.: Johann Wörner's daughter here
       [Elisabeth m. 7 Dec. 1713 Jost Henrich Fischer, son of Conrad
       Fischer, and they were the parents of Elisabetha bp. 5 Sept. 1714,
       first wife of Friederich Gerhard, q.v., 1739 immigrant.]
     4. Henrich, bp. 27 Oct. 1689, died 1698.
       Sp.: Henrich Ruth, Pastor at Selbold.

Died 13 May 1718: Susanna, wife of Melchior Drechssler, master tailor and
Herrschaftl. Fruchtschreiber here; her age 60 years and several months.

Died 29 July 1731: Meister Melchior Dressler, *d. alte Fruchtschreiber*, aged
80 years.

Meister Johannes Dressler, tailor, son of Melchior Dressler, *Herrschafftl. Fruchtschreiber,* m. 24 Jan. 1709 Charlotta Eleonora, daughter of *Meister* Georg ?Pflässer, *Seiler* here. They had a son:

> **Johann Peter,** bp. 11 Nov. 1714
> Sp.: Henrich Lofinck, the child's father's *Schwager, Mitnachbar* here.
> [See his brother, Joh. Henrich Dressler, 1742 immigrant, for more family data.]

AMERICAN RECORDS

Hain's (St. John's) Reformed KB, Berks Co., PA:
John Peter Dresler and wife had:
> 1. Elisabeth, bp. ---- 1747; sp.: William Fischer [q.v.] and wife. (Another translation gives her name as Elisabet Gertrut and the date of bapt. as 1 June 1748.)
> 2. a daughter, bp. 19 Nov. 1749
>   Sp.: Anna Margarette Schatten, daughter of Peter Schatten [?Schad]

In 1744, Peter Dressler patented a tract of 134 A. called "Westphalia" in Lower Heidelberg Twp. Peter Tressler is named as an adjoining land owner in a Warrant dated 30 Nov. 1744 for John Reibert [Johannes Reber?].

Peter Dressler had a warrant for 100 acres in Lancaster Co., *Tulpyhockain* Twp., adjoining land of Joost Hetterick [q.v.], dated 7 Apr. 1744. Return of Survey dated 6 Jan. 1786.

Chalkley's Chronicles, Vol. 3, pg. 383:
Augusta Co., VA, Deed Book 10, pg. 270: 8 May 1762, John Heterich [q.v.] and Susanna to Peter Tresler, £10, 134 acres on Stony Run.

14. ECKERT, JOHANNES
Francis and Elizabeth, 1742
S-H, I: 328

EUROPEAN RECORDS

Langenselbold Reformed KB:
Valentin Hix, son of Henrich Hix, m. 22 Jan. 1711 Magdalena Elisabeth, dau. of the late Wörner Repp. They had a daughter:

> Angelica, bp. 14 Dec. 1712
> Sp.: Christoffel Leiss' wife
> [See immigrant Conrad Hix for more Hix data].

Meister Johannes Eckert, *der Schmid,* son of Peter Eckert, *Mitnachbar* at Streitberg m. 16 Jan 1732 Angelica, daughter of *Meister* Valentin Hix, also smith. Mstr. Johannes Eckert, smith, and Angelica had:

1. Magdalena Elisabeth, bp. 18 Feb. 1733
   Sp.: Mstr. Johann Conrad Hix's (also smith) single daughter.
2. Johann Valentin, bp. 13 Nov. 1735
   Sp.: Mstr. Valentin Hix, *Gemeinsschmid,* the child's grandfather
3. Jonas, bp. 8 Oct. 1738
   Sp.: Niclaus Wacker, the *Burgmüller's* son
4. Johann Conrad, bp. 12 Feb. 1741
   Sp.: Johannes Repp, the *Grissmüller's* son

AMERICAN RECORDS

Hain's (St. John's) Reformed KB, Berks Co., PA:
John Eckert and wife Engel had children:

5? a son bp. 5 Aug. 1750; sp.: John Dautrich.
6? a daughter bp. 10 Feb. 1754.
   Sp.: Anna Maria Ruth, daughter of Jacob Ruth.

Hain's Cemetery, Berks Co.: tombstone inscriptions:
Conrad Eckert, b. 6 Feb. 1741, d. 25 July 1791 (husband of Elisabeth nee Hain).

Elisabeth Eckert, wife of Conrad Eckert, b. 26 May 1750, d. 29 Sept. 1808.

Rev. Boos' Pastoral Records, Burials:
Angelica Eckert, b. 10 Dec.1712; d. 21 Apr. 1786
Had 61 grandchildren and 16 greatgrandchildren.

PA Archives, Sixth Series, Vol. 6, Rev. Waldschmidt's records:
Conf. 26 Mar. 1768 at Cacusy - Anna Maria, daughter of Johannes Eckert.

Host Reformed KB, Tulpehocken, Berks Co., PA:
John Henry Decker, preacher at Cagusi, m. 10 May 1753 Magdalena Elisabeth Eckert.

See Charles H. Glatfelter, *Pastors and People, Volume I: Pastors and Congregations*, page 29 for additional information on John Henry Decker, b. 17 Aug. 1730 at Markoebel, Hanau.

Nat. Autumn, 1765: Conrad Eckert, Heidleberg Twp., Berks Co., PA
Nat. Autumn, 1765: Jonas Eckert, Tulpehoccon Twp., Berks Co., PA

Berks Co., PA, will abstracts:
Nicholas Eckert, Heidelberg, 31 Jan. - 14 Sept. 1824 (trans.) £1000 to children of deceased sister Elizabeth wife of Henry Deckert, same to children ot sister Christina who was married to George Troutman, same to sister Anna Maria married to Fred Hehn. Bequeaths money received of father-in-law Michael Miller to brother-in-law John Miller and his sister married to Daniel Ludwig. Remainder to 3 brothers - Jonas, Conrad, and John and Sarah youngest daughter of brother Valentine in equal shares. £100 to be taken off Conrad's portion for his daughter Barbara. Executors Peter Eckert, son of Conrad; Peter Eckert, son of Jonas; and Peter Adams. Witnesses John von Neida and Daniel Diehl.

Johannes Eckert, Heidelberg, 26 May 1770, 13 Aug. 1770. Provides for wife Angelica. To two youngest sons John Nicholas and Johannes the place whereon I now live and the 50 acres bought of George Halzen at value, when 21. To son Johann Conrad the place I bought of Michael Schauer for £1200. Mentions eldest daughter's husband Decker. Estate to be equally divided but other children not named. Sons Valentine and Jonas, executors. Witnesses George Laick and John George Weiss. Translation.

Angel Eckert, Heidelberg, 12 Aug. 1786. Adm. to Conrad Eckert, 3rd son. Valentin and Jonas elder sons renouncing.

Conrad Eckert, Heidelberg, 5 July 1791 - 12 Sept. 1791. To eldest son John my plantation containing 150 acres also personal property, paying £1400. To daughter Catharina £80. To Peter, George, Barbara, David, Daniel, Solomon and Conrad £100 each. To wife Elisabeth all the land I bought of Jacob Stehely during life to bring up minor children. Wife Elisabeth and brother Nicholas Eckert executors. Witness Jost Fishbach and John Eckert, Esq.

Elizabeth Eckert, widow of Conrad, Heidelberg, 25 Sept. 1808 - 5 Oct. 1808. To children John, Catharine married to Thomas Copeheaver, Peter, George, David, Daniel and Solomon $3.50 to be divided between them. Remainder to my other two children, Conrad and Barbara Eckert. Letters to Conrad Eckert. Witnesses: Ludwig Fisher and William Wood.

George Eckert, Robeson, 17 Aug. 1799, adm. to Abraham, eldest son, Margaret the widow renouncing.

Berks County Newspaper: *Readinger Zeitung:*
12 Sept. 1792 (Sept. 8). Warning against Bonds. The undersigned, Jonas Eckert, of Heidelberg Twp., says that he gave a certain Johann Meyer four Bonds (assigned them) last July 11, all made by his brothers (3 from Nicolas

Eckert and 1 from Johann Eckert) and as the said Johann Meyer came to him with Daniel Ludwig Esq. and it was found that there was a balance of £180 in our reckoning, he now warns all not to purchase said bonds as they will now not be paid until the said Johann Meyer settle with him in an upright manner. "So much from me."

19 Sept. 1792. Notice. Signed: Johann Meyer, Hamburg, 14 Sept. 1792. Dear Printer - I notice in your newspaper no. 187, this Sept. 12th a warning against bonds signed by a certain Jonas Eckert, so now acquaint the public with the following in your next paper: Mr. Henrich Decker's six children are co-heirs in the estate of the deceased Johannes Eckert, late of Berks Co., through a Testament dated 26 May 1770 and the Testament openly mentions £250 for the six children from his real estate, which his sons Johannes and Nicolas fell heir to, as also the 1/8 part of all the remaining portion of his property. The said £250 was payable in portions of £25 per year whereof the first was already due in May 1772. Their share, however of all the remaining was according to law payable after the lapse of one year from the date of the Inventory, and to this Testament the above mentioned Jonas Eckert is one of the administrators. Now, instead of paying off this money, or at least to make an accounting of it and place the money at interest for the benefit of the children like a trusty guardian, he himself held it in hand in order to accomplish his own wishes. It is true that in the year 1777, he gave one of these heirs some Continental money when it stood at 2½ for 1, and here he took receipt for one part and a bond for the other part. But, also, this was already 5 years after the first money was due. After this he paid none of the six heirs one cent until the spring of 1781 when he gave two of them each about £30 each, and the remaining three still have not had a penny to date. As now these children have been led around by such a fool's tether, so they made me their attorney on 19 May 1791, to settle their inheritance with their uncle Jonas Eckert. I agreed with him to let the matter to three men, by whom, on Apr. 3 last it was agreed that Jonas Eckert should pay 309/10/11, that however, Georg Ihle (a man married to one of the heirs) his bond and receipt should be deducted, but did not say if the bond and one of the receipts, which was for Continental money, in all 25/11/3 should be deducted according to the rate of exchange, or as good money, and also, without saying if the Executor should pay interest or not. As now the children saw this, so they rightly again disputed with their uncle Jonas Eckert and said that he had cheated them of their interest and wished to unload on them the poor Continental money.

At last they also began to blame me and openly said they believed I had a hand in it with Jonas Eckert and divided the interest with him and that they were thereby imposed upon, etc. When I heard this I went on the 2nd of July to Jonas Eckert and told him how much the children complained and as I thought with right. I also took with me Daniel Ludwig Esq. to place him under oath in relation to the Continental money if it had been the children's money or not, and if he would do this then I would accept it as cash money (hard gelt) and the children then would also have to accept it as such. This, however, he did not wish to do, but fetched himself a calender containing a table of exchange and told me to figure it out in cash money, and when I asked him about the interest he and his wife answered; they shall have every penny. Hereupon Daniel Ludwig and I reckoned the interest on £250 of the real estate according to the yearly payments due, and taking this for the principal item, then reckoned the interest on the personal property, namely on 11/10/19 (as he then told me that this was all the personal property the children had inherited), and when all this was summed up it came to 507/17/11. After this we reckoned the interest on the money which he had paid and put it underneath the above sum total (it was 224/10/0) and got a balance of 283/7/11. Hereon a commission of 14/3/5/still left 269/4/6 left over for the children and for this sum he gave me the bonds against his brothers. I now thought that Jonas Eckert had acted as an honest man toward his sister's children and with me as their attorney, but how much I found myself cheated, when I looked at the reckoning on getting back to the office I found 141/1/9 had been held back without saying anything to me about it, and of which also the heirs on their part had a right to draw on and that already for 17 or 18 years. Yes, much more I found myself cheated as one of his own brothers related that about £64 were held back that were not in the accounting at all. This may denote how it happens that the children according to his account had no right to 11/10/0 out of the personal property. I have, however, arrested him at last court for this deduction or at least for the as yet unreckoned sum. The esteemed public are requested herewith not to pay the least attention to his warning while the decision on this proceeding is in abeyance. I have settled with the children according to the sum I reckoned with Jonas Eckert and have also already paid them £40 out of my own pocket; I can point to this, that I was ready, in case he himself would settle with the children to withdraw and be satisfied by giving everything up. But this also he did not do. What I now have done, or will do, or also not shall do with the bonds; to this I need neither advice or warning.

Johannes Meyer

Hamburg, Sept. 14, 1792

24 Oct. 1792 (Oct. 18) Notice. Mr. Printer, after I saw a justification in your newspaper no. 188, last Sept. 19 signed by a certain Johannes Meyer in Kerchertown, in which he seeks to deceive the esteemed public by false distortions of the truth. So I wish through further publication to show his character and deceitful proceedings with me, so that the esteemed public will not be further troubled, I dare however show that that which I have written

and that I shall further write has no foundation excepting in honesty and uprightness.

However, without further apology or asking him to repeat himself, I ask the said Justice Johann Meyer in Kerchertown, where and in what I have cheated, or wish to deceive, and, unless he does not do so shortly, he shall experience the further question, etc. etc.

Jonas Eckert

Oct. 12, 1792

31 Oct. 1792 (Oct 26) Notice. Mr. Printer, in your valuable newspaper found in no. 187, under Sept. 12 last, a warning on 4 bonds, that were designated by a certain Jonas Eckert, in which the said Jonas Eckert charged me with deceit. I, however, felt it to be my duty to present an answer to the public to this warning, and I did this in the 188th number last Sept. 19th, and without bringing anything else forward I would only remark, that I am nearing an end to my remarks to the public, that I have arrested him (Jonas Eckert) for the back standing account of the inheritance still due the children of Henrich Deckert and that the result of this process to our quarrel will end the controversy. This is still my intention and his abuse and braying of deception, which he published in no. 193 of your newspaper--etc.

Montgomery's *History of Berks County in the American Revolution*:
"Valentine Eckert was born at Longasalza [sic], in the Kingdom of Hanover, in 1733. He came to America with his parents in 1741, who settled in the Tulpehocken Valley at a point east of where Womelsdorf is now situate. He was naturalized in September 1761. In June 1776, he was one of the ten members of the Provincial Conference who represented Berks County in that important body; and in July following, he was selected as a delegate from the county to the Provincial Convention which was assembled for the purpose of framing a new government founded on the authority of the people. In 1776 and 1779 he represented the county in the Provincial Assembly. He was a resident of Cumru township and a blacksmith by occupation. He offered his services to the Government in the Revolutionary War, which were accepted, and he commanded a company of cavalry Associators for a time. He and his company participated in the Battle of Germantown, in October, 1777, where he was wounded. He was appointed Sub-Lieutenant of the county on March 21, 1777, and served in this office until his promotion to Lieutenant of the County in January, 1781. He continued to act as Lieutenant until the close of the war. While serving as Sub-Lieutenant, he also acted as a commissioner for the purchase of army supplies.

In 1784, he was appointed judge of the Court of Common Pleas of the county and occupied this office for a term of seven years, when, by the

Constitution of 1790, a president judge of all the courts was appointed to take the place of the several judges. In the Pennsylvania Militia, he was brigade inspector for the county from April 11, 1793, for a period of 20 years. About the year 1816, he moved to the State of Virginia, and died at Winchester in December, 1821, in the 88th year of his age."

"Conrad Eckert was born at Longasalza [sic], in the Kingdom of Hanover, on 6 Feb. 1741 [actually 1742]. During that year his father, John Eckert, emigrated from the place named to Pennsylvania, and settled in Heidelberg township, Lancaster (now Berks) County. He was brought up at farming, and when a young man became a blacksmith, which he pursued for some time. When the Revolution began, he was one of the active Associators of the county. As such he commanded a company which was raised in Heidelberg township, and became a part of the 1st Battalion, commanded by Col. Henry Haller. This battalion marched to service in New Jersey in December, 1776, but the companies left and returned home without permission, because they had not been paid according to the terms of their enlistment. Captain Eckert is the "Captain Echard" mentioned by Gen'l Israel Putnam as one of the captains who informed him that "their companies had run away to a man, excepting a lieutenant, sergeant and drummer." His company afterwards formed a part of Spyker's Battalion, and participated in the campaign at and about Germantown and White Marsh during the Fall of 1777. In this service, he was wounded in the battle at the former place, and his health in consequence became so impaired that he never fully recovered. Subsequently, in 1778 and 1780, his company was connected with the 4th Battalion of County Militia.

Upon his return from military service, he carried on farming on the Eckert homestead, near Womelsdorf, until his death, August 25, 1791. He was married to Elizabeth Hain, a daughter of _____ Hain, in Heidelberg township, by whom he had seven sons, John, Peter, George, David, Daniel, Solomon and Conrad, and two daughters, Catharine (married to Henry Copenhaven), and Barbara (married to Daniel Reeser). His remains were buried in the graveyard connected with Hain's Church.

Col. Valentine Eckert was an elder brother."

15. ERMOLD, JOH. PETER
Charming Molly, 1773
S-H, I: 755
                    EUROPEAN RECORDS

Langenselbold Reformed KB:
Wilhelm Ermold, son of Ernst Ermold, m. 23 Feb. 1708 Catharine, widow of the late Ernst Freyman. [Catharina was a daughter of Hans Blos from

Wittgenborn; she m. (1) in 1702 Johan Ernst Freÿman. See their son, Jacob Freÿman, 1746 immigrant.] Wilhelm Ermold and Catharina had a son:
1. Carl Johann Heinrich, bp. 10 Nov. 1709
   Sp.: Carl Johann Heinrich Hedderich

Carl Johann Henrich Ermold, son of Wilhelm Ermold, inhabitant here, m. 12 Jan. 1735 Maria Elisabeth Hübener. They had children:
1. Anna Elisabetha, bp. 26 Oct. 1735
   Sp.: the daughter of Caspar Kirschner
2. Johanna Maria, bp. 15 Sept. 1737
   Sp.: the daughter of Daniel Wagenhörst
3. Magdalena Elisabeth, bp. 31 Jan. 1740; d. 14 Apr. 1793
4. Carl Johann Henrich, bp. 20 Apr. 1745; Sp.: Caspar Hedderich
5. Gertrud, bp. 21 Sept. 1746
6. **Johann Peter,** bp. 7 June 1750
   Sp.: Johann Peter Bloss, single apprentice, son of the late Mstr. Johannes Bloss, linenweber.
7. Johann Adam, bp. 21 Oct. 1753
   Sp.: a son of the deceased Niclaus Ermold.

AMERICAN RECORDS

Hain's (St. John's) Reformed KB, Berks Co., PA:
Peter Ermold and wife Catharina were sp. 12 Dec. 1773 for John Peter, son of George Ermold; and sp. in 1779 for Peter, son of Andrew Bernges.

Peter Ermold (wife not named) had children:
1. Maria Judith, bp. 26 Dec. 1774
   Sp.: John George Ermold and wife Maria Judith
2. Anna Elisabeth, bp. 9 Feb. 1777; sp.: Anna Elisabeth Stouch

First Reformed KB, Reading, Berks Co., PA:
Peter Ermolt and wife Catharine had a son:
   Daniel b. 12 Mar. 1790, bp. 16 June 1793
   Sp.: Hannes Prinz and wife Elisabeth.

Maria Ermoldt m. - Sept. 1792 Friedrich Moers, Reading.
Rosina Ermold m. 19 Aug. 1798 Peter Siegenthal, Reading.

Buried 24 Nov. 1803: Catharine Ermold, daughter of Peter Ermold, age 1 year, 2 months, 2 days.
Buried 20 Sept. 1810: Peter Ermold, age 60 years, 3 months, 15 days.
Buried 21 Sept. 1817: a son of Daniel Ermold, age 3 years, less 7 days.
Buried 18 Jan. 1842: Catharine Ermoldt, age 90 years, 8 months, 9 days.

Berks County, PA, Will Abstracts:
Peter Ermold, Reading, Sept. 8 - Nov. 7, 1810. All estate to remain in hands of wife, Catharine, during life. After her death sold and divided as follows: John, George, Daniel, to grandchild Mary, daughter of Peter Siegendahler, each an equal share in estate. Son-in-law Frederick Mears married to daughter Mary shall have nothing. Friend Christopher Shearer executor. Witnesses: Adam Heyer and Jacob Cake.

16. ERMOLD, MARTIN
Ship data not located
(before 1752)

EUROPEAN RECORDS

Langenselbold Reformed KB:
Hans Ermold and wife Elisabetha had a son:
>   Antonius, bp. 28 Sept. 1694
>   Sp.: Tönges, son of Georg Fuchs.

Anton Ermold, son of Hans Ermold m. 7 Jan. 1712 Anna Maria Roth, daughter of Jörg Roth, *Hoffman* here.
>   1. Anna Catharina, bp. 18 Mar. 1716
>   2. **Johann Martin**, bp. 29 Oct. 1719
>   Sp.: Ludwig Faust's single son from Hüttengesäss

AMERICAN RECORDS

Hain's (St. John's) Reformed KB, Berks Co., PA:
Martin Ermold and wife Margareth were sp. in 1781 for Martin, son of Peter Gerhart and wife; they were sp. again in 1786 for Margareth, daughter of Georg Eirich [q.v.- Eurich].

Johannes Ermold, *Vorst(eher)*, and Anna Elisabeth had a daughter:
>   Anna Margareth b. 31 Jan. 1790, bp. 14 Feb. 1790
>   Sp.: Martin Ermold and Anna Margareth.

Pennsylvania Land Warrants:
Martin Armolt, land warrant 62 ½ Acres, 1752, Lower Heidelberg Twp., Berks County. **Patent Book AA-4-69:** Patent to Martin Armold, 22 Nov. 1762. A Warrant dated 25 Oct. 1752 and surveyed to Martin Armolt, a tract of land in Heidelberg Twp., Berks Co., containing 62½ acres, adjoining land of Peter Treser [Tressler, Dressler?], Joseph [Jost?] Hedrick, William Reiser, George Hedrick.

Bern Reformed KB, Bern Twp., Berks Co., PA:
Martin Ermold and wife had:
>   a son, bp. 9 Aug. 1760
>   Sp.: Anthony Lambrecht and wife.

[Comment by compiler: since no passenger listing has been located for this family, or the next Ermold family, it is possible that both families arrived before 1727 when the passenger lists start; there are no further records for the family after the 1719 birth of Johann Martin Ermold. Also, there are several unidentified Ermolds and Ermels who may be members of these families. For example, an Isaac Ermel (Cumru Twp.) appears in the burial record of Rev. Boos at Schwartzwald, with his dates given: b. 13 Aug. 1756, d. 3 Sept. 1801. The given name Isaac also appears in the Langenselbold Ermold family.]

17. ERMOLD, WILHELM
Ship data not located
EUROPEAN RECORDS

Langenselbold Reformed KB:
Ernst Ermold and wife Margretha had a son:
>   Johan Wilhelm, bp. 17 May 1685
>   Sp.: Wilhelm Roth and Emmanuel Roth.

Wilhelm Ermold, son of Ernst Ermold, m. 23 Feb. 1708 Catharine, widow of the late Ernst Freyman. They had a son:
>   1. Carl Johann Heinrich, bp. 10 Nov. 1709

[See comment above about unidentified Ermolds and Ermels in PA records; the same given names appear in the Langenselbold and Pennsylvania families, and some of the Ermolds disappear from Langenselbold at an early date; there may have been prelist arrivals.]

AMERICAN RECORDS

1754 Berks County tax list, Reading: William Armold

Berks County, PA, Abstracts of Wills & Adm.:
William Ermel, Reading, 19 Jan. 1803, adm. to George House and his wife Elizabeth who is one of the daughters of deceased.

William Ermel, Cumru, 1 Feb. 1819, 13 June 1821. All estate to wife during life, name Sarah. Afterwards to be sold and divided among 5 children - Jacob, Isaac, Susann, Margaret and Daniel. Executors: friends Francis Krick and John Muller. Witnesses: Christian Gaul and Jacob Huffert.

First Reformed KB, Reading, Berks Co.:
Other unidentified Ermolds in the marriage records:
Margretha Ermold m. 19 Mar. 1809 John Bast, Reading.
Johann Ermold m. 24 Apr. 1809 Margretha Ruppert.
George Ermold m. 5 Jan. 1812 Maria Sell.

Creutz Creek Reformed KB, Hellam Twp., York Co.:
One Peter Ermold and wife Catharine had:
> Joh. Georg, b. 26 Aug. ----, bp. 10 Nov.
> Sp.: Georg Ermold and wife Anna Maria
> Susanna, b. 14 Dec. 1799, bp. 22 Mar. 1800.

18. EURICH, CONRAD
EURICH, JOH. GEORG
Chance, 1766
S-H, I: 709
EUROPEAN RECORDS

Langenselbold Reformed KB:
Johan Jörg Eurich, a *?Bender und Bierbrauer*, son of the late Henrich Eurich, *Fassbinds und Inwohner* at Kunzelsau in the Graffschafft Hohenloh, m. 29 Dec. 1711 Maria Gerdraut, daughter of the late Martin Peters, *Inwohner* at Merckenbach *fürstl. Nassau-Dillenburg jurisdiction.*
John Jörg Eyrich, *Binder*, and wife had a son:
> Conrad, bp. 24 Mar. 1715
> Sp.: Conrad Reber, smith, single

Conrad Eürich, son of the late Mstr. Hans Georg Eürich, *Fassbinder* and inhabitant, m. 13 Nov. 1737 Elisabetha, daughter of Mstr. Johannes Winck, linenweaver and also inhabitant here. They had children:
> 1. Anna Sabina, bp. 19 Oct. 1738, d. 30 Dec. 1738
>   Sp.: The child's father's sister.
> 2. **Johann Georg,** bp. 10 Feb. 1740
>   Sp.: Mstr. Johan Georg Winck, linenweaver and
>   the child's mother's brother

   3. Johannes, bp. 22 Apr. 1742
      Sp.: The son of Jacob Kriegsmann
   4. Twin daughter Anna Clara Elisabetha, bp. 4 Jan. 1744
      Sp.: The wife of Georg Winck
   5. Twin daughter **Maria Judith**, bp. 4 Jan 1744
      Sp.: The mother's sister, daughter of Johannes Winck
   6. **Joh. Conrad, bp.** 6 July 1746
      Sp.: Johann Georg Winck's son here
   7. Bastian, bp. 8 Dec. 1748, d. 19 Dec. 1749
      Sp.: Bastian Winterstein
   8. Twin Susanna Elisabetha, bp. 12 Aug. 1750
      Sp.: Grandmother on the mother's side
   9. Twin Maria Catharina, bp. 12 Aug. 1750
      Sp.: Catharina Wacker, single
  10. Sebastian, bp. 28 Nov. 1753
      Sp.: Sebastian Winterstein

Died 18 July 1734: Mstr. Johan Georg Eurich, binder, age 47 y. 4 mo. less
several days.

Died 2 Feb. 1734: Maria Gertraud wife of Mstr. Johan Georg Eurich, age 52
y. 1 mo. several days.

Conrad Eurich m. (2) 12 Feb. 1772 Maria Catharina Stamm.

AMERICAN RECORDS

PA Archives, Sixth Series, Vol.6, Waldschmidt's Records:
Daniel Ermold m. 29 Oct. 1766 Judith ?Eyrricker, daughter of Conrad
?Eigereicher. At the same time a son was baptized. Another translation
gives her surname as Eyerich.

Johann Georg Eurich m. 20 Dec. 1769 Anna Maria, dau. of Dietrich Sohl.

Conrad Eyerich, son of Conrad Eyerich, m. 18 Feb. 1771 Juliana, daughter
of Michael Lauer.

Bern Reformed KB, Bern Twp., Berks Co., PA:
Conrad Eurich and wife had a son:
        Michael, b. 9 June 1774, bp. 3 July 1774
        Sp.: Michael Lauer

Hain's (St. John's) Reformed KB, Berks Co., PA:
Conrad Eurig and wife had;
> Conrad, bp. 17 May 1778
> Sp.: Georg Ermold and Maria Judith.

Conrad Eurig and wife Juliana were sp. in 1778 for Conrad, son of Henrich Lauer and wife.

Georg Eurich and wife had children:
> 1. Johannes, bp. 23 Oct. 1774
> Sp.: Johannes Sohl and Rosina
> 2. Johannes, bp. 2 June 1776; same sponsors.
> 3. Susanna, bp. 24 Oct. 1779
> Sp.: Susanna Schäfer

Another Georg Eurich had children:
> 1. Anna Maria, b. 7 Apr. 1785, bp. 16 Apr. 1785
> Sp.: Anna Maria Ermold
> 2. Margaretha, b. 2 Oct. 1786, bp. 4 Nov. 1786
> Sp.: Martin Ermold
> 3. Magdalena, b. 21 Mar. 1788, bp. 23 Mar. 1788
> Sp.: Magdalena Ermold

Rev. Boos' Burials, Schwartzwald Reformed KB, Berks Co., PA:
Georg Eurich
b. 12 Oct. 1739 - d. 14 Mar. 1784

Berks County, PA, Abstracts of Wills & Adm.:
George Eirich, Heidelberg, 19 Aug. 1812 - 02 Nov. 1815. Plantation in Heidelberg where I live to be sold, 47 acres. All personal estate to wife Margaret and 1/3 remainder to children, viz: John, George, Daniel, Mary, Margaret, Elizabeth, Catharine, Rebecca and Magdalena. Son John and son-in-law Daniel Meierly executors. Witnesses: Benjamin Hain and Joseph Hain.

19. EŸGELBÖRNER, JOH. DANIEL
(Danl Igelbourner, age 45)
Queen Elizabeth, 1738
S-H, I: 217, 219, 220

EUROPEAN RECORDS

Langenselbold Reformed KB:
Johann Caspar Eichelburner, son of Clos Eichelburner, m. 11 Feb. 1686
Magdalena, daughter of Hans Fuchs.

Died 20 Nov. 1736: Magdalena, widow of the late Johann Caspar
Eÿchelbörner; age 74 y. less 1 mo. and __ days.

Johann Daniel Eÿgelbörner, son of the late Hans Caspar Eÿgelbörner,
former *Mitnachbar* here, m. 23 Feb. 1724 Maria Margretha, daughter of
Hans Conrad Lach, inhabitant at Langendiebach. They had children:
1. Johann Henrich, bp. 12 Nov. 1724
   Sp.: Joh. Henrich Wacker, single, from the Obermühl
2. Johann Jacob, bp. 1 May 1726
   Sp.: Joh. Jacob Lach, the child's mother's brother from
   Langendiebach
3. Johann Conrad, bp. 16 Mar. 1729
   Sp.: Johann Conrad ?Hess from Schlichtern, a citizen
   and hatmaker
4. Anna Catharina, bp. 13 Feb. 1735, d. 26 Mar. 1736
   Sp.: the wife of Johannes Kirschner
5. Johann Gottfried, bp. 27 Jan. 1737
   Sp.: The child's mother's sister and her bridegroom

AMERICAN RECORDS

Rev. John Waldschmidt's Marriage records; PA Archives, Sixth Series, Vol. 6, p. 217:
Gottfried Eichelbrenner, son of Daniel Eichelbrenner, m. (no date) 1760
Juliana, dau. of Caspar Raush.

Host Reformed KB, Tulpehocken, Berks Co., PA:
Jacob Eichelbrönner m. 27 Dec. 1753 Maria Numann from Mühlbach.

Tabor First Reformed KB, Lebanon, PA.:
Godfried Eichelberner and wife Juliana were sp. in 1775 for a child of
Johann Umberger, and again in 1775 for a child of Georg Grupensch; they
sp. in 1779 a child of the schoolmaster Johannes Reiter, and in 1780 a child
of Johannes Steger.

Jacob Eichelberner and wife Catharina (nee Zimmerman) had children:
1. Jacob, b. 6 Nov. 1780, bp. 26 Nov. 1780
2. Catharina, bp. 29 Sept. 1782

3. Elisabetha, bp. 14 Feb. 1785

Peter Eichelberner and wife Margaretha had children:
    1. Peter, b. 13 Oct. 1784, bp. 14 Nov. 1784
        Sp.: Jacob Eichelberner and Catharina
    2. Joh. Jacob, b. 12 Oct. 1785, bp. 1 Jan. 1786
        Sp.: Gottfried Eichel*berger* and wife Juliana
    3. Elisabetha, [surname given as *Eichelberger*] b. 30 Feb. 1787

Half-timbered house in Langenselbold

20. FAUST, ANTON
Francis and Elizabeth, 1742
S-H, I: 329

EUROPEAN RECORDS

Langenselbold Reformed KB:
Johann Faust, son of the late Johann (Hans) Faust, m. 25 Feb. 1706 Anna
Rosina [nee Dieterich], widow of Christoffel Schieser. Data on the Dieterich
family is presented here, since this family had several connections with
emigrant families Faust, Kirschner and Grauel.
Johann Dieterich, son of Henrich Dieterich, m. 26 Feb. 1680 Cathar. Rüger,
daughter of Hans Rüger, former *Herrschaftl. Müller* at Birstein. They had:
   1. Anna Rosina Dieterich, bp. 28 Nov. 1680; [she m. Johann Faust,
      above.]
   2. Caspar Dieterich, twin, bp. 25 June 1682
   3. Stoffel Dieterich, twin, bp. 25 June 1682
   4. Gertraud Dieterich, bp. 17 Nov. 1683; [she m. (1) in 1704
      Johannes Schuffert. They were divorced and she m. (2) 11 Feb.
      1717 Johannes Kirschner.]
   5. Helena Dieterich, bp. 10 May 1685; sp.: Helena, daughter of the
      late Henrich Dieterich. [This sponsor m. Conrad Grauel, q.v.]

Hans Faust, in Oberdorff, and wife Anna Rosina had children, surname
Faust:
   1. Joh. Peter, bp. 17 June 1707
   2. Anna Gertraud, bp. 13 Feb. 1710
   3. Elisabetha, bp. 15 Jan. 1713
   4. **Antonius**, bp. 1 Dec. 1715
      Sp.: Tönges Hübener
   5. Joh. Henrich, bp. 10 Mar. 1718
   6. Helena, twin, bp. 23 Mar. 1721
   7. Anna Gertraud, twin, bp. 23 Mar. 1721

AMERICAN RECORDS

St. Michael's and Zion Lutheran KB, Philadelphia, PA:
Antony Faust from Oley m. 28 Apr. 1749 by liscense Elisabeth Fischer from
Tulpehocken. Wit: Paul Geiger and Jürg Ernst Loechler from Ohley.

1754 Berks County tax list, Heidelberg Twp.: Antony Foust

Hain's (St. John's) Reformed KB, Berks Co., PA:
Antonius Faust and wife were sp. in 1754 for Maria Elisabeth, daughter of

Michael Grauel [q.v.]. Anthony Faust and Elizabeth were sp. in 1777 for John, son of John Yost Stamm [q.v.].

Rev. Boos' Burial Record, Schwartzwald KB, Berks Co., PA:
Antoni Faust b. 1715, d. 9 Apr. 1806. Had 38 grandchildren and 26 great-grandchildren.

PA Archives, Sixth Series, Vol. 6, Rev. John Waldschmidt's records:
Elisabeth Faust, daughter of Anthon Faust, m. 2 Nov. 1768 Joh. Jost Stamm, son of Adam Stamm [q.v.].

Conf. Easter 1765 - Anthon Faust's daughter Maria Elisabeth.
Conf. 15 Apr. 1770 -   Maria Margretha, daughter of Anthon Faust
      at Cacusy: Anna Maria, daughter of Anthon Faust

1767 Berks County tax list, Heidelberg Twp.: Anthony Faust, 100 acres.

21. FAUST, JOH. GEORG
Francis and Elizabeth, 1742
S-H, I: 329
                    EUROPEAN RECORDS

Langenselbold Reformed KB:
Johannes Faust m. 4 Jan. 1666 Künigunda, daughter of the late Hans Mohn. [See Johann Peter Faust, 1733 em., for a complete list of their family.] They had a son [Philips (Lips)], bp. 4 May 1679.

Philipp Faust, son of the late Johann Faust, m. 14 Jan. 1706 Elisabeth Rack, daughter of Paul Rack, *Gemeinsmann* here. They had children:
    1. Joh. Peter, bp. 5 Aug. 1708
    2. Magdalen Elisabeth, bp. 23 Mar. 1710
    3. **Joh. Jörg,** bp. 18 Sept. 1712
    4. Maria Kunigunda, bp. 18 Feb. 1714
    5. Joh. Michael, bp. 21 May 1716
    6. Johannes, bp. 13 June 1719

Meister **Johann Georg Faust,** linenweaver, son of Lips Faust, inhabitant here, m. 16 Sept. 1739 Elisabetha Catharina, daughter of the deceased Mstr. Martin Weÿs, also former inhabitant and mason here. {Martin Weiss from Parish Brande? in *Bischthum Auchspurg*, m. 19 Jan. 1713 Anna Kniss, daughter of Caspar Kniss.}

Johann Georg and Elisabetha Catharina (Weiss) Faust had one child before
emigrating:
  1. Johannes, bp. 6 July 1740
     Sp.: Mstr. Johannes Dein, the carpenter from Langendiebach.

AMERICAN RECORDS

Berks County, PA, tax lists, George Foust, 1760-1779, in Tulpehocken Twp.

Pennsylvania Land Warrants:
George Faust, land warrant dated 28 Oct. 1746.

Rev. John Caspar Stoever's Pastoral Records, PA:
Georg Faust (Northkill) had children:
     A daughter, b. 12 Apr. 1747, bp. 10 May 1747
        Sp.: Philip Faust [1733 imm., q.v.] and wife
     Magdalena Elisabeth, b. Sept. 1749, bp. 15 Oct. 1749
        Sp.: the wife of Casper Hetterich [q.v.]
     John George, b. 22 Nov. 1757, bp. 8 Dec. 1757
        Sp.: John George Haag and Catarina Muench

Host (St. John's) Reformed KB, Tulpehocken, Berks Co., PA:
George Faust and wife Elisab. Cathar. had:
     John Philip, b. 9 Feb. 1760, bp. 30 Mar. 1760
        Sp.: John Philip Faust

22. FAUST, JOH. PETER age 40
    FAUST, JOH. PHILIP age 20
Elizabeth, 1733
S-H, I: 113, 114, 115, 765, 766, 767
    Also on ship: Anna Eliza Foust, 40; Micol Foust, 13; Johannes Foust, 11;
              John Peter Foust, 9; Ann Eliz. Foust, 5; Matelina, dead, 3;
              Johan Hendrick Foust, 2.

EUROPEAN RECORDS

Langenselbold Reformed KB:
Hans Faust and Elisabeth had twin sons:
     1. Johann, bp. 3 weeks before Easter 1643, at Selbold
        Sp.: Johann Ermuth?

2. Wörner, bp. 3 weeks before Easter 1643, at Selbold
   Sp.: Wörner Moon [Mohn]

Johannes Faust m. 4 Jan. 1666 Künigunda, daughter of the late Hans Mohn.
They had children:
  1. Anna Barbara, bp. 21 Jan. 1667.
     She m. Joh. Melchior Mell [see Mell].
  2. Caspar, bp. 2 June 1668
  3. Johannes, bp. 2 Sept. 1672
  4. Michael, bp. 9 May 1675. He m. in 1707 Helena, widow of
     Conrad Grauel [see Grauel].
  5. A son [Weigel], bp. 26 Aug. 1677
  6. A son [Philipp], bp. 4 May 1679
  7. Anna Maria, bp. 13 May 1683; she m.
     Joh. Heinrich Braunmüller [see Braunmüller]
  8. Magdalena, bp. 10 Oct. 1684; she m. Johann Hübener
  9. Elisabetha, bp. 5 Apr. 1686; she m. (1) Heinrich Henkel; she m.
     (2) Andreas Lerch [q.v.].
 10. Anna Barbara, bp. 7 Aug. 1688
 11. **Johan Peter**, bp. 22 Dec. 1689

[There may be other children - there are two Johann Fausts having children
at the same time; this one seems to be designated "the younger" in most
entries].

Died at Selboldt 4 Sept. 1694 - Johann Faust, age 51 years and several
weeks.

Johann Peter Faust, son of the late Johann Faust, m. (1) 5 Jan. 1713
Magdalena, dau. of Philipps Adam. They had:
  1. **Philips**, bp. 22 Feb. 1714
     Sp.: Johann Conrad Adam

Johann Peter Faust, widower and inhabitant here, m. (2) 14 Jan. 1717 Anna
Elisabeth, daughter of the late Joh. Conrad Grauel, former baker and
Gemeinsmann here. [See 1733 immigrant Michael Grauel for more complete
Grauel data].
Johann Peter and Anna Elisabeth (Grauel) Faust had children:
  2. Michael, bp. 20 Jan. 1718
     Sp.: Michael Faust, the child's father's brother
  3. Johannes, bp. 27 Sept. 1719
     Sp.: Hans Faust, the child's father's brother
  4. Johann Henrich, bp. 21 Sept. 1721
     Sp.: Henrich Kirschner's eldest single son

   5. Johann Peter, bp. 17 May 1723
      Sp.: Michael Faust's single son
   6. Anna Maria, bp. 1 Oct. 1724
      Sp.: Mstr. Joh. Henrich Braunmüller's second
      daughter, single
   7. Anna Elisabetha, bp. 21 July 1728
      Sp.: The wife of Anton Wacker, the *Riedmüller*
   8. Magdalena Elisabetha, bp. 6 Nov. 1729
      Sp.: Single daughter of Lips Faust
   9. Joh. Henrich, bp. 24 Apr. 1731
      Sp.: Joh. Henrich Braumüller, linenweaver

Buried 29 Oct. 1721 - Kunigunda, widow of Joh. Faust. She was the
community midwife for more than 20 years and delivered over 800 children.
Age 74 years less several weeks.

AMERICAN RECORDS

1754 Berks County tax list, Bern Twp.: Philip Foust

Philadelphia, Book F, page no. torn off, Est # 1745
Peter Ffaust, Last Will & Testament, dated 22 Jan. 1745: Mentions mother
of (son) Peter. Peter shall have plantation; Peter shall give to mother every
year 15 bushels of wheat, 4 bushels of rye, 15 pounds of flax, etc. and every
year 5 shillings of money. Johannes shall have £15 paid by Peter in 1750, £5
in 1751, £6 in 1752. Michel shall have the £30 which he had of his father
for his portion but the money he borrowed of Johannes Schneider's widow
he shall pay if he comes again.
Wit: Christoph Beyer   Peter Ffaust
     Hans Martin Gerigh   Trans. by Conrad Weiser,
     Martin Altstatt   Heidelberg twp.
     Martin X Zwealler

Bern Reformed KB, Bern Twp., Berks Co., PA:
Philip Faust and wife had:
        1. John, bp. 18 May 1739; sp.: John Wegenschmit.
           [Buried at Belleman's Cemetery, Berks Co.:
           Johannes Faust, b. 3 Mar. 1739, died 6 May 1792.]
        2. Catharine Elisabeth, bp. 5 Apr. 1752
           Sp.: Jacob Albrech and wife.

John Faust and wife had:
        1. John Christian, bp. 16 Nov. (1750).
           Sp.: Christian Altbrech (Albrecht) and wife.

2. Barbara, bp. 9 Feb. 1752; sp.: Barbara Albrech.

Michael Faust and wife had:
1. John, bp. 27 June 1754
Sp.: John Faust and wife.

Stoners (Steiner's) Church, Alamance Co., NC: tombstone inscriptions:
(Jo)Hannes Faust
(1)789 age 70 (years) 3 m.
[stone broken]

Barbara Foust
b. 1719 (d) 1802

From the burial records of this churchbook:
Widow Foust, named Barbara, a born Albright, died March 1, 1802 aged 82 years, 4 months and several weeks. In her marriage, she had 10 children, but 2 are dead. She has 75 grandchildren and 48 great-grandchildren. She lived in widowhood 12 years and near 3 months.
  [Record kindly supplied by Grace Thompson of Burlington, NC, along with photographs of tombstones. John Foust was one of the earliest elders of this congregation.]

Berks County Administrations: Vol. 4: 59:
Philip Faust of Bern Twp. His widow Magdalena renounced her right to administer. Letters of Adm. were granted to John Faust, eldest son, and Henry Moll, son-in-law, on 3 July 1786.

St. Michael's Union Church cemetery, Tilden Twp., Berks Co., PA:

P------- Faust   Magdalena Faust
b. ----- 1713   wife of P------ Faust
d. 19 Apr. 1786   b. Feb. 20, 1716
                                d. Apr. 5, 1789
                                married 48 years, had 6 sons, 4 dau.

23. FAUST, PETER
Francis and Elizabeth, 1742
S-H, I: 329
                    EUROPEAN RECORDS

Langenselbold Reformed KB:
Johann Faust, son of the late Johann (Hans) Faust, m. 25 Feb. 1706 Anna

Rosina [nee Dieterich], widow of Christoffel Schieser. [See immigrant Anton Faust for further detail on the Dieterich family.]

Hans Faust, in Oberdorff, and wife Anna Rosina had children:
  1. **Joh. Peter,** bp. 17 June 1707
  2. Anna Gertraud, bp. 13 Feb. 1710
  3. Elisabetha, bp. 15 Jan. 1713
  4. Antonius [q.v.], bp. 1 Dec. 1715
  5. Joh. Henrich, bp. 10 Mar. 1718
  6. Helena, twin, bp. 23 Mar. 1721
  7. Anna Gertraud, twin, bp. 23 Mar. 1721

AMERICAN RECORDS

Hain's (St. John's) Reformed KB, Berks Co., PA:
Johan Peter Faust and wife Anna Maria had children:
  1. Magdalena, b. 1 Mar. 1747
     Sp.: Adam Hain and wife
  2. a son, bp. 9 Apr. 1749
     Sp.: Johan Henrich Hen and wife Anna Christina
  3. a daughter, bp. 14 July 1751
     Sp.: Anna Elisabetha Faust

PA Archives, Sixth series, Vol 6, Rev. John Waldschmidt's records:
Magdalena Faust, daughter of Peter Faust, m. 24 Mar. 1767 Christen Theel.

Elisabeth Faust, daughter of Peter Faust, m. 12 June 1769 Daniel Maurer, son of Christofel Maurer; in the Pastor's house.

Heinrich Faust, son of Peter Faust, m. 12 June 1769 Magdalena, daughter of Nicolaus Weimer.

1754 Berks County tax list, Heidelberg Twp.: Peter Foust.

Berks County, PA, Abstracts of Wills & Adm.:
Peter Faust, Heidelberg 28 Dec. 1788 - 31 Jan. 1789 (translation). To sons Peter and Anthony my plantation where I live, and shall pay to my other children £205, viz: To children of dau. Anna Elisabeth, to children of dau. Anna Barbara, and to my four daughters Magdalena, Maria, Catharina and Christina, and sons Henry, Philip and John. To son Henry 7 acres of land where he lives. Provides for wife Anna Maria. Wife Anna Maria and John van Ried, executors. Witnesses: Peter Hetterick and Bastian Berlet.

24. FEUERSTEIN, JOHANNES
Edinburgh, 1750
S-H, I: 430

EUROPEAN RECORDS

Langenselbold Reformed KB:
The earliest Feuerstein record at Langenselbold is the marriage on 19 Apr.
1688 of Philipps Henrich Fewerstein, an apprentice carpenter, son of Conrad
Fewerstein, miller at Heldenberg, and Anna, dau. of the late Caspar Raidel.

Mstr. Johannes Feuerstein, the smith, and wife Augusta Maria had children,
[their marriage not recorded at Langenselbold]:
1. Maria Catharina, bp. 2 Apr. 1749
   Sp.: A daughter of the late Herr Joh. Jacob Holtzener of
   Neu Hanau.
2. Johan Jacob, bp. 1 Apr. 1750
   Sp.: Joh. Jacob Pfundt, apprentice shoemaker *aus der Schweitz.*

AMERICAN RECORDS

PA Archives, Sixth Series, Vol. 6, Rev. Waldschmidt's marriages:
Anna Feuerstein, daughter of Johannes Feuerstein, m. 16 Jan. 1781 Jacob
Britsch, son of Jacob Britsch, dec'd.

Daniel Feuerstein, son of Johannes Feuerstein, m. 5 Aug. 1783 Anna,
daughter of Görg Lang.

Görg Feuerstein, son of Johannes Feuerstein, m. 5 Feb. 1782 Salome,
daughter of the dec'd. Christofel Bercker [?Becker].

Magdalena Feuerstein, daughter of Johannes Feuerstein, m. 12 Sept. 1773
Johannes Lufft, son of Peter Lufft, dec'd.

Johannes Feuerstein settled in Cocalico Twp., Lancaster Co., PA.

Lancaster Will Abstracts, Book H-1:102:
Johannes Feuerstein, Will dated 18 May 1801, prob. 21 Aug. 1801;
Wife: Justina Maria and 5 children.

See also George Ely Russell, *"Founders of the American Firestone Family"*
National Genealogical Society Quarterly, Vol. 52 (1964) 241-244.

For other Firestone [Feuerstein] immigrants, see Annette K. Burgert, *Eighteenth Century Emigrants from the Northern Alsace to America,* (1992) and George Ely Russell, F.A.S.G., *Firestone Family of Frederick Co., MD* in Western Maryland Genealogy, Vol 9, No. 1 (Jan. 1993).

25. FILTZMEYER, PHILIP

Emigrated ca. 1733 [last entry in German records 7 Sept. 1732; first entry in PA, land warrant dated 1 Apr. 1734].
He is likely the Philip (M) Mire, age 36 (did not sign) on the ship:
Richard and Elizabeth, 1733
S-H, I: 127, 129, 130
Other passengers on ship: Anna Margaretha Mire, age 40 (probably Anna Margretha (Stam) Filtzmeyer); Anna Barbara Stamm, age 26 [q.v.] (sister of Anna Margretha Filtzmeyer); children: Anna Maria (no surname given), age 4; and Anna Catharina (no surname given) age 1½.

EUROPEAN RECORDS

Langenselbold Reformed KB:
Died 31 Mar. 1743: Mstr. Dieterich Filtzmeyer the smith, age about 80 years.
Died 29 May 1743: Margaretha, wife of Mstr. Dieterich Filtzmeyer, age 72 years, 4 months and some days.

Dieterich Felsmaÿer, *Gemeinschmied*, and wife Margretha had children:
1. **Philippus**, bp. 3 Jan. 1697
   Sp.: Hans Faust's single son of this name.
2. Joh. Caspar, bp. 15 Feb. 1698
3. Rachel, bp. 30 Aug. 1699; she m. 1726 Joh. Adam Stamm [q.v.]
4. Joh. Michael, bp. 30 Sept. 1701
5. Hieronymus, bp. 21 Jan. 1703
6. Anna Rosina, bp. 11 Oct. 1705
7. Johanna Maria, bp. 27 Apr. 1708

Meister **Philips Filtzmeyer**, smith, son of *Meister* Dieterich Filtzmeyer, also a smith, m. 4 Feb. 1728 Anna Margretha, daughter of the late David Stamm [q.v.: Stamm], former cartwright here. They had children:
1. Johanna Maria, bp. 1 Aug. 1728
   Sp.: The child's father's sister, single.
2. Catharina, bp. 7 Sept. 1732. Sp.: The wife of Hennerich Adam.

AMERICAN RECORDS

Pennsylvania Land Warrants, Film 3.75, Book F-126:
Philip Filtzmeyer, warrant for 150 acres near Tulpehoccon, adj. Hugh Jones' land. Dated 1 Apr. 1734.

1754 Berks Co. tax lists, Heidelberg: Philip Fitzmier.

PA Archives, Sixth Series, Vol. 6, Rev. John Waldschmidt's records:
Johann Jost Filtsmeyer, son of Philip Filtzmeyer m. 5 Apr. 1757 a daughter of Gabriel Rietscher.

Born 9 Nov. 1773, an illegitimate son of the widow of Jost Filtzmeyer; bp. 23 Nov. 1773. The father of the child was Filip Wehrheim, a married man. Sp.: Henry Hetterich and wife Catharina.

Catharina Fellsmeyer m. William Hetterich [son of Carl Hedderich q.v.].

Reading Lutheran KB, Burials:
Died 2 June 1768: Anna Maria Seisinger, wife of Nicolas Seisinger, nee Filsmayer. Mother of 3 sons and 3 daughters, age 38 years. [See *Historical Review of Berks County,* Vol. V, No. 1, pg. 24 (Oct. 1739), "The Seitzinger Family" by J. Crawford Hartman for details about Seitzinger descendants.]

1767 Berks County tax list, PA Archives, Third Series, Vol. 18:
Heidelberg Twp.: Jost Filsmeyer, 200 acres.

Berks County, PA, Abstracts of Wills & Adm.:
Philip Filsmeyer, Heidelberg, 23 Mar. 1769 - 28 Sept. 1775.
To grandchild Margaretha Seitzinger £10. To grandchildren, viz: Maria Magdalena, Nicholas, Alexander and Michael, children of deceased daughter Maria £10 to be divided, giving a considerable sum to their parents Nicholas [Seitzinger] and Maria. All remainder to son Jost, who is also executor. Letters to Verner Stam, nephew of the deceased, the executor named being deceased. Witnesses William Reeser and Conrad Wirheim. Translation.

Hain's (St. John's) Reformed KB, Berks Co., PA:
John Jost Filtzmeyer and wife Anna Maria had:
　　　Maria Elisabeth, b. 15 Oct. 1768, bp. 30 Oct. 1768
　　　Sp.: Casper Bräuning and wife Maria Elisabeth

Berks County, PA, Abstracts of Wills & Adm.:
John Jost Fitsmeyer, Heidelberg, 15 Oct. 1771. Adm. to Anna Maria Fitzmeyer, the widow.

Abstracts of Berks Co. Orphans Court Records:
Dated 13 Dec. 1771:
Petition of Mary Filzmeyer, widow and Admr. of Yost Filzmeyer of Heidelberg, deceased, Yeoman. Petitioner states that Yost Filzmeyer died intestate about 3 months since, leaving three children: Catharine, age 12 years; Margaret, age 8 years; and Elizabeth, 3 years. Prays for guardians. Court appoints John Heckert and David Bright.

Dated 12 Dec. 1782:
Petition of Adam Ruth and Catharine his wife (eldest daughter of Yost Filtzmeyer, late of Heidelberg, Yeoman, decased). That Yost Filtzmeyer died intestate about 11 years since, seized of three tracts of land in Heidelberg, containing about 331 acres, leaving a widow (Anna Maria) and 3 daughters, to wit: Catharine, Margaret and Elizabeth, the last two in their minority. Prays for an inquest to divide or value. So ordered.

Dated 6 Apr. 1785:
Elizabeth Filtzmeyer (above 14) daughter of Yost Filtzmeyer of Heidelberg, Yeoman, deceased, chooses Conrad Kershner, Jr., for guardian.

Petition of Adam Ruth and Catharine his wife (late Catharine Filtzmeyer, eldest daughter of Yost Filtzmeyer of Heidelberg, deceased). Jacob Shaffer and Margaret his wife (late Margaret Filtzmeyer, another daughter of deceased), and Conrad Kershner, guardian of Elizabeth Filtzmeyer, the other daughter of deceased. That Jost Filtzmeyer died intestate about 14 years since leaving a widow (Anna Maria) and 3 children to wit: Catharine, Margaret & Elizabeth, who is yet in her minority. That intestate died seized of four contiguous tracts of land in Heidelberg of 330 acres. The petitioner pray the Court to appoint and order John Bulman, Peter Fisher, John Hehn (son of Adam Hehn) and Jacob Haak to make partition of the premises above mentioned or value. So ordered.

Nat. Sept./Oct. 1749, Philip Filchmir, Lancaster Co., PA.

26. FISCHER, JOH. HENRICH age 38
Samuel, 1733
S-H, I: 107, 111, 112
   with Anna Lydia Fischer 36, Anna Maria 11, Susanah 3, Hans Jacob 2

EUROPEAN RECORDS

Langenselbold Reformed KB:
Conrad Fischer, son of Johannes Fischer, m. 13 Jan 1687 Anna Veronica, daughter of Caspar Schuffert. Conrad Fischer and Anna Veronica had:
1. Anna Catharina, bp. 18 Mar. 1688
   Sp.: The father's sister, daughter of Johannes Fischer
2. Anna Barbara, bp. 25 Sept. 1690
   Sp.: The wife of Johannes Fischer, the child's grandmother
3. Henrich, bp. 24 Feb. 1692
   Sp.: Jost Henrich Weber, a servant at Hans Roth's, born in *Bicken aus dem Fürstenthumb Dillenburg.*
4. **Henrich,** bp. 21 Mar. 1694
   Sp.: Henrich Herger from ?Gonschrod
5. Joh. Melchior, bp. 26 Feb. 1696
   Sp.: M. Melchior Tressler, tailor and *Herrschaffl. Fruchtschreiber.*
6. Anna Maria, bp. 13 June 1698; [she m. Caspar Koch and she emigrated in 1746 as a widow, q.v.]
   Sp.: Johan Conrad Fischer's wife
7. Magdalena, bp. 27 June 1700
   Sp.: daughter of Joh. Faust
8. Anna, bp. 8 Oct. 1702
   Sp.: Anna, daughter of Johannis Döll
9. Johannes [q.v.], bp. 6 June 1706
   Sp.: the child's grandfather, Johannes Fischer

Joh. Henrich Fischer, son of Conrad Fischer, m. (1) 23 Nov. 1717 Elisabetha Reichert, daughter of the late Friedrich Reichert. [See 1733 em. Ludwig Reichert for her family records.] They had children:
1. Johannes, bp. 9 Jan. 1721. Sp.: Johannes Koch.
2. Anna Maria, bp. 3 Dec. 1721
   Sp.: The child's father's single sister.

Died 28 Aug. 1724, Joh. Henrich Fischer's wife named Elisabetha, age 23 years less several days.

Johann Henrich Fischer, widower, m. (2) 6 Dec. 1724 Anna Elisabetha, daughter of the late Johann Lerch. They had:
3. Anna Elisabetha, bp. 13 Jan. 1726
   Sp.: Wife of Joh. Georg Kirschner
4. Joh. Melchior, bp. 14 Jan. 1728
   Sp.: the child's father's brother, Joh. Melchior Fischer
5. Susanna Elisabetha, bp. 1 Jan. 1729
   Sp.: Wife of Mstr. Michael Gliem, the shoemaker
6. Joh. Jacob, bp. 19 July 1731
   Sp.: The son of Christian Neidert, the baker

AMERICAN RECORDS

Heidelberg Moravian KB, Berks Co., PA:
Family Register:
Nicolaus Glat from Waltersbach in Lower Alsace was born in November
1713, son of Johann and Barbara Glat. He was married in Conestoga in
Pennsylvania on 28 Dec. 1740 by Emmanuel Zimmermann, a justice of the
peace, to Anna Maria Fischer, a daughter of Heinrich Fischer, a citizen of
Langenselbot [sic] in Isenburg, and his wife Elisabeth. Nicolaus Glat and
wife Anna Maria, nee Fischer, had children:
1. Elisabeth, b. 27 Oct. 1742 in Bern Twp.; bp. 23 Dec. in a private
   house in Heidelberg. Sp.: Friedrich Gerhart [q.v.] & Barbara.
   (Elisabeth Glad, daughter of Nicholas and Anna Maria Glad,
   married 13 Sept. 1763 Johannes Votring of Manacosie.)
2. Anna Maria, b. 14 Dec. 1744 in Bern, bp. 16 Dec. in Heidelberg.
   Sp.: Johannes Fischer [q.v.] in Kakusy [Cacoosing, Cacusi] and
   his wife Anna Maria.
   (Anna Maria Glad, 2nd daughter of Nicholas Glad, married 23
   Apr. 1764, Johannes Keller, only son of Johannes Keller, Sr.)
3. Georg, b. 4 Nov. 1746 in Bern, bp. 13 Nov. in the meeting house.

Died 20 Nov. 1748 Anna Maria Glad, wife of Nicolaus, a born Fischer. She
was a faithful member of this small congregation.

Died 1751 (burial #16): Elisabeth Brecht, widow of Stephan Brecht.
[She was nee Lerch, widow of Joh. Henrich Fischer.] One child to her
marriage with Stephan Brecht:
1. Maria Magdalena Brecht, b. 11 Nov. 1744

Lancaster County, PA, Orphans Court Records:
Held at Lancaster, 8 Aug. 1744. Before Samuel Smith, Conrad Weiser,
Emanuel Carpenter, Esqrs. Justices:
Upon settling account of Addimistrators of estate of **Henry Fisher**, ordered
to be distributed to the Widow, Jacob Fisher, eldest son, Anna Mary,
Susanna and Christian.
Dated 5 Mar. 1747/48: Upon settling the account of Elizabeth Brecht,
widow, (formerly Elizabeth Fisher, widow) Addimistratrix of **Henry Fisher**.
It appears there is a balance to be distributed to said Elizabeth, the Widow,
Jacob Fisher, eldest son, John Christian Fisher and Maria *Cloam*, [?Glad]
the Eldest daughter, by Virtue of a Codocil, Susanna Keen, another
Daughter. John Fisher, Uncle of Jacob Fisher and John Christian Fisher, is
appointed their Guardian.

Dated 6 Mar. 1749/50: Jacob Fisher and Christian Fisher, Orphan children of **Henry Fisher**, late of Heidelberg Twp., Nominated Andrew Boyer to be their Guardian (John Fisher their late guardian being dead.)

David Brecht and Wendell Brecht, the older sons of Stephen Brecht, are appointed guardians over George, Adam, Margaret, Catharine, Mary, Elizabeth and Magdalena, the younger and Orphan children of the said Stephan Brecht, deceased.

27. FISCHER, JOH. WILHELM age 26
Samuel, 1733
S-H, I: 107, 111, 112

EUROPEAN RECORDS

Langenselbold Reformed KB:
Weigel Fischer, son of Jörg Fischer, m. (1) 23 Feb. 1681 Künigunda, daughter of Conrad Adam. They had children:
> 1. Elisabeth, bp. 6 Dec. 1685
>   Sp.: Hans Ruth's daughter, here.
> 2. Philipps, bp. 28 Mar. 1687
>   Sp.: Philipps Adam, son of Conrad Adam, the child's
>   mother's brother.
> 3. Jörg, bp. 3 Feb. 1689; Sp.: Jörg Fuchs.

Weigel Fischer, widower, m. (2) 29 Jan. 1691 Anna, daughter of Johannes Lerch. Children of the second marriage:
> 4. Johan Henrich, bp. 3 Feb. 1692
>   Sp.: Henrich Leimbach, schoolmaster at Alten Hasel
> 5. Johan Conrad, bp. 17 Feb. 1693
>   Sp.: Peter Blum's single son.
> 6. Johannes, bp. 24 May 1696
>   Sp.: the son of Conrad Adam, Sr.
> 7. Johan Henrich, bp. 17 Apr. 1701
>   Sp.: Johannes Leimbach from Alten Haselau, the Organist.
> 8. **Johann Wilhelm,** bp. 11 Apr. 1706
>   Sp.: Wilhelm Roth
> 9. Johan Caspar, bp. 20 Dec. 1709
>   Sp.: Johan Lerch's single son.

Buried 2 July 1719: Anna, wife of Weigel Fischer, age 50 y. 7 mo.
Buried 8 Nov. 1725: Weygel Fischer, age 71 y. 30 mo.

AMERICAN RECORDS

Berks County, PA, Abstracts of Wills & Adm.:
William Fischer, Heidelberg, 2 Nov. 1768, 21 Nov. 1771. To son Peter 4 several pieces of land contiguous in Heidelberg as shown in draught or plan signed with my hand 15 Jan. 1763, paying therefore £270. To son Philip 3 several pieces of land in same township, paying £130 to the executors. To son John 3 tracts in the same township paying to executors £290. To son Michael 3 pieces of land being my present dwelling place, paying £600 to executors. Personal estate to be sold and whole proceeds divided into eleven equal parts - Sons Peter, Philip, John, Henry, Michael, Frantz, Frederick and George, and daughters Elizabeth, Susanna, Rosina all to have one share each. Son Peter and son-in-law John Heckert, executors. Witnesses Michael Schmöhl, Peter Ruth, Frederick Weitzel. Translation. [7 page will].

Hain's (St. John's) Church, Berks Co., Published History:
William Fischer, b. 11 Apr. 1706 in Langenselbold, County of Ronnenburg (Release pub. on pg. 24 of 1916 History of Hain's Church); arrived on ship *Samuel*, 1733. Married 1733 Elisabeth Gertrude Hain, daughter of Georg and Veronica Hain. She was b. 1711 and d. 4 June 1768. William Fisher d. 23 Oct. 1771. Children:

1. Elisabetha Gertrude, b. ca. 1734; m. John Heckert
2. Peter, b. 8 Sept. 1735, d. 23 Nov. 1787; m. 1758 (Waldschmidt) Appollonia Heckert, daughter of Michael Heckert. His will 11 Mar. 1788, Berks Co.
3. Philip, b. 22 Sept. 1736; m. Anna Maria _____ His will dated 12 July 1803. Burial recorded Reading Reformed.
4. John, b. ca. 1738, d. 1812; m. Anna Catharina _____ His will proven 19 Mar. 1812.
5. Henry, b. 1739, d. 1822; m. 28 Sept. 1761 (Waldschmidt) Christina, dau. of the late Casper Durst
6. Michael, b. 1741, d. 1822; m. Catharina Bollman
7. Susanna, b. 1743
8. Rosina, b. 1745; m. 10 Apr. 1764 (Waldschmidt) Peter Grauel, son of Michael Grauel [q.v.]
9. Frantz, bp. 7 June 1747 at Hain's Church Sp.: Frantz Krick and wife
10. Frederick, bp. 11 Mar. 1750 at Hain's Church, d. 17 Oct. 1828; m. Gertrude Faust, b. 15 Feb. 1751
11. Joh. Georg, bp. 3 May 1753; m. Catharine _____

Pennsylvania Archives, Sixth Series, Vol. 6, Rev. Waldschmidt's Records:
Confirmed 4 May 1760 at Cacusy: Wilhelm Fischer's son and daughter.
Confirmed 3 Apr. 1763: Frantz, son of Wilhelm Fischer;

Confirmed 3 Apr. 1763: Wilhelm Fischer's son Friedrich.
Conf. at Cacusy 26 Mar. 1768: Joh. Gorg, son of Wilhelm Fischer.

[NOTE by compiler: It has been assumed that the Joh. Henrich Fischer [q.v.] who also arrived on the ship *Samuel* in 1733 was a brother of Wilhelm, since Weigel Fischer had two sons with that name. However, research in the Langenselbold records revealed that the Joh. Henrich Fischer, 1733 immigrant, was a son of Conrad Fischer. This is proven by the birth of the daughter of Joh. Henrich Fischer in Langenselbold, Anna Maria, bp. 3 Dec. 1721; she later appears in PA, married to Nicholas Glat; the 1733 immigrant Joh. Henrich Fischer, was a brother of other immigrants: see Johannes Fischer, below, 1731 emigrant, and Anna Maria Koch, 1746 emigrant.]

See *Journal of the Berks County Genealogical Society*, Vol. 14, no. 4, Summer, 1994 for article titled "Johan Wilhelm Fischer" by Kenneth L. Fischer, for additional descendants of this large family.

28. FISCHER, JOHANNES
Samuel, 1731
S-H, I: 39, 41, 42
    others on ship: Women: Anna. Children: Fleny.

EUROPEAN RECORDS

Langenselbold Reformed KB:
Conrad Fischer, son of Johannes Fischer, m. 13 Jan 1687 Anna Veronica, daughter of Caspar Schuffert. Conrad Fischer and Anna Veronica had:
1. Anna Catharina, bp. 18 Mar. 1688
     Sp.: The father's sister, daughter of Johannes Fischer
2. Anna Barbara, bp. 25 Sept. 1690
     Sp.: The wife of Johannes Fischer, the child's grandmother
3. Henrich, bp. 24 Feb. 1692
     Sp.: Jost Henrich Weber, a servant at Hans Roth's, born in *Bicken aus dem Fürstenthumb Dillenburg.*
4. Henrich [q.v.], bp. 21 Mar. 1694
     Sp.: Henrich Herger from ?Gonschrod
5. Joh. Melchior, b. 26 Feb. 1696
     Sp.: M. Melchior Tressler, tailor and *Herrschaffl. Fruchtschreiber.*
6. Anna Maria [q.v., Koch], bp. 13 June 1698; [she m. Caspar Koch and she em. in 1746 as a widow.]
     Sp.: Johan Conrad Fischer's wife

7. Magdalena, bp. 27 June 1700
   Sp.: daughter of Joh. Faust
8. Anna, bp. 8 Oct. 1702; [she m. Johann Jörg Kirschner, q.v.]
   Sp.: Anna, daughter of Johannis Döll
9. **Johannes**, bp. 6 June 1706
   Sp.: the child's grandfather, Johannes Fischer

Johannes Fischer, shoemaker's apprentice, son of Conrad Fischer, m. 20 Mar. 1726 Johanna Maria Leimbach, daughter of the late Johann Henrich Leimbach, former Schoolteacher at Kleindorfelden, *Hochgraffl. Hanauischer Jurisdiction.* They had children:
   1. Anna Elisabetha, bp. 26 Feb. 1727
      Sp.: the wife of Henrich Fischer, the father's brother
   2. Anna Veronica, bp. 15 Dec. 1728
      Sp.: daughter of Johannes Koch
   3. Johann Henrich, bp. 1 Oct. 1730
      Sp.: son of Mstr. John. Caspar Belser, shoemaker at Hanau

AMERICAN RECORDS

Heidelberg Moravian Member Catalog, 1746:
Johannes Fischer, Jr. and wife Anna Maria had:
   1. Elisabetha
   2. Heinrich

Heidelberg Moravian KB, Berks Co.:
Died Jan. 1749 Anna Maria Fischer, wife of Johannes Fischer, Jr.

Researchers working on these Fischer families should note that there were two Johannes Fischers who emigrated from this region and became members of the congregation at Heidelberg. When the congregation was organized on 8 Apr. 1745 there were 23 present, including:
   Johannes and Sybilla Fischer [designated in the records as Sr.]
      (see appendix for this emigrant from Eckhartshausen)
   Johannes and Anna Maria Fischer [designated in the records as Jr.]

Johannes Fischer in Kakusy (Cacoosing) and his wife Anna Maria were sp. in 1744 for Anna Maria, daughter of Nicolaus Glat and his wife Anna Maria, nee Fischer, daughter of Heinrich Fischer [q.v.].

Christ "Little Tulpehocken" Church, Berks Co.:
Johannes Fischer and wife had children:
   4. Joh. Heinrich, b. 5 Oct. 1734, bp. 8 Jan. 1735
      Sp.: Joh. Heinrich Adam.

5. Catharina, b. 8 Sept. 1740, bp. 14 Sept. 1740
   Sp.: Johannes Kürschner [q.v. Kirschner] and wife.

[Note: this John Fischer died ca. 1749/50, since a new executor was named for his brother Henry Fischer's estate on 6 Mar. 1749/50, and it is mentioned in Henry's probate records that John Fischer had died.]

29. FREYMAN, GEORG age 33
Samuel, 1739
S-H, I: 256, 259, 261

EUROPEAN RECORDS

Langenselbold Reformed KB:
Leonhard Freÿman, son of Jacob Baltzar Freÿman *von St.----?*, m. 1663 [no other date given] Anna Christina, daughter of Michael Phaar?, former citizen *aus Frankreich.* They had children:
   1. Johannes, bp. 19 Feb. 1665
      Sp.: Hans, son of Görg Schadt
   2. Peter, bp. 10 Feb. 1667
      Sp.: Peter, son of Peter Fuchs
   3. Johan Jacob, bp. 16 Aug. 1668
   4. Adam [?Ernst], bp. - Nov. 1670
   5. Anna Maria, bp. 23 Mar. 1673

Peter Brüning and wife Anna had a daughter Elisabeth, bp. 12 June 1671.

Hans Freÿman, son of the late Lenhard Freÿman, linenweaver, m. 30 Jan. 1696 Elisabeth Brüning, daughter of the late Peter Brüning.
Hans Freymann and Elisabetha had a son:
   Johann Jörg, bp. 10 July 1707
   Sp.: Herr Joh. Jörg Jost, *Bierbrauer* here

Died 25 Jan. 1733: *Meister* Hans Freymann, linenweaver, age 68 y. less 1 mo.

Johann Georg Freÿman, a linenweaver, son of the late Hans Freÿman, master linenweaver and inhabitant here, m. 23 Jan. 1737 Anna Sabina, daughter of Andreas Lörch [q.v.] inhabitant here. [The father Andreas Lerch em. 1738]. They had:
   1. Anna Maria, bp. 21 Sept. 1738, d. 4 Nov. 1738
      Sp.: Joh. Adam Lörch's dau.

AMERICAN RECORDS

Lower Saucon Reformed KB, burial records:
Anna Sabina Freyman, wife of George Freyman, buried 18 Apr. 1802, age 91 years, 4 months, 9 days.
Cemetery Inscription: Sawina Freiman, nee Lerch, daughter of Andreas Lerch, born in Germany 7 Dec. 1710, died 16 Apr. 1802, widow of Georg Freiman.

Tohickon Reformed KB, Bucks Co.:
Georg Fryman and wife were sp. for Anna Sabina, b. 27 Mar. 1760, daughter of Philip Mann and wife Magdalena.

Married 1 Dec. 1761, Jacob Mayer and Elisabeth Freymann.

Northampton County Will Book 4: 424:
George Freyman, Lower Saucon Township, Northampton County; dated 6 Mar. 1790, proven 13 May 1812. Names dear and beloved wife Sabina. Daughters: Catharine, wife of William Baker [Becker]; Elizabeth, wife of Jacob Meyer; Margaret, wife of Michael Beyer; Ann Sabina, wife of Christian Ruch. Wit: John Stout and Peter Lerch.

For more data on Johann Georg and Anna Sabina (Lerch) Freymann, see article by David Green, C.G., F.A.S.G., "The Parents of Nicholas Michel of Northampton County, Pennsylvania: Using Circumstantial Evidence in Pennsylvania German Research" in *The Pennsylvania Genealogical Magazine,* Volume XXXVIII, No. 4, Fall/Winter 1994, pages 322-324.

30. FREYMANN, JACOB
Ann Galley, 1746
S-H, I: 360, 362

EUROPEAN RECORDS

Langenselbold Reformed KB:
Lenhard Freÿman, linenweaver, and wife Christina had a son:
        Ernst, bp. 6 Feb. 1675
        Sp.: Ernst Ermoldt, son of Wörner Ermoldt.

Johan Ernst Freÿman, son of the late Lenhard Freÿman, linenweaver here, m. 3 Jan. 1702   Anna Catharina Bloss, daughter of Hans Bloss from

Wittgenborn. They had a son:
>   Joh. Jacob, bp. 17 Dec. 1702
>   Sp.: Joh. Jacob Hulsinger from Büdingen

Jacob Freÿman, son of the late Ernst Freÿman, m. (1) 13 Feb. 1726
Kunigunda, daughter of the late Friederich Reichhart, former *Mitnachbar*.
[See 1733 em. Ludwig Reichert for her family records.]

Died 19 June 1741 - Jacob Freyman's wife Kunigunda, age 45 y. less 2 mo.

Johann Jacob Freymann, widower here, m. (2) 24 Jan. 1742 Anna
Magdalena Elisabetha, daughter of Johann Georg Koch, also formerly
Unterthanens here.

Johann Jacob Freymann and wife Anna Magdalena Elisabetha had:
>   1. Johann Philipps, bp. 7 Oct. 1742
>   Sp.: Johann Philipps Hartmann, the butcher here
>   2. Johann Henrich Carl, bp. 24 June 1744
>   Sp.: Carl Ermold

AMERICAN RECORDS

Williams Twp. Congregation, Northampton Co., PA:
Joh. Jacob Freyman and wife Magdalena Elisabetha had:
>   a child, b. 28 June 1752, bp. 26 July
>   Sp.: Maria Catharina Kleinhans and Johann Georg Laubach

Tohickon Reformed KB, Bucks Co., PA:
Jacob Freyman and wife Maria Elisabetha had:
>   Maria Sophia, bp. 1 Apr. 1750
>   Sp.: Christopher Wagner and wife

Conf. 1757 in Lower Saucon twp.: Elisabeth Freyman

Jacob Mayer m. 1 Dec. 1761 Elisabeth Freymann.

31. FUCHS, ANTHON
Minerva, 1769
S-H, I: 727
EUROPEAN RECORDS

Langenselbold Reformed KB:
Antonius Fuchs, son of Jörg Fuchs, *Gerichtsschöffen,* m. 15 Feb. 1700
Juliana Mohn, daughter of the late Tönges Mohn, *Mitnachbar* here. Their
son:
>   Johann Peter, bp. 14 Apr. 1709

Joh. Peter Fuchs, son of Tönges Fuchs, inhabitant here m. (1) 17 Feb. 1734
Elisabetha, daughter of the late Conrad Mohn.

Johann Peter Fuchs, widower and inhabitant here, m. (2) 3 Feb. 1740 Anna
Elisabetha, daughter of Wörner Hamburger, (he m. 9 Feb. 1703 Elisabetha
Schieser) also inhabitant here. They had:
>   1. Wörner, bp. 26 Oct. 1740
>   Sp.: Wörner Scherer
>   2. **Antonius**, bp. 5 Sept. 1742
>   Sp.: Wörner Leyss' son here
>   3. Johann Peter, bp. 17 Feb. 1745
>   Sp.: Johann Peter Hamburger, the mother's brother
>   4. Anna Maria, bp. 22 Mar. 1747
>   Sp.: Michael Roht's daughter here
>   5. Johann Michael [q.v.], bp. 12 Jan. 1749
>   Sp.: Wörner Hamburger, the child's mother's youngest brother
>   6. Johann Philips, bp. 25 June 1753
>   Sp.: Johann Philips Döll

AMERICAN RECORDS

Zion's Church (Old Red Church), Orwigsburg, Schuylkill Co., PA:
Anton and Elisabetha Fuchs were sp. for Johann Henrich Hix, bp. 11 July
1773, son of Conrad Hix [q.v.] and wife Anna Maria.

Blue Mountain Reformed KB, Berks Co., PA:
Anthony Fuchs was sp. in 1775 for Anthony Hahn, son of John Hahn [q.v.].

32. FUCHS, JOH. MICHAEL
Charming Molly, 1773
S-H, I: 754
                        EUROPEAN RECORDS

Langenselbold Reformed KB:
Antonius Fuchs, son of Jörg Fuchs, *Gerichtsschöffen,* m. 15 Feb. 1700

Juliana Mohn, daughter of the late Tönges Mohn, *Mitnachbar* here. Their son:
> Johann Peter, bp. 14 Apr. 1709

Joh. Peter Fuchs, son of Tönges Fuchs, inhabitant here m. (1) 17 Feb. 1734 Elisabetha, daughter of the late Conrad Mohn.

Johann Peter Fuchs, widower and inhabitant here, m. (2) 3 Feb. 1740 Anna Elisabetha, daughter of Wörner Hamburger, (Wörner Hamburger m. 9 Feb. 1703 Elisabetha Schieser) also inhabitant here. They had:
1. Wörner, bp. 26 Oct. 1740
   Sp.: Wörner Scherer
2. Antonius [q.v.], bp. 5 Sept. 1742
   Sp.: Wörner Leyss' son here
3. Johann Peter, bp. 17 Feb. 1745
   Sp.: Johann Peter Hamburger, the mother's brother
4. Anna Maria, bp. 22 Mar. 1747
   Sp.: Michael Roht's daughter here
5. **Johann Michael**, bp. 12 Jan. 1749
   Sp.: Wörner Hamburger, the child's mother's youngest brother
6. Johann Philips, bp. 25 June 1753
   Sp.: Johann Philips Döll

AMERICAN RECORDS

Bernville, Berks Co., PA, tombstone inscriptions:

Johan Michael Fuchs	Anna Margaret, his wife
b. in Germany 9 Jan. 1749	b. 9 Dec. 1760
d. 3 Mar. 1815	d. 17 June 1843
	(nee Schwartzhaupt - see below)

Bern Reformed KB, Bern Twp., Berks Co., PA:
John Schwartzhaupt and wife had a daughter:
> Anna Margaretta, bp. 21 Dec. 1760

Berks County, PA, Will Abstracts:
Michael Fuchs, Tulpehocken, 25 Jan. -11 Apr. 1815 (trans). Provides for wife Margaret. To son Peter his farm containing 230 acres; other children mentioned: John, Peter, Catharine. Executor wife Margaret and sons John and Peter. Witnesses John Buchs and John Riegel.

33. FUCHS, JOST
Francis & Elizabeth, 1742
S-H, I: 327, 329

EUROPEAN RECORDS

Langenselbold Reformed KB:
Jörg Fuchs, son of Niclas Fuchs, *Gemeinsmann* here, m. 24 Apr. 1704
Magdalena, daughter of the late Paul Koch. They had a son:
    Jost Henrich, bp. 12 Aug. 1708

Died 19 Dec. 1709: Magdalena, wife of Jörg Fuchs, age 27 y. 2 mo.

Jost Henrich **Fuchs,** son of Georg Fuchs, inhabitant here, m. 30 Jan. 1737
Elisabetha Herchenröder, dau. of Johannes Herchenröder, *Mitnachbar* at
Fischborn. Children:
    1. Johannes, bp. 3 Nov. 1737
        Sp.: Georg Fuch's son, the child's father's brother
    2. Johann Adam, bp. 11 Sept. 1740
        Sp.: Adam Hedderich

AMERICAN RECORDS

Hain's (St. John's) Reformed KB, Berks Co., PA:
Yost Fox (Jost Fuchs) was a sp. in 1755 for a child of Frederick Swartz.

PA Archives, Sixth Series, Vol. 6, Rev. Waldschmidt's Records:
Joh. Adam Fuchs, son of the late Jost Fuchs, m. 20 Mar. 1764 Anna Maria,
daughter of Görg Hain.

Sybilla Fuchs, dau. of the late Jost Fuchs, m. 3 Jan. 1769 Johann Michael
Euler, son of the late Adam Euler.

Berks County, PA, Abstracts of Wills and Adm.:
Yost Fox - Heidelberg, 27 July 1761-25 May 1764.
To son Adam, plantation, horse geers, etc., he paying to dau. Phillipina on
her marriage £30 etc. and household goods. Also provides for wife Elisabeth
during life. Letters c.t.a. to Adam Fox, the widow renouncing. Wit: Jonas
Seely, Johann Gasper Diehl, Abraham Brosius. Letters of Adm. 25 May 1764
to Adam Fox, only son, the widow Anna Elisabeth Fox having renounced.

Adam Fox of Heidelberg; Adm. to Anna Maria Fox, the widow, 16 Apr.
1771.

Berks County Abstracts of Orphans' Court Records:
dated 11 Aug 1781 - John Fuchs (above 14) son of Adam Fuchs of
Heidelberg, dec'd, chooses John Faust for guardian.
Peter Fuchs (above 14) chooses Peter Reedy for guardian.

dated 16 Apr. 1788 - Petition of John Fuchs, eldest son of John Adam Fuchs
of Heidelberg, yeoman, deceased. That his father died intestate about 18
years since, leaving a widow Anna Maria (since married to Jacob Lerch) and
2 children, to wit: the petitioner and Peter, who is yet in his minority. That
intestate was seized of a tract of land in Heidelberg of 130 acres. Prays for
partition or valuation. So ordered.

34. GERHART, CONRAD
Francis & Elizabeth, 1742
S-H, I: 329

EUROPEAN RECORDS

Langenselbold Reformed KB:
The marriage record of Michael Gerhart is not recorded at Langenselbold;
the sponsorship of one of his children indicates that his wife was a daughter
of Johann Görg Stichel from Neuhassel. [Possibly the marriage is entered in
the Neuenhasslau KB].
Michael Gerhart and his wife (NN) had a son:
1. **Johann Conrad,** bp. 7 Mar. 1714
   Sp.: Johannes Schad's son, a single person
2. Susanna Catharina, bp. 6 Sept. 1716
   Sp.: Caspar Lerch's wife
3. Anna Margretha (surname Gereth) bp. 29 Aug. 1719
4. Johann Georg (Gereth), bp. 29 May 1724
   Sp.: Johann Görg Stichel, the child's
   mother's brother from Neuhassel.

AMERICAN RECORDS

Lancaster Co. Land Records, Warrants, Surveys & Patents:
25 Nov. 1743: Conrad Gerhard warranted 100 Acres in Tulpehocken Twp.
between lands of Mathias Wagoner and Mathis Smith.
Return of survey: 22 Dec. 1783 to Jacob Smith.

Quittopahilla Reformed KB, near Annville, Lebanon Co., PA:
Johann Conradt Gerhart and his wife had a son:
      Johann Conradt bp. 14 June 1747
      Sp.: Henrich Köllicker and wife.

Johann Conradt Gerhart and his wife were sp. for Anna Maria, bp. 12 Nov. 1745, dau. of Heinrich Koellicker and wife; and they again sp. in 1748 Maria, dau. of Hans Ulrich Jaegeli and Liesbeth.

35. GERHARD, WILHELM
GERHARD, FRIEDRICH
Samuel, 1739
S-H, I: 256, 259, 261

EUROPEAN RECORDS

Niedermittlau Reformed KB:
Georg Gerhardt from Langen Selbold, surviving son of Georg Gerhard, deceased *Nachbar*, married (1) 26 Feb. 1673 Anna, daughter of Carl Ruppert, *Nachbar* at Nieder Mittlau. They had children:
1. Johannes, twin, bp. 26 Nov. 1673
   Sp.: Johannes, son of Carl Ruppert.
2. Catharina, twin, bp. 26 Nov. 1673
   Sp.: Catharina Gerhard, sister of the father.
3. Johannes Georg, bp. 27 Jan. 1675
   Sp.: Johannes Ruppert, son of Carl Ruppert.
4. Joh. Henrich, bp. 28 Jan. 1677
   Sp.: Henrich Gerhard, brother of the father.

Georg Gerhardt's [first] wife died 29 Dec. 1678.

Georg Gerhart, *Nachbar* at Mittlau, widower, m. (2) 14 May 1679 Anna, daughter of Thomas ?Lufft, former *Nachbar* at Schlierbach. They had:
5. Joh. Henrich, bp. 25 Feb. 1680
   Sp.: Henrich Ruppert, son of Carl Ruppert.
6. A son **[Wilhelm]**, b. 24 Feb. 1683, bp. 4 Mar. 1683
   Sp.: Joh. Wilhelm Klosterman
7. Peter, b. 1 Jan. 1686, bp. 5 Jan. 1686
   Sp.: Peter Helmud
8. Catharina, b. 30 Dec. 1692; bp. 5 Jan. 1693
   Sp.: Catharina, wife of the swineherd at Nieder Mittl(au).

Langenselbold Reformed KB:
Died 1 Apr. 1711, Hans Jörg Gerhard, *Gemeinsman* here, age 67 years.
Died 12 Mar. 1727 at Langenselbold: Master Georg Gerhard's widow from Nied(er)Mitlau, named Anna. Her age about 66 years.

Wilhelm Gerhard, master cartwright from Nieder Mittlau, son of Jörg Gerhard, m. at Langenselbold 17 Nov. 1707 Anna Elisabet(h), widow of the deceased Johann Faust. Her first marriage, recorded 23 June 1701, reveals that she was a daughter of Johannes Keÿser, master cartwright and inhabitant at Langenselbold. Wilhelm Gerhart (surname also spelled Geret, Geerdt) and wife Anna Elisabeth had children:

1. Anna Elisabeth, bp. 14 Dec. 1710
   Sp.: Peter Döll's single daughter here
2. Johann Henrich, bp. 30 July 1712, d. 23 May 1714
   Sp.: Joh. Henrich Gerhard at Neuenhassel
   (Neuenhasslau), the child's father's brother
3. **Friderich,** bp. 31 Mar. 1715
   Sp.: Joh. Friedrich Richter, *der Pfarrknecht*
4. Anna Maria, bp. 24 July 1718, d. 29 Apr. 1725
   Sp.: Peter Lamb's wife, the child's mother's sister

Died 10 Dec. 1733 - Anna Elisabetha, wife of Wilhelm Gerets, the master cartwright, age 57 years less 1 month and several days. [See **Keÿser** for additional data on her lineage].

Friederich Gerhard, cartwright, son of Wilhelm Gerhard, master cartwright here, m. (1) 2 Jan. 1737 at Langenselbold Anna Elisabeth, daughter of Jost Henrich Fischer, master shoemaker here. She was bp. 5 Sept. 1714, daughter of Jost Henrich Fischer (son of Conrad Fischer) and his wife Anna Elisabeth nee Drechssler (daughter of Melchior Drechssler).
Friederich Gerhard and wife Anna Elisabetha had:

1. Johann Peter, bp. 3 Nov. 1737
   Sp.: Peter Lamm's son here

AMERICAN RECORDS

Heidelberg Moravian KB, Berks Co., PA:
Friedrich Gerhard from Langensel*bot*, Amt Ronnerburg in Graffschaft Ÿsenburg, was born at that place 26 Mar. 1715 new style and baptized on 31 Mar. by the pastor at that place, d. 30 Nov. 1779. His father was Wilhelm Gerhart from Graffschaft Ysenburg - Merhols .... and his mother Elisabeth, born Keyser. He was married in Jan. 1737 to Miss (Elisabeth and Barbara both crossed out) daughter of Jost Heinrich Fischer, citizen of Langensel*bot* and his wife Elisabeth. They had a child:

1. Peter, born in Langensel*bot* on 28 Oct. 1737 and bp. on 30 Oct.
   by Pastor Ruth of that place. Sp. was Peter Lamm.

Friedrich Gerhard was married, 2nd, on 14 Feb. 1740 in the Tulpehocken Reformed church by Pastor Johann Philipp Böhm, to Miss Barbara Reiger, born 5 Apr. 1719, in Bicken [Benken, Canton Baselland, Switzerland], daughter of Anton Reiger and wife Judith Schaub. In this marriage they had the following children:

1. Conrad, born in Bern twp., Lancaster Co., 11 Nov. [o.s.] 1740. Bapt. in the Reformed church in Bern 22 Nov. by Pastor Rieger. Sp. were Conrad Kirschner and his mother Barbara Kirschner.
2. Elisabeth, born in Heidelberg, 29 Sept. 1742, [o.s.] bp. by Philipp Maurer, Lutheran Pastor in Tulpehocken, on 1 Nov. in the parents' home. Sp.: Johannes Zerbe and Sybilla Fischer.
3. Friedrich, born in Heidelberg, 12 Sept. [o.s.] 1744?, bp. in Tobias Beckel's house on 23 Sept. by Brother Paul Daniel Brizelio. Sp. were Friedrich Bekel and his wife Anna Elisabeth.
4. Johannes, born in Heidelberg, 1 Feb. [o.s.] 1747, Sunday evening at six o'clock and bp. 3 Feb. at public song service by Brother Johannes Brucker ?, Lutheran minister at the Tulpehocken church. Sp.: Tobias Bekel, Johannes Meyer, Stephan Brecht, Nicolaus Glat, Johannes Keller and G. Heisser.
5. Anna Maria, b. in Heidelberg, 2 June [o.s.] 1749, bp. 18 June, the 4th Sunday after Trinity, by Christian Rauch in the meeting house of the Brethren. Sp.: Christina Beckel, Margaretha Meyer, Barbara Stoer and Hanna Heibert.
6. Jacob, born in Heidelberg 21 Dec. 1751, and bp. on Christmas Day, o.s., by Brother Matthes Reüs after the public service. Sp.: Tobias Boeckel, Johannes Meyer, Jacob Conrad, Peter Frey, Henrich Stör and Jacob Müller.
7. Anton, born in the evening of 10 Feb. 1754, bp. 12 Feb. by Brother Anton Wagner. Sp.: Tobias Böckel, Johannes Meyer, Niclaus Glät and Jacob Creter. Anton died on 26 Nov. 1754 and was buried on the 27th in our God's acre in Heidelberg, age 40 weeks less one day.
8. Anna Rosina, b. early in the day on 29 Oct. 1755 and was bp. 2 Nov. by Brother Antony Wagner. Sp.: Christina Böckel, Maria Margaretha Meyer, Barbara Creter and Barbara Stöhr.
9. Catharina, born on Monday, 2 Oct. 1758 and bp. 5 Oct. by Brother Anton Wagner. Sp.: Elisabeth Wagner, Christina Bökel, Maria Margaret Meyer, Eva Catharina Brandel.

Burial record, # 71: Friedrich Gerhard was born in the Wetterau in County Ysenberg, in Langen-Selbot [sic], Mar. 26, 1715. He married, first, on Jan. 28, 1737, and in this marriage had a son Peter. After being a widower, he married (his now) widow Barbara born Rieger, on Feb. 14, 1740, and soon thereafter came to this land [note here a discrepancy in a primary source record.]. He came to Heidelberg in 1742. In his second marriage he had 5 sons and 4 daughters, and he was survived by 24 grandchildren. He died Nov. 30, 1779.

Burial record, # 95: Barbara Gerhard, born Rieger, was born 5 Apr. 1719 in Binken [Benken, Canton Baselland, Switzerland]. On Feb. 14, 1740, she married widower Friedrich Gerhard here in America. [note discrepancy with above burial record; this one is correct.] They were blessed with 5 sons and 4 daughters, of whom one son died. When her husband died on Nov. 30, 1779, she already had 24 grandchildren, since then some died, but when she died she was survived by 36 grandchildren and 3 great-grandchildren. She died Feb. 9, 1794, age 75 years, 10 months and 3 days.

It is also recorded in the Heidelberg Moravian KB that a grown-up boy, Conrad Gerhard, moved to Bethlehem on 26 Oct. 1758.

Land Warrant, Penn Twp., Berks Co., PA:
Frederick Gerhard, 69 acres. Surveyed 22 Apr. 1754 on a warrant dated 4 Sept. 1751. Patented 25 May 1765 to Jacob Miller.

Berks County, PA, Abstracts of Wills:
Frederick Gerhart, Heidelberg, 26 Nov. 1779 - 27 Dec. 1779.
Provides for wife Barbara. To son Jacob my land and plantation and all belonging to it after 4 years at appraised value. All estate in equal shares to nine children: Peter, Conrad, Elisabeth, Frederick, John, Mary, Jacob, Rosina and Catharine. Sons Frederick and John executors. Wit: George Brendle, John Meyer (trans.).

Philadelphia Moravian KB, deaths:
Conrad Gerhard, hatter, b. 22 Nov. 1740 in Heidelberg, Berks Co.,
d. 24 Feb. 1815.

Nat. by affirmation, 24 Sept. 1755, Frederick Gerhart, Heidleburgh Twp., Berks Co., PA.

[It will be noted that the European data given above disproves the statements concerning the descent of this family from the noted hymnist Paul Gerhardt, as found in Morton Montgomery's *Genealogical and Biographical History of Berks County* published in 1909, and copied many times since by descendants.]

36. GLEBER, MICHAEL
Ann Galley, 1746
S-H, I: 360 [appears on list as Klawer]

EUROPEAN RECORDS

Langenselbold Reformed KB:
Johan Henrich Kleber, *Ochsenhirt,* m. 18 Apr. 1695 Gerdraut, daughter of
Christoffel Spindler, *Fasbinder* here. They had a son:
1. Johan Michael, bp. 26 Jan. 1696
   Sp.: Michael Spindler, *der Fassbinder* here
2. Andreas, bp. 10 Oct. 1699; sp.: Andreas Schneider

Johann **Michael Gleber,** *Schäfferknecht,* son of the late Joh. Henrich Gleber,
former *Gemeinenhirt* here, m. 12 June 1726 Anna Magdalena, daughter of
the late Melchior Mell, former inhabitant and *Landreuther* here. (Melchior
Mell, son of Conrad Mell, m. 30 Nov. 1687 Anna Barbara Faust, daughter
of Johan Faust.) Michael Gleber and wife Anna Magdalena had:
1. Johannes, bp. 23 Feb. 1727, d. 23 Mar. 1727
   Sp.: the child's father's brother
2. Anna Rosina, bp. 1 Sept. 1728
   Sp.: The child's mother's younger single sister
3. Anna Elisabetha, bp. 22 Apr. 1731
   Sp.: The daughter of Johannes Hebener here
4. Maria Elisabetha, bp. 29 Nov. 1733
   Sp.: A servant girl
5. Magdalena, bp. 6 July 1738
   Sp.: daughter of Georg Scherer
6. Johann Henrich, bp. 18 Apr. 1742
   Sp.: J.Henrich Isler
7. Johann Melchior, bp. 9 Feb.1746
   Sp.: Johann Henrich Eckert's son

AMERICAN RECORDS

Michael Tepper, Ed., *Emigrants to Pennsylvania 1641-1819,* an article titled
"Account of Servants Bound and Assigned Before James Hamilton, Mayor
of Philadelphia.":
dated 29 Sept. 1746:
Anne Elizabeth Klevering in consideration of thirteen pistoles and a half
paid Benjamin Shoemaker for her passage from Holland with consent of her
father indents herself servant to Henry Van Aken his Exc. for seven years
from this date to have customary dues.

dated 30 Sept. 1746:
Maria Elizabeth Cleverin in consideration ten pistoles paid Benjamin
Shoemaker for her passage from Holland indents herself servant to
Elizabeth Holton of Philadelphia widow, her Exc. for eight years from this
date when free to have customary dues and half a pistole.

Trinity (Reading) Lutheran KB, Berks Co., PA:
Dietrich Sinn of Heidelberg twp. m. 2 Oct. 1754 Anna Elisabeth Kloeberin,
daughter of Michael Kloeber.

Hain's (St. John's) Reformed KB, Berks Co., PA:
Michael Kleber and wife were sp. in 1748 for Magdalena, daughter of
Ludwig Mohn [q.v.].

37. GLEIM, JOH. MICHAEL
Samuel, 1731
S-H, I: 39, 40, 41, 42
   others on ship: Susan (wife) and Elisabeth (child)

EUROPEAN RECORDS

Langenselbold Reformed KB:
Mstr. Joh. Michael Gliem, shoemaker, son of Mstr. Philip Gliem also
shoemaker, m. 20 Feb. 1726 Anna Susanna Elisabetha Weber, daughter of
the late Mstr. Friederich Weber, former carpenter at Ravoltzhausen. They
had children:
   1. Magdalena Elisabetha, bp. 12 Jan. 1727
      Sp.: The wife of Mstr. Philips Gliem, shoemaker,
      the child's grandmother
   2. Anna Margretha, bp. 9 Oct. 1729
      Sp.: The wife of Joh. Georg Tag from Ravoltzhausen

AMERICAN RECORDS

A History of the Beginnings of Moravian Work in America, **Publications of The
Archives of the Moravian Church, No. 1 (1955), pg. 136:**
"John Adam Gruber joined the "Inspired" on the estate of Count Ernst
Casimir von Isenburg-Buedingen, in Wetteravia, where such places as
Marienborn, Herrnhaag and the Ronneburg Castle are located."

"A group of *Inspirierte* came to Pennsylvania, led by Gruber, Gleim and Blasius Mackinet, settled in Germantown probably in 1731, for Gleim "qualified" as an inhabitant on August 17, 1731. (See Hinke, *Life and Letters of John Philip Boehm*, pg. 257.) John Michael Gleim or Cleim is listed as a deacon of the Whitemarsh Reformed Church, 28 Oct. 1734; in 1747 became a trustee for this church's Whitpain land, and in 1749 acted as a bondsman for John Philip Boehm, Jr."

38. GRAUEL, MICHAEL age 32
Elizabeth, 1733
S-H, I: 113, 114, 115, 765-767
with Ann Eliza, age 23 and Anna Catharina age 3½, Conrad, age 3½ (error in age?)

EUROPEAN RECORDS

Langenselbold Reformed KB:
Conrad Grauel, born in Schlüchtern, a baker here, m. 7 June 1688 Helena, daughter of Henrich Dieterich, former resident here. [See Dieterich data under immigrant Anton Faust]. They had children:
1. Johan Peter, bp. 5 Mar. 1692 at Selbold
   Sp.: Johan Peter Muth, schoolteacher.
2. Anna Elisabeth, bp. 7 July 1693; she m. 1717 Joh. Peter Faust
   [q.v., em. 1733]; Sp.: the wife of Clos Schieser.
3. Johan Heinrich, bp. 1 Apr. 1696
   Sp.: Henrich Kirschner, single son of Joh. Kürschner here.
4. Elisabeth, bp. 20 July 1698; she m. 1728 Anton Wacker.
   Sp.: the single daughter of Clos Schieser.

Conrad Grauel, the baker here, d. 30 June 1700, age 44 or 45 years. One child was born to his widow after his death:
5. **Johan Michael**, bp. 16 Jan. 1701, son of Helena,
   the widow of the late Conrad Grauel.
   Sp.: Michael Faust, single son of the late Johan Faust.

Helena, widow of Conrad Grauel, m. (2) 18 May 1701 Michael Faust, son of the late Johann Faust. They had one child:
1. Joh. Peter Faust, bp. 25 Nov. 1704

Joh. Michael Grauel, son of the late *Meister* Conrad Grauel, baker here, m. 9 Feb. 1729 Anna Elisabetha, daughter of Emanuel Roth, inhabitant here. They had:

1. Anna Catharina, bp. 6 Nov. 1729
   Sp.: The child's mother's eldest single sister, daughter of Emanuel Roth.
2. Johann Conrad, bp. 7 Oct. 1731
   Sp.: The son of Tönges Schiesser.

AMERICAN RECORDS

Hain's (St. John's) Reformed KB, Lower Heidelberg Township, Berks Co.:
Michael Grauel and wife had:
   A son, bp. 1 Jan. 1752; sp.: John Eckert [q.v.] and wife
   Maria Elisabeth, bp. 20 Mar. 1754
      Sp.: Antonius Faust [q.v.] and wife
   A son, bp. 24 Jan. 1756; sp.: Conrad Hart and wife

1754 Berks County, PA. Tax List: Cumru Twp., Michael Crowl.

PA Archives, Sixth Series, Vol. 6: Rev. John Waldschmidt's records:
(Reformed Pastor serving congregations in Lancaster and Berks counties):
Peter Grauel, son of Michael Grauel, m. 10 Apr. 1764 Rosina, daughter of Wilhelm Fischer [q.v.].

Conf. 28 Apr. 1765 in Bern twp. at Eppler's Church: Michael Grauel's daughter Maria Sara.
Conf. 28 Apr. 1765: Johannes Dauber, Michael Grauel's step-son.

Elisabeth, daughter of Michael Grauel, was sp. in 1765 for a child of Daniel Zacharias.

First Reformed KB, Philadelphia, Pa:
There was a Peter Grauel buried 25 Feb. 1791, aged 52 years, 2 months. It is not known if this was a member of this Grauel family or another.

Christ (Little Tulpehocken) Lutheran KB, Jefferson Twp., Berks Co.:
Catharine Krauel was a sponsor in 1746 for a daughter of Philip Petry and his wife. Johann Michael Krauel and his wife were sp. in 1736 and 1741 for children of Joh. Georg Petry and his wife [Sabina Roth, q.v., also from Langenselbold. She was a sister of Michael Grauel's wife.]

Michael Growl, Cumru Twp., Berks Co., PA, Nat. 24-25 Sept. 1761.

[A quarterly newsletter titled *Crowl Connections* is published by the Crowl Family Association. For additional information on this publication, contact Gail Komar, 9603 Bel Glade St., Fairfax, VA 22031-1105.]

39. HAHN (HAAN), JOH. THOMAS
HAHN (HAAN), JOHANNES
Ann Galley, 1746
S-H, I: 359, 361

EUROPEAN RECORDS

Langenselbold Reformed KB:
Died 7 May 1748: Conrad Han, age about 85 or 86 years.
Died 5 Jan. 1747: *Meister* Conrad Hoyn, *Schneider*, age 66 y. less about 3 mo.

Conrad Han from ?Wallroth ___?Esslischer jurisdiction m. 3 Nov. 1698
Margaretha, dau. of Wörner Repp, the *Bürckmüller*. They had children:
   1. **Johan Thomas**, bp. 25 Aug. 1699
      Sp.: Thomas Götz from Mittelgründau
   2. Johannes, bp. 25 May 1702
      Sp.: Johannes Reyel, linenweaver at Wächtersbach
   3. Anna Margretha, bp. 9 Aug. 1705
      Sp.: the wife of Anton Repp, the young *Bürckmüller*.
   4. Johanna Magdalena, bp 20 May 1708
      [She m. 1736 immigrant Johannes Reber, q.v.]
      Sp.: The child's father's brother and mother's sister
   5. Johann Henrich, bp. 24 Dec. 1712
      Sp.: Henrich Rep, the mother's brother

Johan Thomas Hähn, son of Conrad Hahn, m. 21 Feb. 1731 Anna
Catharina, daughter of the late Johannes Keyser.
   1. **Johannes,** bp. 8 Aug. 1731
      Sp.: Johannes Repp, the *Geissmüller*
   2. Johann Henrich, bp. 7 Apr. 1734
      Sp.: The child's father's younger brother, single
   3. Augusta Maria, bp. 14 Dec. 1738
      Sp.: *Herr von Eÿsenbergs Jungfrau Haushälterin Augusta Maria Mohr von Dillenberg.*
   4. Angelica, bp. 1 May 1743
      Sp.: The wife of Niclaus Wacker, *Burgmüller*.

AMERICAN RECORDS

St. Michael's Lutheran KB, Germantown, PA:
Thomas Hahn and wife Catharina, Reformed, had a son:
      Daniel, b. 30 Sept. 1746

Blue Mountain KB, Berks Co., PA:
John Hahn and wife (not named) had children:
   1. Justina Maria, b. 17 Nov. 1767, bp. 26 Dec. 1767
      Sp.: John Rohn and wife.
   2. Maria Catharina, b. 10 Apr. 1770, bp. 24 June 1770
      Sp.: Catharina Hahn, widow.
   3. John Jacob, bp. 12 Apr. 1772; sp.: Jacob Lang and wife.
   4. Anthony, bp. 14 May 1775; sp.: Anthony Fuchs [q.v.] & wife.

Abstracts of Berks County Wills & Adm.
Thomas Hahn, Tulpehocken, 6 Mar. 1758, adm. to Catharine Hahn, the widow and John eldest son.

John Hahn, Tulpehocken, 25 July 1776, adm. to Maria Christina Hahn, the widow.
[Maria Christina, wife of John Hahn, is named as a daughter of Henry Shuckert of Heidelberg Twp. in Shuckert's will dated 24 Apr. 1772, probated 13 Aug. 1773. See immigrant Heinrich Schuchert from Eckartshausen in Appendix C.]

Abstracts of Berks County Orphan's Court Records:
Dated 22 Aug. 1782: petition of Mary Christina Hahn, admx. of John Hahn of Tulpehocken, Yeoman, deceased. She states that John Hahn died intestate seized of considerable real and personal estate, leaving 4 children, one of whom Anna Mary is yet under 14 years of age. Prays for guardian. Court appoints Tobias Schucker. Justina Hahn (above 14) chooses John Albert for guardian. Michael Hahn (above 14) chooses Michael Hornberger. Catharine Hahn (above 14) chooses Jacob Long.
[John Hahn had 140 acres of land in Tulpehocken.]

In 1787, another entry in the Orphan's Court records indicates that Anna Maria Hahn (now above 14), daughter of John Hahn of Bern, deceased, chooses her husband William Berger for guardian.

40. HAHN, JOHANNES
Several in S-H
Possibly on S-H, I: 668, 670, 671

EUROPEAN RECORDS

Langenselbold Reformed KB:
Conrad Han m. 3 Nov. 1698 Margretha, daughter of Wörner Repp. [See

immigrant Joh. Thomas Hahn for more detail on their family.] Their son:
Johannes, bp. 25 May 1702

Mstr. Johannes Hoÿn, shoemaker, son of Conrad Hoÿn, tailor, m. __ Feb.
1731 Anna Maria Elisabetha, (she d. 19 June 1741, age 37 y. less 4 mo.)
daughter of Hans Freÿmann, linenweaver. (Hans Freÿman m. 30 Jan. 1696
Elisabetha Brüning). Children, surname Han, Hoÿn, Hahn:
  1. Anna Catharina, bp. 14 June 1733, d. 17 June 1733
     Sp.: Eldest daughter of Michael Gereth
  2. Anna Philippina, bp. 29 Aug. 1734, d. 22 Aug. 1741
     Sp.: The wife of Johan Henrich Hübener
  3. Johann Adam, bp. 23 Sept. 1736, d. 19 Mar. 1742
     Sp.: *Mstr.* Joh. Adam Stamm, *Wagner* here
  4. **Johannes**, bp. 11 June 1738
     Sp.: The son of Mstr. Joh. Henrich Braumüller, linenweaver

Mstr. Johannes Hoÿn, widower and shoemaker here, m. 3 Jan. 1742 Anna
Margretha, daughter of the late Mstr. Jost Caspar Wolff, also inhabitant and
tailor. Several more children to this second marriage.

AMERICAN RECORDS

Pastoral Records, Rev. Thomas Pomp, Northampton County, PA:
Johannes Hain, son of Johann & Maria Hain, b. 15 June 1740 in Langen-
Sel*burg*; married to A. Maria Rihel for 29 years; only 1 daughter survives
and 3 grand children. Died Wed. at 4 a.m., age 63 years less 7 days., buried
10 June 1803 in Williams Township.

41. HAMBURGER, MICHAEL
Edinburgh, 1750
S-H, I: 429

EUROPEAN RECORDS

Langenselbold Reformed KB:
Johannes Hamburger, son of the late Herman Hamburger, former citizen of
Steinau an der Strasse, m. (1) 25 Feb. 1675 Maria, daughter of Conrad Mell.
No children listed in baptismal record.
Johannes Hamburger, widower, m. (2) 30 July 1678 Anna Elisabeth,
daughter of Bastian Leis. They had a son:
  1. Wörner, bp. 27 Apr. 1679; sp.: Wörner Schieser.

Johannes Hamburger m. (3) 10 Jan 1684 Margretha, daughter of Clos Eychelbörner. They had:
2. Anna Catharina, bp. 15 Oct. 1688
3. Joh. Peter, bp. 2 Sept. 1691; sp.: son of Lenhard Freyman.

Buried 10 Sept. 1741: Johannes Hamburger, an old married man, *u. Christr. Mitbruder*, age 87 y. 4 mo.

Wörner Hamburg(er), son of Johann Hamburger, m. 9 Feb. 1702 Elisabetha Schieser, daughter of Nicklas Schieser. They had children:
1. Johann Peter, bp. 11 Mar. 1703
   Sp.: single son of Tönges Schieser
2. Wörner, bp. 1 Jan. 1706
   Sp.: Wörner Leiss, single son of Christoffel Leiss.
3. Johannes, bp. 17 Jan. 1709
   Sp.: Johannes Hamborger, the child's grandfather.
4. Anton, bp. 11 Oct. 1711; sp.: Anton Rep.
5. Anna Elisabeth, bp. 25 Nov. 1716
   Sp.: the child's mother's sister, wife of Conrad Mohn.
6. Conrad, bp. 11 June 1719; sp.: Conrad Mohn.
7. **Johan Michael**, bp. 25 Oct. 1722
   Sp.: Michael Faust, church *Baumeister* here.

AMERICAN RECORDS

1754 Berks County tax list, Tulpehocken Twp.: Michael Hambarger

Christ "Little Tulpehocken" Church, Berks Co.:
Michel Hamburger (& wife) had a daughter:
   Catharina Margretha, b. 10 Sept. 1751, bp. 17 Sept. 1751
   Sp.: Joh. Georg Münch and Catharina Gütmann

Blue Mountain (Zion) Reformed KB, North Tulpehocken Twp., Berks Co.:
Michael Hambarger and wife had:
   Catharina, bp. 25 Feb. 1753; Sp.: William Giesseman and wife

Michael Hamberger and wife sp. in 1766 a child of John Rohn; in 1767 a child of Michael Braun; Michael Hamberger sp. in 1772 a son of Simon Kern.

Rev. Daniel Schumacher's Pastoral Records:
Michell Hamburger and Anna Catharina had a daughter:
   Justina Maria, bp. 7 Nov. 1756, 14 days old, at the Northkill Church
   Sp.: Johannes Rohn and Anna Justina.

Abstracts of Berks County Wills & Adm.:
Michael Hamburger, Tulpehocken Twp., Feb. 28, 1803 adm. granted to John Riegel, son-in-law.

Naturalized Fall, 1965, Michael Hambergher, Tulpehoccon Twp., Berks Co.

42. HEDERICH, JOH. ADAM
Francis & Elizabeth, 1742
S-H, I: 327, 329 (John Adam (+) Heydrig)

EUROPEAN RECORDS

Langenselbold Reformed KB:
Michael Haderich and wife Anna Maria had:
    1. Johan Adam, bp. 31 Oct. 1703
        Sp.: Adam Schad, *Schlosser* here

Johann Adam Hederich, son of the late Michael Hedderich, former swineherder here, m. 12 Jan. 1724 Anna Catharina, daughter of Ernst Ermold. They had:
    1. Elisabetha, bp. 8 Nov. 1724
        Sp.: Johannes Rudel's daughter

Died 20 Apr. 1727: Anna Catharina, wife of Joh. Adam Hederich (in childbirth), age 28 y. less 3 mo. and some days.

Joh. Adam Hedderich, widower, m. (2) 3 Mar. 1728 Anna Margretha, daughter of the late *Herr* Joh. Henrich Leimbach, former schoolteacher at Kleindorfelden, Graffschaft Hanau.

AMERICAN RECORDS

Lower Heidelberg Twp. (today Berks Co. PA), Land Warrants:
Adam Hetrich, tract called "Hermanton" containing 105 acres, 96 perches, 1749. Book C-78-232.

Rev. John Caspar Stoever's marriage records:
John Ermentrout m. 22 May 1743 Anna Elizabetha Hedderich, Bern, (also recorded in Christ "Little Tulpehocken" Lutheran KB)

Chalkley's Chronicles, Vol. 3, pg. 141:
Augusta County, VA, Will Book V: 362:
Dated 5 Jan. 1775- Adam Hadrick's will, farmer. (Legacies) to grandson
John Ermontrout; to daughter, Elisabeth Coutts; to great grandson, George
Ermontrout; to aforesaid John Ermontrout's brother, Henry Ermontrout.
Exec: above named John Ermontrout. Wit: Jacob Nicholas, Felix Gilbert and
3 Germans. Proved: 20 June 1775 by Nicholas & Gilbert. John Armentrout
qualifies with Jacob Nicholas.

Chalkley's Chronicles, Vol. 1, pg. 321:
Augusta Co., VA, county court judgments: August, 1760:
Hetrick vs. Counts and wife. Adam Hetrick, in 1742 [sic; note record above
1743], then living in PA, married his daughter Elizabeth to John
Harmantrout, deceased by 1759. In 1752 Adam (Hetrick) came to VA and
purchased land of Jacob Pence. John (Ermentrout) died in 1753 leaving a
widow and two children. Elizabeth (Hetrick, Ermentrout) intermarried with
John Counts.

Chalkley's Chronicles, Vol. 1, pg. 336:
Augusta Co., VA, county court judgments: August, 1762:
Nicholas and Hetrick vs. Pence and Pence. Jacob Nicholas and Adam
Hetrick, in 1747, came to Augusta from PA. Jacob Pence left a son Jacob,
his eldest, and heir-at-law. Jacob, Sr. and Valentine Pence were brothers.
Valentine left Adam, his eldest son and heir, an infant 14 years old (in
1762). Jacob also had a son George.

---

43.   HEDDERICH, CARL
          with HEDDERICH, CASPAR [q.v.]
          and HEDDERICH, GEORG [q.v.]
Ann Galley, 1746
S-H, I: 360, 361
                    EUROPEAN RECORDS

Langenselbold Reformed KB:
Jörg Roth, son of the old *Hoffman* Conr. Roth, m. (1) 9 Nov. 1681 Anna
Maria, dau. of Henrich Hoffmann of Büdingen.

Jörg Roth m. (2) 28 Apr. 1692 Anna Catharina Niedenthal.

Died 1 Nov. 1736 - Anna Maria widow of the late Michael Hedderich,
herdsman, age about 80 years. [He is mentioned in various records as *Hirt,*

Rosshirt, Schweinhirt].

Carl Johan Henrich Hädderich, son of Michael Hedderich *aus Sachsen*, now herdsman at Neuen Hasslau, m. 15 Jan. 1705 Elisabeth, daughter of Jörg Roth, *Hoffman* here. They had:
1. Joh. Caspar [q.v.], bp. 5 May 1706
   Sp.: The mother's brother, single son of Jörg Roth
2. Joh. Jörg, b. 8 Mar. 1708
   Sp.: Joh. Jörg M-----? from Coburg
3. Conrad, bp. 30 June 1709
   Sp.: Conrad Reber, single son of Michael Rebert
4. Johan Jörg [q.v.], bp. 21 Oct. 1711
   Sp.: Joh. Jorg Niedenthal, smith and innkeeper at Closterberg
5. Christian Ludwig, bp. 24 Dec. 1713, d. 28 Nov. 1734, age 21
6. Anna Elisabetha, bp. 13 Sept. 1716
   Sp.: The wife of Carl Hedderich, the child's father's brother
7. Maria Catharina, bp. 10 Mar. 1719
   Sp.: The child's father's single sister
8. Johannes, bp. 26 Dec. 1720 [em. 1738, q.v.]
   Sp.: Hans Reber
9. Joh. Adam, bp. 23 July 1724; died 10 May 1725, age 1 year less 2 months and several days.
   Sp.: The father's youngest brother

AMERICAN RECORDS

Abstracts of Berks County Wills & Adm:
Charles Hedrick, Heidelberg, 24 Oct. 1757, adm. to George Hedrick, second son, Casper Hedrick oldest son having left the province three years ago.

Chalkley's Chronicles, Vol. 1, pg. 360:
Augusta Co., VA, county court judgments: March, 1770:
Hetrick vs. Hetrick- Chancery. Filed 28 Aug. 1768. In 1752-53, John Hetrick [q.v.], defendant, brother of Caspar Hetrick [q.v.], orator, went from PA to the back part of this Colony (VA) and purchased land from John Bombgardner and then returned to PA where the orator then lived. Land was cheap and the range for cattle good and fresh. Orator and defendant came to VA and settled on the land bought by John. William Frazer had entered a piece of land near which he gave to orator, but John sold to Peter Tresser [elsewhere Tresler; see Dressler]. This caused trouble between the brothers and orator built his own house on first piece of land. Orator heard defendant would not give him the land and removed his family to the house of Adam Hetrick [q.v.] and sent his neighbors, Valentine Pence and Frederick Harmentrout, to defendant to know his intentions. Orator moved

back on the land and had been living there 14 years in 1768. Bill to compel John to convey to him.

44. HEDDERICH, GEORG
Ann Galley, 1746
S-H, I: 360, 361
EUROPEAN RECORDS

Langenselbold Reformed KB:
Johan Melchior Mell, son of Conrad Mell, m. 30 Nov. 1687 Anna Barbara, dau. of Johan Faust. Their daughter:
>   Anna Rosina, bp. 3 Feb. 1709
>   Sp.: the wife of Hans Faust, the child's mother's brother.
>   [Another daughter of the Mells married Joh. Michael Gleber [q.v.], also an immigrant on the *Ann* Galley in 1746.]

Joh. George Hederich, son of Carl Hederich, inhabitant here, m. 24 Feb. 1734 Anna Rosina, daughter of the late Melchior Mell. They had:
>   1. Anna Sabina, bp. 3 July 1735, d. 13 Oct. 1735
>   Sp.: Daughter of Andreas Lerch
>   2. Anna Elisabetha, bp. 6 Nov. 1736
>   Sp.: The child's father's sister
>   3. Johann Henrich, bp. 24 July 1740
>   Sp.: Johann Henrich Eckert
>   4. Maria Magdalina, bp. 3 June 1744
>   Sp.: The wife of Caspar Hedderig, the child's father's brother
>   5. Carl Johann Henrich, bp. 11 July 1745
>   Sp.: Caspar Hedderig's son

AMERICAN RECORDS

Abstracts of Berks County Wills & Adm:
Charles Hedrick, Heidelberg, 24 Oct. 1757, adm. to George Hedrick, second son, Casper Hedrick oldest son having left the province 3 years ago.

45. HEDDERICH, CASPAR
Ann Galley, 1746
S-H, I: 360, 361

EUROPEAN RECORDS

Langenselbold Reformed KB:
Johan Henrich Braumüller, linenweaver, son of M. Johan Nicklas Braumüller from Ziegenhan in Hessen, m. 15 Nov. 1703 Anna Maria, daughter of the deceased Johan Faust. Their daughter:
> Magdalena, bp. 17 Aug. 1704
> Sp.: the child's mother's sister, daughter of the late Johan Faust

Joh. Caspar Hedderich, son of Carl Hedderich, m. 28 Jan 1733 Magdalena, dau. of *Mstr.* Johannes Henrich Braumüller, linenweaver. They had:
> 1. Carl Johann Henrich, bp. 14 Mar. 1734
> Sp.: The child's grandfather on the father's side.

AMERICAN RECORDS

Chalkley's Chronicles, Vol. 1, pg. 360:
Augusta Co., VA, county court judgments: March, 1770:
Hetrick vs. Hetrick- Chancery. Filed 28 Aug. 1768. In 1752-53, John Hetrick, defendant, brother of Caspar Hetrick, orator, went from PA to the back part of this Colony (VA) and purchased land from John Bombgardner and then returned to PA where the orator then lived. Land was cheap and the range for cattle good and fresh. Orator and defendant came to VA and settled on the land bought by John. William Frazer had entered a piece of land near which he gave to orator, but John sold to Peter Tresser [elsewhere Tresler; see Dressler]. This caused trouble between the brothers and orator built his own house on first piece of land. Orator heard defendant would not give him the land and removed his family to the house of Adam Hetrick and sent his neighbors, Valentine Pence and Frederick Harmentrout, to defendant to know his intentions. Orator moved back on the land and had been living there 14 years in 1768. Bill to compel John to convey to him.

46. HEDDERICH (HETRICH) CARL
Elizabeth, 1733
S-H, I: 113, 114, 115, 765, 766; names on list: Coblin Hetrick, age 40; Elizabeth age 35, John Onst 17, Willaim 10, Catrina 8½, Johan Henrick 2, Anna Margret, dead, 3.

EUROPEAN RECORDS

Langenselbold Reformed KB:
Carl Hederich, *Gerichtsdiener,* and wife Elisabetha nee Ermold had:
[Note: it is mentioned in the bp. record of his brother's child in 1716 that

this Carl Hedderich is the brother of Carl Johann Henrich Hedderich, 1746 immigrant; therefore, both immigrants named Carl were sons of Michael Hedderich *aus Sachsen.*]
1. Johannes Justus, bp. 18 May 1714; sp.: Johannes Justus Stoffel
2. Johann Wilhelm, bp. 13 Apr. 1717
   Sp.: Wilhelm Ermold, the child's mother's brother
3. Catharina Elisabetha, bp. 13 July 1721
   Sp.: The mother's youngest single sister, dau. of Ernst Ermold
4. Anna Catharina, bp. 3 June 1725
   Sp.: The wife of Wilhelm Ermold, the mother's brother
5. Anna Margretha, bp. 10 Apr. 1727
   Sp.: the wife of Mstr. Nicolaus Keller, carpenter.
5. Georg Henrich, bp. 15 June 1729; sp.: Georg Henrich Isler.

AMERICAN RECORDS

Bern Reformed Church, Berks County, PA, burials:
William Hetterich, b. 3 Apr. 1717 in Langenselbold, husband of Catharina Fellsmeyer. Had 2 daughters. Died 8 Oct. 1769.

Lower Heidelberg Township (today Berks County), Land Patents:
William Hetrig, A-46-73, 231½ A., 1737. Survey 1738; Patent (part) A-19-493.

Joost Hetrig, A-46-78, 160 A., 1742; Patent to Jost Hetrig, 1761 (Patent Book AA-1-406.

Land Warrants, Penn Twp., today Berks County, PA:
Jost Hydrig, 161 acres, Warrant 12 Oct. 1737, survey 22 Apr. 1737; Patent 13 Apr. 1761 to William Hydrick.

1754 Berks County tax list, Heidelberg Twp.:
Henry Hetterick and Yost Hederick

1754 Berks County tax list, Bern Twp.:
William Hatrick

Philadelphia County Adm. Book D., pg 102: #25
Letters of Adm. to Elizabeth Hederick, widow of Charles Hederick, dec'd. 18 Oct. 1739.

Philadelphia estate records, packet # 25, 1739:
Elisabeth Hederich, widow of Charles Hederich, deceased, and Jacob Frymeyer and Adam Shrove [he signed Adam Schroff] in the twp. of

Heidelberg, county of Lancaster. Dated 18 Oct. 1739.
Inventory of the est. of Caroll (sic) Hederich, deceased, dated 18 Oct. 1739
near Tulpehocken. 2 pages of inventory exhibited 21 Nov. 1739.

Rev. John Casper Stoever's Pastoral Records:
Wilhelm Hedderich (Northkill) had:
> Anna Elisabetha, b. 27 Dec. 1743, bp. 1 Apr. 1744
> Sp.: Heinrich Greber and wife

Christ [Little] Tulpehocken KB, Berks Co., PA:
Jost Heddrich had a daughter:
> Anna Margaretha, b. 26 July 1745, bp. 26 Sept. 1745
> Sp.: Anna Margaretha, on account of whose minority Magdalena
> Hetderichin.

Hain's (St. John's) Reformed KB, Berks County, PA:
Henrich Hetrich had children:
> 1. a daughter, bp. 20 Dec. 1751; sp.: Frederich Ermentrout
> 2. a son, bp. 16 Dec. 1753; sp.: William Hetrich and wife.

Henrich Hetterich and Catharina had children:
> 3. Elisabetha, b. 5 Nov. 1758, bp. 25 Nov. 1758
>   Sp.: Elisabeth, dau. of Wilhelm Hetterich, and
>   Johann Peter, son of Peter Ruth.
> 4. Johann Peter, b. 28 Feb. 1767, bp. 7 Mar. 1767
>   Sp.: Peter Zöller and Elisabetha Schmöll.

Pastoral Records of Rev. Boos, Burials [also known as the Schwartzwald Reformed KB], Berks Co., PA:

Georg Henrich Häderich	Widow of Henrich Hederich
b. 15 June 1729 d. 18 Sept.1785	b. 1724 d. 22 May 1786

Pennsylvania Patent Book AA-4, pg. 475:
Thomas Penn and Richard Penn; whereas a warrant under the seal of our
Land Office, dated 28 Nov. 1737, there was surveyed to William Hetrig land
situate part in Heidelberg and part in Bern Twp., county of Berks,
containing 231 A. Said William Hetrig sold 76 A. of the said tract to Adam
Baver and the remaining 155 A. William Hetrig sold on 7 June 1760 to
Hans Peter Haass of Heidelberg Twp. Now a Patent for 155 A. is granted
to Hans Peter Haass, 1764.

Abstracts of Berks County Wills & Adm.:
William Hetrick, Bern, 18 Oct. 1769, adm. to Magdalene Hetrick, the widow.

William Hetterick, Bern, 12 Mar. 1820 Adm. Philip Kershner and John Himmelberger, friends, the widow renouncing.

Naturalized 10 Apr. 1761, William Headrick and Yost Headrick (Hedrick), Bern Twp., Berks Co., PA.

47. HETERICH, JOHANNES age 18
Queen Elizabeth, 1738
S-H, I: 217

EUROPEAN RECORDS

Langenselbold Reformed KB:
Carl Hederich, swineherd, and wife Elisabeth, had a son:
    Johannes, bp. 26 Dec. 1720
[See 1746 immigrant Carl Hedderich for additional family data].

AMERICAN RECORDS

Rev. John Casper Stoever's Records:
Johannes Hedderich (Cacoosing) had:
    Johannes Wirner, b. 7 July 1744, bp. 26 Aug. 1744
    Sp.: Wirner Weitzel
[This baptism also recorded in the Christ (Little Tulpehocken) Lutheran Church, Jefferson Twp., Berks Co., PA.]

Chalkley's Chronicles, Vol. 1, pg. 360:
Augusta Co., VA, county court judgments: March, 1770:
Hetrick vs. Hetrick- Chancery. Filed 28 Aug. 1768. In 1752-53, John Hetrick, defendant, brother of Caspar Hetrick, orator, went from PA to the back part of this Colony (VA) and purchased land from John Bombgardner and then returned to PA where the orator then lived. Land was cheap and the range for cattle good and fresh. Orator and defendant came to VA and settled on the land bought by John. William Frazer had entered a piece of land near which he gave to orator, but John sold to Peter Tresser [elsewhere Tresler; see Dressler]. This caused trouble between the brothers and orator built his own house on first piece of land. Orator heard defendant would not give him the land and removed his family to the house of Adam Hetrick and sent his neighbors, Valentine Pence and Frederick Harmentrout, to defendant to know his intentions. Orator moved back on the land and had been living there 14 years in 1768. Bill to compel John to convey to him.

Chalkley's Chronicles, Vol. 3, pg. 383:
Augusta Co. Deed Book 10: 270: dated 8 May 1762.
John Heterick and (wife?) Susanna to Peter Tresler, £10, 134 acres on Stony Run on north side Shanando (sic) River, part of 285 acres patented to John Heterick on 2 June 1760; cor. Jacob Man and land of said Hetrick. Delivered: Gabriel Jones, November Court, 1778.

48. HIX, CONRAD
[It is not certain whether the father Johan Henrich Hix, or the son Conrad Hix is the immigrant.] (Not in S-H) Conrad Hix in PA by 1768.

EUROPEAN RECORDS

Langenselbold Reformed KB:
Johan Henrich Hix, smith from Rotenberg, m. 25 Apr. 1688 Anna Maria, daughter of Mstr. Johannes Heÿliger, *Siebmacher* and citizen at Gelnhausen. They had a son:
    1. Valentin, bp. 20 Dec. 1688
       Sp.: Valentin Heÿliger from Gelnhausen,
       the child's mother's brother.

Johann Valentin Hix, apprentice smith, son of Henrich Hix, master smith [*Gemeinenschmied*] m. 22 Jan 1711 Magdalena Elisabeth, daughter of the late Wörner Repp, former miller. They had a son:
    Johann Henrich, bp. 8 Mar. 1716
    Sp.: Johann Henrich Fuchs

Died 6 Jan 1737, Magdalena Elisabetha, wife of Mstr. Valentin Hix, age 49 years, 8 months.

Died 5 Oct. 1738, Mstr. Valentin Hix, smith, age 50 years.

Johan Henrich Hix, smith, son of Mstr. Valentin Hix, smith, m. 6 Mar. 1737 Anna Catharina, daughter of Caspar Faust, inhabitant here. They had:
    1. Johannes, bp. 16 Feb. 1738
       Sp.: Caspar Faust's second son, the child's mother's brother
    2. **Johan Conrad**, bp. 13 July 1740
       Sp.: Mstr. Johann Conrad Hix, also smith here.
       [Marginal note that an extract of record was sent to America
       21 May 1789.]

3. Anna Elisabetha, bp. 18 Nov. 1742
   Sp.: The wife of Mstr. Jacob Neidert, the baker
4. Johann Henrich, bp. 18 Oct. 1744
   Sp.: Joh. Conrad Hix, smith *"auf dem Closterberg."*

Meister Johann Henrich Hix, smith and widower here, m. (2) 9 Feb. 1746
Anna Catharina, daughter of the late Herr Johannes Kleiss, former *Cintgraff*
at Altenhasslau. Children:
5. Anna Maria, bp. 9 July 1747
   Sp.: The wife of Henrich Neidert
6. Anna Clara, bp. 16 Feb. 1749
   Sp.: Wife of master shoemaker Michael Rut
7. Anna Catharina, bp. 28 Oct. 1750
   Sp.: daughter of Johannes Barthel

AMERICAN RECORDS

Salem (Hetzel's) Lutheran Church, Pinegrove Twp., Schuylkill Co., PA:
Conrad Hix, b. in Europe 13 July 1740, died 21 Dec. 1814, age 75 years, 5
months, 3 days.

PA Archives, Series 6, Vol. 6, Rev. John Waldschmidt's records:
Conrad Hix, son of Heinrich Hix, m. 15 May 1768 Anna Maria, dau. of
Georg Heyer.

Abstracts of Berks County Wills & Adm.:
John Hicks, Tulpehocken, 31 July 1804.
Adm. to Conrad Hicks, his father, Nancy the widow renouncing.

Zion's (Old Red Church), West Brunswick Township, Schuylkill County, PA:
Conrad Hix and wife Anna Maria had:
      Johann Henrich, bp. 11 July 1773, 3 weeks old
      Sp.: Anton Fuchs [q.v.] and wife Elizabeth
[This same baptism is also recorded in Daniel Schumacher's baptismal
register, where Pastor Schumacher refers to the location as "Blue Mountain".

Schuylkill County Will Book 1, pg. 249:
HIX, Conrad, registered, 14 Feb. 1840, mentions wife, not named, mentions
to children of Anna Maria Kerschner, mentions to children of Henrich Hix,
heir, Elizabeth Seman not to have as long as her husband Seman lives, (does
not state the relationship, but probably a daughter). Mentions: Conrad,
Michael, Rebecca Schumacher, "now comes George Hix, he shall have an
English shilling but nothing more because he has treated his father and
mother in an unbecoming manner." Executors, Conrad Kerschner, Michael

Hix, Hannes Shumacker. Witnesses, Adam Wagner and Henry W. Conrad.
Codicil, Appointed son Michael Hix, son-in-law Conrad Kerschner and son-in-law John Schumacher, Exrs., 20 December 1814. Witnessed by: Adam Wagner, Henry W. Conrad, Will Dated, 4 Dec. 1814, Probated 19 Jan. 1815.

Hain's (St. John's) Reformed KB, Berks County, PA:
Georg Hix was sp. in 1792 for Johann, son of Conrad Kirschner and wife.
Henrich Hix was sp. in 1798 for Wilhelm, son of Conrad Kirschner and wife.
Conrad Hix was sp. in 1800 for Samuel, son of Conrad Kirschner and wife.

Henrich Hix and wife had children:
1. Elisabetha, b. 18 Apr. 1799, bp. 19 May 1799
   Sp.: Ludwig Fischer and Elisabetha
2. Daniel, b. 24 Sept. 1800, bp. 26 Oct. 1800
   Sp.: Conrad Kirschner and Anna Maria.

[Note: There are other records in PA and MD that indicate perhaps other members of the Hix family also emigrated; a Johan Görg Hyx arrived on the *Townsend,* in 1737, with Peter Schad and a Johan Adam Filtzmeior. (One Johan Jörg Hix was bp. 31 Jan. 1687 in Selbold; no further records were located there for him.) The surnames Hix, Schad and Filtzmeier all appear in the Langenselbold records, but these specific emigrants could not be conclusively identified there; perhaps their records will be found in a nearby village. There was a Jacob Hix with wife Barbara in the Salem Reformed KB, Hagerstown, MD. They had a daughter Anna Maria, b. 9 July 1775, bp. 5 Nov. 1775; sp.: Johannes Kirschner and wife Anna Maria.]

KEŸSER
[Although no immigrant with this surname has been verified from Langenselbold, family data is included here because of the frequent relationships of established immigrant families with the Keÿsers of Langenselbold. See Kirschner, Gerhard, Lamm, etc.]

EUROPEAN RECORDS

Langenselbold Reformed KB:
Johannes Keÿser, an apprentice cartwright, son of the late (n.n.) Keÿser, *Gerichts* and *Wagner* at Rohrbach, Eckartshausen, m. 17 Jan. 1672 Anna Catharina, daughter of Nickel Döll, *Gemeinsmann und Nachbahr* here, after 3 proclamations. Children:
1. Margaretha, bp. 23 Feb. 1673
   Sp.: Margaretha, wife of Friedrich Hoin.

[Margaretha Keÿser m. 16 Feb. 1699 Joh. Conrad Kirschner; their
son Martin Kirschner emigrated.]
2. Anna Maria, bp. 24 May 1675
Sp.: Anna Maria, daughter of Martin Lamb.
[Anna Maria Keÿser m. 1709 Peter Lamm; their son Peter Lamm
emigrated.]
3. Anna Elisabeth, bp. 28 Jan. 1677
Sp.: Anna Elisabeth, daughter of Tönges Droit.
[Anna Elisabeth Keÿser m. 10 Jan, 1709 Henrich Scherer. One
Henrich Scherer and wife were sp. at Hain's Church, Berks Co.,
Pa. in 1750 for a child of one Adam *Kieser* and wife.]
4. Johannes, bp. 8 Aug. 1678, died 1688.
Sp.: the mother's brother.
5. Anna Elisabeth, bp. 21 Mar. 1680
Sp.: Anna Elisabeth, wife of Clos Schieser.
[This Anna Elisabeth Keÿser m. 1707 Wilhelm Gerhard; Wilhelm
Gerhard and their son Friedrich Gerhard emigrated in 1739.]
Note: two daughters, both named Anna Elisabeth, born into this
Keÿser family, and both lived to be adults.
6. Catharina, bp. 25 Dec. 1681, died 1688.
Sp.: the child's grandmother, wife of Nickel Döll.
7. Anna Regina, bp. 17 Nov. 1683
Sp.: daughter of Johannes Fischer.

Johannes Keÿser, cartwright and widower here, m. (2) 15 Jan. 1685 Juliana,
daughter of the late Paul Gerhard. They had children:
8. Joh. Conrad, bp. 23 Jan. 1687.
9. Johann Peter, bp. 26 Jan. 1689;
Sp.: Joh. Peter Koch, a smith from Streitberg.
[Joh. Peter Keÿser m. 1716 Anna Margretha Stamm.]
10. Johannes, bp. 15 May 1691 [mother's name given in this record
as Giel, used in these records for Juliana.]
Sp.: Johannes Mohn, single son of the late Tönges Mohn.
[Johannes Keÿser m. 1718 Anna Elisabeth Hübener.]

Juliana, wife of Johannis Keÿser, died 15 Oct. 1693.

Johannes Keÿser m. (3) 30 Jan. 1710 Anna Maria, widow of the late Conrad
Mohn.

Johannes Keÿser, master cartwright, was buried 10 Apr. 1711, age 63 years.

Johann Peter Keÿser, master cartwright, son of the deceased Johannes Keÿser, m. 9 Jan. 1716 Anna Margretha Stamm, daughter of the late Hans Jörg Stamm. Children:

1. Anna Maria, bp. 17 Jan 1717
   Sp.: eldest single daughter of Conrad Betz
2. Anna Elisabetha, bp. 17 June 1718
   Sp.: the wife of Henrich Scherer
3. Anna Maria Barbara, bp. 13 May 1720
   Sp.: the child's mother's sister, wife of Johannes Ruppel
4. Anna Catharina, bp. 11 Jan. 1722
   Sp.: the wife of Hans Huber, mason
5. Joh. Conrad, bp. 21 Jan. 1724
   Sp.: the son of Peter Lamm
6. Anna Elisabetha, bp. 4 June 1725; she m. 1750 the immigrant Johann Georg Kirschner [q.v.]
7. Johanna Maria, bp. 25 Apr. 1728
8. Johann Peter, bp. 19 July ?1731

Johannes Keÿser, son of the late Johannes Keÿser, m. 9 Dec. 1717 Anna Elisabetha Hübener, daughter of Tönges Hübener, *Gemeinsmann* here. Children:

1. Anna Maria bp. 16 Apr. 1719
   Sp.: single daughter of Tönges Hübener, the mother's sister
2. Antonius, bp. 9 Mar 1722
3. Rosina, bp. 11 Feb. 1725
4. Elisabetha, bp. 21 May 1726
   [She m. 25 Feb. 1750 Johannes Kniess. One Johannes Kniess emigrated, arriving on a ship with other Langenselbold immigrants, but this couple had children born in Langenselbold after the date of his departure.]

49. KIRSCHNER, JOH. JÖRG
Samuel, 1731
S-H, I: 39, 41, 42
   other passengers on ship: Women, Anna: Children, Martin, Elisabeth and Barbara.

EUROPEAN RECORDS

Langenselbold Reformed KB:
Johann Kirschner, son of Peter Kirschner, *Gerichtsschöffen,* m. 26 Jan.1660
An Els [Anna Elisabeth] Ermoldt, daughter of Hans Ermoldt, also
Gerichtsschöffen. Their son:
    Johann Conrad, bp. not located in KB

Johann Conrad Kürschner, son of Johan Kürschner, *Gerichtsschöffen,* m. (1)
23 Feb. 1693 Maria, widow of Hans Bernhard Schad. She was bp. 28 Feb.
1669, daughter of Caspar Knies. She died 21 Nov. 1697. They had children:
    1. Johannes, bp. 26 Nov. 1693 [q.v. - Em. 1733]
        Sp.: the child's grandfather
    2. **Joh. Jörg,** bp. 9 May 1695
        Sp.: Hans Schad

Johann Conrad Kirschner m. (2) 16 Feb. 1699 Anna Margretha Keÿser [q.v.],
daughter of *Meister* Johannes Keÿser, *Wagner.* They had:
    3. Joh. Caspar, bp. 18 Sept. 1700
    4. Joh. Martin, bp. 4 Nov. 1703 [q.v. - em. 1742]

Johann Jörg Kirschner, son of Johann Conrad Kirschner, m. 28 Jan. 1722
Anna, daughter of Conrad Fischer [She was bp. 8 Oct. 1702, daughter of
Conrad Fischer and Anna Veronica.] Their children were:
    1. Joh. Martin, bp. 3 Dec. 1722
        Sp.: the child's father's youngest brother
    2. Anna Elisabeth, bp. 25 Mar. 1725
        Sp.: Friederich Fischer's single daughter
    3. Anna Barbara, bp. 26 Jan. 1727
        Sp.: Johannes Fischer's wife
    4. Johannes, bp. 24 Feb. 1729
        Sp.: the father's brother, Johannes Kirschner.

AMERICAN RECORDS

St. John's Reformed KB, Host, Berks Co., PA:
Peter Laucks married 1743 Anna Barbara Kürschner.

Monocacy Lutheran KB, Frederick Co., MD:
Martin Kirschner had a son:
    David, b. ___ Feb. 1750; bp. 29 July 1750
    Sp.: David John and wife.

Anna Kirschner was a sp. in Aug. 1750 for a child of Henrich Wehage.

Colonial Maryland Naturalizations:
Oct. (20), 1747: Jonathan Isagar (probably Hager), and Martain Keisner (probably Kirschner). [Note: they are said to be brothers-in-law, with Jonathan Hager's wife being Elisabeth Kirschner, b. in Langenselbold. She d. 16 Apr. 1765.] For more data on Hager, see *Der Kurier,* publication of the Mid-Atlantic Germanic Society, Vol. 15, No. 1 (March, 1997), p. 6-8. Article titled "Our German Heritage: Jonathan Hager and the Hager House".

Frederick County (MD) Wills, Book A1, abstracted by Donna Valley Russell, C.G., F.A.S.G, and published in *Western Maryland Genealogy, Vol. 3, No. 2, Apr. 1987:*
Martin Kirshner of Frederick Co. Will dated 30 Nov. 1769, sick. To wife Margretha: list of foodstuffs, etc. to be distributed to her yearly (incl. 5 gallons of "rie" liquor), she to live in the shopp, which is to be reboarded and have a chimney and stove. Mentions mulatto Coxley, who is to stay for term of her indenture. If wife dies before that, Anna Coxley should become part of the estate. Land to be sold, house and mill on *Battemak* (Potomac), and a tract in the Big Coof(?), Cumberland Co., Pa., and a 151a tract, formerly belonging to Peter Pringley. Exec. to give lawful deeds to John and George Kirshner and George Kirshner, Senr., William Kelly, Jacob Kirshner, George Shultz, and George Beak. Also to settle matter with William Paul about a tract of land. Residue to children as follows: oldest son Martin: £50. Second and third sons David and George, one part; daughters Madalina and Margreth, two parts. To three grandchildren, Joseph, Martin, and John Baum: £50 each. To two daughters of George Ritinawer, dec'd., Margreth and Elizabeth: 50a of my land. If any of my children marry into Conrad Miller's family, he/she to have no more than 5 sh. My youngest son George to learn Dutch and English and be bound to trade. Capt. Jonathan Hagar and my son Martin exec. /s/ Martin Kirshner. Wit: Henry Ridenawer, Henry Shnebely, John Casner. Proved 30 Dec. 1769 by 3 wit. (pp 351-3)

[Additional records on the distribution of this estate are found in Washington Co. Land Records, Liber A, pp 4-7, and pp. 131-135; also Liber D: pp. 31-35 and pp. 108-111. *Western Maryland Genealogy, Vol. 1, & Vol. 5].*

50. KIRSCHNER, JOHANN GEORG
Edinburgh, 1750
S-H, I: 429
EUROPEAN RECORDS

Langenselbold Reformed KB:
Henrich Kirschner, son of Johann Kirschner, *Gerichtsschöff(en)*, m. 7 Jan.
1697 Anna Catharina Dieterich. They had children:
   1. Johannes, bp. 24 Oct. 1697; sp.: Johannes Döll
   2. Johan Henrich, bp. 20 June 1700
       Sp.: Johan Kirschner, the child's grandfather
   3. Wörner, bp. 28 May 1702; sp.: Wörner Hamburger
   4. Johan Bernhard, bp. 28 Sept. 1704; sp.: son of Caspar Knies
   5. Johann Jörg, bp. 9 Sept. 1708
       Sp.: single son of the late Stoffel Koch
   6. Anna Catharina Elisabetha, bp. 7 Jan. 1711
       Sp.: daughter of Joh. Conrad Fischer
   7. Anna Catharina, bp. 10 Jan. 1713
       Sp.: the child's mother's sister, wife of Caspar Hübener.

Johan Henrich Kirschner, son of Henrich Kirschner, m. 14 Jan. 1722 Maria
Häffner, daughter of Tönges Häffner. They had children:
   1. **Johan Georg**, bp. 25 Nov. 1723
       Sp.: the child's father's youngest single brother.
   2. Anton, bp. 12 June 1726
   3. Johann Henrich, bp. 4 Nov. 1728; sp.: Joh. Henrich Lohfinck
   4. Rosina, bp. 4 July 1731
       Sp.: the child's maternal grandmother, widow of Tönges Häffener
   5. Johanna Catharina, bp. 18 Dec. 1732
       Sp.: Johannes Kirschner's wife.
   6. Johann Henrich, bp. 19 Oct. 1734
       Sp.: Henrich Kirschner, grandfather
   7. Johan Conrad, bp. 13 May 1736; sp.: son of Johannes Döll
   8. Anna Elisabetha, bp. 6 Mar. 1738
       Sp.: daughter of Johannes Keÿser.
   9. Anna Margretha, bp. 6 Dec. 1739
       Sp.: daughter of Melchior Herchenröder.

Johann Georg Kirschner, son of Johann Henrich Kirschner, inhabitant here,
m. 22 Apr. 1750 Anna Elisabetha, daughter of *Meister* Johann Peter Keÿser,
Wagner und Mitnachbar here. Anna Elisabetha Keÿser was bp. 4 June 1725,
daughter of Johann Peter Keÿser and wife Anna Margretha (nee Stamm).
[See **KEÿSER** for more family records. No further records for this Georg
Kirschner in Langenselbold. Since a Georg Kirshner appears in the ship lists
later the same year (as this marriage) along with several others from this
town, it is concluded that he may be this immigrant.]

AMERICAN RECORDS

Distinguishing between the several Johan Georg Kirschners is difficult. One George Kershner was naturalized Apr. 1761 in Saucon Twp., Northampton Co., PA. Several George Kirshners appear in records of Frederick and Washington Counties in MD. See immigrant family # 49, Johan Jörg Kirschner in 1731, whose son Martin also had a son George mentioned in his 1769 will in Maryland, along with a George Kirschner, Sr. See the following immigrant Johannes Kirschner with son George, b. 1722.

51. KIRSCHNER, JOHANNES age 40
Elizabeth, 1733
S-H, I: 113, 114, 115 and 765-767
  with Kertroudt age 50, Conrut age 14, Johan Yerek age 12

EUROPEAN RECORDS

Langenselbold Reformed KB:
Johann Kirschner, son of Peter Kirschner, *Gerichtsschöffen,* m. 26 Jan.1660 An Els [Anna Elisabeth] Ermoldt, daughter of Hans Ermoldt, also *Gerichtsschöffen.* Their son:
  Johann Conrad, bp. not located in KB

Johann Conrad Kürschner, son of Johan Kürschner, *Gerichtsschöffen,* m. (1) 23 Feb. 1693 Maria, widow of Hans Bernhard Schad. She was bp. 28 Feb. 1669, daughter of Caspar Knies. She died 21 Nov. 1697. They had children:
  1. **Johannes,** bp. 26 Nov. 1693
     Sp.: the child's grandfather
  2. Joh. Jörg, bp. 9 May 1695 [q.v. - em. 1731]
     Sp.: Hans Schad

Johann Conrad Kirschner m. (2) 16 Feb. 1699 Anna Margretha Keÿser [q.v.], daughter of Johannes Keÿser, cartwright. They had children:
  3. Joh. Caspar, bp. 18 Sept. 1700
  4. Joh. Martin, bp. 4 Nov. 1703 [q.v. - em. 1742]

Johannes Kirschner, son of Conrad Kirschner, m. 11 Feb. 1717 Gertraud, daughter of the late Johann Dieterich, divorced wife of Johann Schuffart.

[See data on the Dieterich family under Anton Faust.]
They had children:
1. Joh. Conrad, bp. 17 Sept. 1717
   Sp.: Joh. Conrad Kirschner, the child's grandfather
2. Joh. Peter, bp. 15 Oct. 1719, d. 29 Dec. 1725
   Sp.: single son of Hans Faust from Oberdorff
3. Anna, bp. 15 May 1722, twin, d. 26 Dec. 1722
4. Joh. Georg, bp. 15 May 1722, twin
   Sp.: Joh. Jörg Kirschner and his wife
5. Anna Philippina, bp. 20 Aug. 1724, d. 12 June 1725
   Sp.: Joh. Peter Schad's single daughter
6. Anna Catharina, bp. 5 Nov. 1727
   Sp.: single daughter of the late Christoph Schiesser

AMERICAN RECORDS

Philadelphia Wills, 1742:
Abstract from the original will Johannes Kirshner/John Kerssoner, Philadelphia, 1742, will #293, Bern twp., Lancaster Co., PA.
Dated 19 Apr. 1742, proved 10 Sept. 1742 at Tulpehocken, before Conrad Weiser.
[Will written in English with very poor spelling; testator made his mark]

1. To son Connrat Kerrssoner the plandation containing 200A for £150. He is also ordained as the "only and solo executor of this my last will and testement"
2. To son George a trackt of woodland "living near Goolshill in the said downship above mensoned conddnig 400 acers"
"Conrat is to give his brother George only £20 and ?234 buskell of wheat."
3. Connratt is to give his mother £40 "and to kip her with him in his house" and give her 20 shillings plus other stipulated amounts of flax, cows, wool, corn, etc.
4. Sons Connratt and George are to equally divide the remainder of Est, and Connratt is to have £15 "to bild a hous for him on his land."
Wit. by John Reesar (who appears to have written the will) and Johannes Meyer, Friderich Böckel (both signed, German script).

1754 Berks County tax list, Windsor Township.:
Conrad Kirschner and George Kersner

Berks County Orphan's Court Records, dated 12 Feb. 1768:
Petition of Conrad Kerchner, age 14 years and 2 months, and Anna Maria Kerchner, age 16, two of the children of George Kerchner, late of Windsor,

yeoman, dec'd. Prays for guardians. They select Conrad Kerschner, Sr. of Windsor Township, Berks County, PA.

Moselem Lutheran KB, Richmond Twp., Berks County, PA:
Johan Conrad Kirschner and wife Catharina Beck had children:
> 1. Joh. Conrad b. 1 Aug. 1744, bp. 12 Aug. 1744
>   Sp.: Martin Kirschner and wife Anna Margretha
> 2. Johan Peter, b. 7 May 1749, bp. Festo Trinitat.

Abstracts of Berks County Wills and Administrations:
Conrad Kershner, Windsor, 31 May 1791. Adm. to Conrad, eldest son, and Thomas Reber of Bern Twp., son-in-law, Catharina, the widow, renouncing.

Conrad Kerschner, Windsor, 2 Nov. 1813. Adm. to Catharine, the widow and sons John and Conrad.

Catharine Kerschner, widow of Conrad, 2 Nov. 1813. Adm. to George Hinkle, son-in-law.

John Kerschner, Manheim, 3 July - 7 Aug. 1810 (trans) All to be sold and money divided among children, viz: Catharine, John, Jonathan, Elisabeth, John George, Christian, John Peter, Sara, Anna Maria, Magdalena and Daniel as they come of age. Magdalena to have £50 beforehand. Brother Jonathan and brother-in-law Thomas Reber of Bern executors. Witnesses: Jacob Krebs and Abraham Schneider.

Heidelberg Moravian KB, North Heidelberg Twp., Berks Co., PA:
Conrad Kirschner and his wife Catharina Heck [this name is given as Beck at Moselem Church] were sp. in 1738 for Anna Catharina, daughter of Johannes Meyer. The child was baptized in Bern in Lancaster County by Pastor Schmidt.

Christ "Little Tulpehocken" Lutheran KB, Berks Co., PA:
Joh. Cunradt Kürschner sp. a son of Cunradt Messerschmidt in 1741.

Naturalized by affirmation 10 Apr. 1753: Conrad Kearsner, Windsor Twp., Berks Co., PA.

52. KIRSCHNER, MARTIN
Francis and Elizabeth, 1742
S-H, I: 329
                    EUROPEAN RECORDS

Langenselbold Reformed KB:
Johann Kirschner, son of Peter Kirschner, *Gerichtsschöffen,* m. 26 Jan.1660
An Els [Anna Elisabeth] Ermoldt, daughter of Hans Ermoldt, also
Gerichtsschöffen. Their son: Johann Conrad, bp. not located in KB.

Johann Conrad Kürschner, son of Johan Kürschner, *Gerichtsschöffen*, m. (1)
23 Feb. 1693 Maria, widow of Hans Bernhard Schad. She was bp. 28 Feb.
1669, daughter of Caspar Knies. She died 21 Nov. 1697. They had children:
1. Johannes, bp. 26 Nov. 1693 [q.v. - Em. 1733]
   Sp.: the child's grandfather
2. Joh. Jörg, bp. 9 May 1695 [q.v. - Em. 1731]
   Sp.: Hans Schad

Johann Conrad Kirschner m. (2) 16 Feb. 1699 Anna Margretha Keÿser [q.v.],
daughter of Johannes Keÿser, cartwright. They had:
3. Joh. Caspar, bp. 18 Sept. 1700
4. Joh. **Martin**, bp. 4 Nov. 1703.

Joh. **Martin Kirschner,** son of Johann Conrad Kirschner, m. 26 Nov. 1732
Anna Elisabeth, daughter of Johann Schuffert. (Anna Elisabeth Schuffert
was bp. 29 Dec. 1711, daughter of Johannes Schuffert who m. 17 Apr. 1704
Gertraud Dieterich.) Martin Kirschner and wife Anna Elisabeth had:
1. Anna Catharina, bp. 11 Oct. 1733; she d. 1733.
   Sp.: the daughter of Joh. Peter Scherer
2. Joh. Conrad, bp. mid Oct. 1734. Sp.: Peter Schad's son
3. Joh. Peter, bp. 27 May 1736; he died 1737.
   Sp.: Elder son of Conrad Schuffert
4. Anna Maria, bp. 17 Oct. 1737
   Sp.: the wife of Joh. Henrich Neidert, the young baker
5. Joh. Caspar, bp. 10 June 1739
   Sp.: Joh. Caspar Kirschner, father's brother
6. Johannes, bp. 9 Apr. 1741. Sp.: Johannes Alt's son

AMERICAN RECORDS

Bern Reformed KB, Bern Township, Berks County, PA:
Martin Kirschner (also Kuersner) and wife Elisabetha had children:
7. John, (elsewhere b. 2 Aug. 1743), bp. 20 Aug. 1745
   Sp.: John Meth and Margaret Laux
8. Gertrude, b. 29 Dec. 1744; sp.: Gertrude Faust.
9. Peter, b. 17 Apr. 1747; sp.: Peter Laucks.
   [This Peter Kirschner is buried in the Bern Reformed Church
   cemetery in Bern Twp. Dates from tombstone: b. 17 Apr. 1747;
   d. 11 Sept. 1809].

1754 Berks County tax list, Bern Township, Berks County, PA:
George Kerschner and Martin Kershner.

Land Warrants and Patents, Penn Twp., Berks Co., PA:
Conrad Kersner - 30 acres, called "Heckenheim". Warrant dated 25 Sept.
1753; surveyed 22 Apr. 1754; patented 20 Nov. 1766 to John Heck.
Conrad Kersner - 14¾ acres, called "Heckenheim". Same dates as above.

Martin Kersner - 59 acres. Warrant dated 5 Oct. 1743; surveyed 26 Oct.
1743; patented 7 Oct. 1763. Also a 230 acre tract, same dates.

Reading Reformed KB, Berks County, burials:
Buried 19 Dec. 1820 Conrad Kershner, age 86 years, 2 months, 21 days.

Abstracts of Berks County Wills & Administrations:
Martin Kirschner, Bern, 10 June 1771 - 6 Dec. 1782. Provides for wife
Elisabeth. To son Conrad £15, having received a large sum in his lifetime.
To son Philip £170 to be paid from the sums my sons Peter and Nicholas
are indebted to me for land I have sold them. To daughter Gertraut Rigel
£115. Wife Elisabeth and friend Conrad Kirschner executors. Witnesses:
Peter Brecht and Wm. Reeser (trans.)

John Kershner, farmer, Bern, 14 Mar. - 12 Apr. 1823. Provides for wife
Christina. Children not named. Executor friend Philip Filbert of Bern and
son Peter S. Kershner. Also appoints his brother Philip Kershner guardian
of his 6 youngest children. Witnesses: Abraham Klopp and Jacob Schneider.

Readinger Zeitung: **Newspaper dated Jan. 11, 1793:**
Kirschner, Conrad, 16 Jan. 1793 (Jan. 11) Private sale, Valuable plantation
grist and saw mill with oil and "Reib" mill, in Manheim twp. on the little
Schuylkill, 330 A (100 A cleared), 22 A good meadow and never failing
stream. Has two story house, barn and stables, good well at house, orchard,
is on the great road from Lickens Valley to Shamokin. Apply to the
undersigned, Conrad Kirschner, living on the place or to Frederich Maurer
in Maiden Creek twp.

Berks Co. Deed Book 29: 111:
15 July 1816, Jacob Kershner of Canocojick [sic] Hundred, MD, one of the
heirs of Peter Kershner, late of Bern twp., Berks Co. acknowledges receipt
of inheritance from John Kershner, Exr.

Berks Co. Deed Book 29: 198:
1 July 1817, Jacob Kershner, late of Washington Co, Md, son and heir of Peter Kershner of Berks Co., dec'd, acknowledges receipt of legacy from Philip Kershner, Exr.

Berks Co. Deed Book 29: 439:
8 Apr. 1818, George Zacharias of Washington Co., Md., guardian of his children: Catharine, Peter, Elizabeth and Daniel, heirs of his father-in-law Peter Kershner, late of Bern twp., Berks Co., dec'd, acknowledges receipt of share of estate from John Kershner, executor of Peter Kershner.

Naturalized Apr. 1761, Martin Kersener, Bern Twp., Berks Co., PA.

KLEBER, see GLEBER

53. KOCH, ANNA MARIA widow of Joh. Caspar Koch
Emigrated 1746
Probably on *Ann Galley* with others from area.

EUROPEAN RECORDS

Langenselbold Reformed KB:
Conrad Fischer, son of Johannes Fischer, m. 13 Jan. 1687 Anna Veronica, daughter of Caspar Schuffert. Their daughter:
      Anna Maria, bp. 13 June 1698

Caspar Koch, son of Burckhard Koch, m. (1) 26 Jan. 1708 Elisabeth, daughter of Ludwig Adolff Roth. They had children:
    1. Andreas, bp. 10 Mar. 1709
        Sp.: Andreas Lerch, son of Joh. Conrad Lerch
    2. Johannes, bp. 22 May 1712. Sp.: Johannes Adam
    3. Johann Peter, b. 6 Jan. 1715
        Sp.: Joh. Peter Koch, the child's father's brother
    4. Adolph, b. 26 Jan. 1718
    5. Joh. Conrad, b. 12 July 1719
        Sp.: M. Joh. Conrad Hix, smith here.

Joh. Caspar Koch, widower and inhabitant here, m (2) 25 Feb. 1722 **Anna Maria**, daughter of Conrad Fischer. They had:
1. Anna Catharina, bp. 25 Nov. 1722
    Sp.: single daughter of Johannes Mell
2. Anna Elisabetha, b. 18 Feb. 1725
    Sp.: single daughter of Johannes Mohn
3. Johann Justus, bp. 31 Mar. 1727
    Sp.: Mstr. Jost Fischer, shoemaker, the child's mother's brother. (This child was a twin, the other son was stillborn).
4. Johann Caspar, bp. 30 May 1728; d. 26 June 1731, age 3.
    Sp.: Johann Peter Koch's surviving son, single.
5. Anna Catharina, bp. 22 Feb. 1731
    Sp.: Johannes Koch's wife, the childs' mother's sister.
[Note: both daughters named Anna Catharina lived and married in PA.]

Died 23 Oct. 1731 Johann Caspar Koch, age 50 years.

AMERICAN RECORDS

Heidelberg Moravian KB, North Heidelberg Twp., Berks Co., PA:
Family Register: Anna Maria Koch, widow of Johann Caspar Koch. She was born June 13, 1698 in Langensel*bot* in Ysenberg. She died 4 Mar. 1762, age 63 years, 8 months, and 19 days, and was buried on our God's acre. She left three daughters living in Bethlehem:
1. -------
2. Anna Elisabeth, b. 18 Feb. 1725
3. Anna Catharina, b. 22 Feb. 1731

Burial records # 36: Anna Maria Koch, b. June 13, 1698 in Isenburg. In her 21st year she married Caspar Koch. They were married twelve years and had six children, of whom three daughters are living. In 1746 she came to this land as a widow. She died Mar. 4, 1762.

Bethlehem Moravian Cemetery, Bethlehem, Northampton Co., PA:
Catharine Moeller, nee Koch (1722-98) from Selbold, principality of Isenburg. She was the wife of Joseph Moeller who died 1778.

Anna Catharina Ziegler, nee Koch (1732-1805) born at Selbold, County Isenburg. She came here with her widowed mother and married J. Fred. Ziegler. She was widowed in 1786.

Joseph Moeller (1713-78) born at Zittau, Saxony. He came here with the first "sea congregation" in 1742 and was employed at Nazareth, Gnadenthal and Bethlehem as a gardener. He married Catharine Koch and had two sons.

Elizabeth Schneider (1725-63) from the Wetteravia, Germany. She was married to Adam Schneider and left several children. Since 1762 they lived south of the Lehigh River. The cause of her death was cancer.

John Adam Schneider (1716-1801) born at Hanau, Bavaria; a shoemaker, came to Bethlehem in 1747 with his first wife Elizabeth, maiden name Koch, and served in the Economy. After her death he married Catharina Luckenbach and moved to Upper Saucon.

54. LAMM, PETER
Francis & Elizabeth, 1742
S-H, I: 329

EUROPEAN RECORDS

Langenselbold Reformed KB:
Martin Lamb had a son:
> Peter, bp. 17 May 1663; sp.: Peter Scherer.

Peter Lamb, son of Martin Lamb, married (1) 12 Feb. 1691 Catharina, daughter of Daniel Reber. They had:
> 1. Johan Conrad, bp. 25 Oct. 1693
>   Sp.: Joh. Conrad Reber
> 2. Johan Lenhard, bp. 27 Oct. 1695
> 3. Johannes, bp. 18 Sept. 1698
>   Sp.: the son of Melchior Trechsler
> 4. Michael, bp. 20 Jan. 1702
>   Sp.: Michael Reber

Peter Lamb, widower, married (2) 11 Apr. 1709 Anna Maria, daughter of *Mstr.* Johannes Keyser, *Wagner*. They had children, surname given as Lamm or Lamb in various records:
> 1. Elisabeth, bp. 12 Jan. 1710
> 2. **Johann Peter**, bp. 7 Oct. 1711
>   Sp.: Peter Keisser [Keyser], single & cartwright
> 3. Anna Margretha, bp. 17 Sept. 1713
>   Sp.: the wife of Joh. Conrad Kirschner, sister of the child's mother.
> 4. Johann Philips, bp. 8 Dec. 1715. Sp.: Johannes Schneider.

Died 26 Oct. 1740, Anna Maria, wife of Peter Lamm, age 65 years, 5 mo.

Died 20 Dec. 1743, Peter Lamb, age 80 years, 7 months.

AMERICAN RECORDS

Rev. Boos' Pastoral Record, Schwartzwald Reformed KB, Berks Co.:
Died 7 June 1787: Peter Lamm, b. ---- 1715.

Johannes Moser married 11 June 1793 Elisabeth Lamm of Bern, Berks Co.

Hain's (St. John's) Reformed KB, Berks Co., PA:
Johann Peter Lamm was sp. in 1751 for a son of Fritrich Ermentraut [q.v.].
Peter Lamm was a sp. in 1755 for a son of Henrich Gerlitz.

Peter Lamm and wife Anna Margaretha had children:
      1. Appollonia, b. 23 Nov. 1757, bp. 11 Dec. 1757
        Sp.: Peter Fischer and Apollonia Heckert
      2. Johannes b. 1 Dec. 1759, bp. 25 Dec. 1759
        Sp.: Johannes Heckert and Elisabeth Barbara
      3. Peter, bp. 4 Apr. 1774
        Sp.: Peter Fischer and Apollonia
      4. Philipp, bp. 5 Oct. 1776
        Sp.: Philip Heckert and Anna Maria.

Johann Peter Lamm and Anna Margaretha were sp. in 1784 for a son of
Friedrich Stein and his wife.

[The immigrant Peter Lamm was a first cousin of Friedrich Gerhart and
Martin Kirschner, both immigrants from Langenselbold.]

Abstracts of Berks County Wills & Adm.:
Peter Lamm, Heidelberg; 9 May 1787 - 20 Oct. 1787 (translation). Provides
for wife Anna Margaret. Land to be divided after 10 years among the
children as they may agree upon. Eldest son John only one named. Friends
Jacob Gerhart and John Miller executors. Witnesses John Smith and Martin
Kissling.

**Hain's (St. John's) Reformed KB, Berks County, cemetery: tombstone
inscription:**
      Peter Lamm, b. 1 June 1715; d. 5 June 1787, age 72 years, 5 days.

Pennsylvania Patent Books:
Tract of land called "Lamb's Pasture" in Heidelberg Twp., (now Berks Co.):

Warrant dated 19 June 1741 granted to Frederick Gerhart; warrant dated 15 May 1751 to William Spatz; warrant dated 10 Apr. 1754 to Martin Mull. These 3 warrants containing a total of 169 acres, 24 perches by sundry conveyances to John Lamb [Lamm]. Patent dated 29 Mar. 1810.

Naturalized 10 Apr. 1761, Peter Lamb, Heidleberg Twp., Berks Co., PA.

55. LEINBACH, JOHANNES
   prelist, 1723
                    EUROPEAN RECORDS

Langenselbold Reformed KB:
Married 6 Dec. 1672 at Selbold, Henrich Leinbach born in Gerthenroth [?Gerterode] *aus dem Ried-Eselischen,* linenweaver and Barbara, daughter of Johannes Lehrch [Lerch], shopkeeper and *Gemeinsmann* here. They had children:
1. **Johannes,** bp. 15 Mar. 1674
   Sp.: Johannes Lerch, the maternal grandfather
2. Anna Margreth, bp. 26 Dec. 1677
   Sp.: Margretha, daughter of Hans Fuchs
3. A son, bp. 29 Feb. 1680
   Sp.: Johan Christoffel, son of Bast Leis
4. Anna Elisabeth, bp. 25 Dec. 1681
   Sp.: Peter Lohefinck's daughter
   [She m. 1 Mar. 1708 in Oberdorfelden, Michael Leimbach.]
5. Eva, bp. 2 May 1684
   Sp.: The child's grandmother on the mother's side
6. Anna Margreth, bp. 30 June 1686
   Sp.: Margretha, wife of Hans Schad
   [She m. 3 Mar. 1728 Joh. Adam Hedderich, q.v.]
7. Andreas, b. 20 Feb. 1689, bp. 24 Feb. 1689
   at Hochstadt Reformed KB; the father's occupation is given as schoolteacher or school-sexton.

Oberdorfelden, Kreis Hanau, KB:
Buried 5 Apr. 1716: the schoolmaster Mr. Leinbach, age 67 years.

Hochstadt [Hessen] Reformed KB:
Johannes Leinbach and wife Elizabeth had:
1. Johann Frederick, bp. 22 Aug. 1703
   Sp.: Johannes Schwartz, blacksmith and church elder.

    2. Johann Heinrich, bp. 29 Nov. 1705
       Sp.: Heinrich Leinbach, school sexton in Dorfelden
         [Oberdorfelden]
    3. Johanna Elisabeth, bp. 18 Oct. 1708, d. 28 Nov. 1712
    4. A son [Johannes], bp. 18 Feb. 1712
       Sp.: Johannes Heckerth
    5. A daughter, bp. 10 Dec. 1714, d. 3 Aug. 1716
    6. Johanna Maria, bp. 13 Feb. 1718
       Sp.: Johannah Maria Leinbach of Langenselbold
    7. Maria Barbara, bp. 11 Sept. 1722

AMERICAN RECORDS

Family Register, Oley Moravian KB, Berks County, PA, [published in *Der Reggeboge*, Quarterly of the Pennsylvania German Society, Vol. 14, No. 1 (Jan. 1980):

Johannes Leinbach, Senior was born in the Wetterau in Germany at Langen Selbolt in the year 1674, March 9, and was baptized there immediately after his birth by the pastor of the place in the Reformed religion, in which he was raised by his parents, Henrich Leinbach and Barbara, nee Lerch. In Germany he was an organist. He married Anna Elisabeth Kleiss on 2 Oct. 1700, and emigrated with his wife 11 Sept. 1723. In 1742 he was received into the congregation. He died 20 Nov. 1747, aged 73 years, 7 months, and 11 days.

Anna Elisabeth Leinbach, nee Kleiss, was born in Germany at Eidengesäss in the Wetterau in the year 1680, 2 Feb., and baptized there right after her birth by the pastor of the place in the Lutheran religion, in which she was also raised by her parents, Adam Kleiss and Elisabeth, nee Schillinger. She had five children:
    1. Friedrich Leinbach
    2. Johann Henrich Leinbach
    3. Johannes Leinbach
    4. Johanna Maria Leinbach
    5. Maria Barbara Leinbach

Johannes Leinbach born in Hochstadt in the Wetterau in Germany on 18 Feb. 1712, and at once baptized in the Reformed religion in which he was also raised by his parents; his father was Johannes Leinbach, organist, his mother Elisabeth, nee Kleiss. He emigrated with them in 1718 [corrected to read 1723]. Here he devoted himself to the soil as a farmer. On 12 Aug. 1735, he married Catharina, nee Riem, and joined the Moravians in 1743.

Catharina Leinbach, nee Riem, was born in Germany in the Upper
Palatinate [Leimen near Heidelberg; see *Der Reggeboge X,* No. 3-4, p. 11],
1 Jan. 1712, and baptized eight days after her birth in the Reformed religion.
She emigrated in 1717 with her parents Eberhard Riem and Elisabeth, nee
Schwab. Children [surname Leinbach]:

1. Elisabeth, born in Oley, 7 June 1736, bp. 19 Nov. 1737
   by Pastor Goetschy; moved to Bethlehem 1755.
2. Friedrich, born in Oley in 1737, bp. 19 Nov. 1737
   by Pastor Goetschy; moved away 1749.
3. Maria Barbara, born in Oley 14 June 1739, bp. 15 July 1739
   by Pastor Goetschy. Sp.: Stephan Schlaunecker, Maria
   Martin; moved to Bethlehem 30 Apr. 1759.
4. Johannes, born in Oley 5 Dec. 1740, unbaptized.
5. Ludwig, born in Oley 2 Jan. 1743, bp. 10 Jan. 1743
   by Brother Pyrlaeus. Sp. were the parents.
6. Abraham, born in Oley 26 Oct. 1744, bp. by Brother
   Kohn 4 Nov. 1744 in the church. Sp.: the father.
7. Joseph, born 12 Sept. 1746, died at once.
8. Benjamin, born 12 Sept. 1746, bp. in the middle of
   September by Brother Christian Rauch. Sp.: Michler,
   Johannes Leinbach, Sr.
9. Johanna, born in Gnadenthal 9 June 1748, bp. 11 June
   by Leonhard Schnell, died in Germantown 27 Apr. 1749.
10. Johanna, born in Bethlehem 7 Apr. 1750, bp. 7 Apr. 1750
    by Johann Nitschmann.
11. Joseph, born in Oley 3 Apr. 1752, bp. 4 Apr. 1752 by Brother
    Uthley. Sp.: the father.
12. Catharina, born in Oley 27 Nov. 1755, bp. 5 Dec. 1755 by
    Brother Krogstrup. Sp.: Rosina Müller, Johanna Leinbach,
    Gertraud Neukirch, Catharina Börstler.

Friedrich Leinbach was born at Hochstadt in Germany 15 July 1703, and
baptized right afterwards by Pastor Bender, the pastor there, in the
Reformed religion. His parents were Johannes Leinbach and Elisabeth, nee
Kleiss. He learned the trade of tailor in his youth. He emigrated to
Pennsylvania with his parents in 1723. He married 2 June 1737, Elisabeth
Frey. In 1742 he was received into the congregation at Oley.

Elisabeth Leinbach, nee Frey, was born in Skippack 1 July 1719. She was
left unbaptized in her youth and was baptized by Brother Ludwig 6 May
1742. Her parents were Henrich Frey, a turner, and Maria Catharine, nee
Levering. Was received by the Moravians with her husband. Children
[surname Leinbach]:

1. Johannes, born 1738 in Skippack, unbp., d. 10 Jan. 1746

    in Oley.

2. Henrich, born in Skippack, Worcester twp., 2 Feb. 1739, unbp.; moved to Bethlehem 21 Mar. 1758.
3. Jacob, born in Skippack, Worcester twp., 2 Apr. 1740, unbp.
4. Benjamin, born in Worcester twp., 20 Sept. 1741, unbp.
5. Elisabeth, born in Exeter 7 Apr. 1743, bp. at ten days by Eschenbach. Sp. the parents. Moved to Bethlehem 5 Sept. 1760.
6. Anna, born in Exeter twp. 11 Jan. 1745, bp. at eight days by Brother Peter Böhler.
7. Johanna, born in Exeter 9 Feb. 1746, bp. soon thereafter by Brother Christian Rauch. Sp. the parents.
8. Son born dead and buried 17 June 1747.
9. Joseph, born in Oley 25 Aug. 1748, bp. 20 Dec. 1748 by Brother Uthley. Sp. the parents.
10. Maria, born in Oley 3 Mar. 1750, bp. 20 Dec. 1750 by Brother Uthley.
11. Magdalena, born in Oley 11 Aug. 1751, bp. 18 Aug. 1751 by Brother Christoph Francke.
12. Johannes, born in Oley 21 June 1753, bp. 8 July 1753 by Brother Brandmüller.
13. Rosina, born in Oley 9 Mar. 1755, bp. 11 Mar. 1755 by Brother Soelle. Sp. Catharina and Johanna Leinbach, Gertraud Neukirch, and Rosina Müller.
14. Catharina, born in Oley 8 Jan. 1757, bp.16 Jan. 1757 by Brother Brandmüller.
15. Friedrich and
16. Daniel, born in Oley at 10 a.m. 23 Mar. 1760, bp. on the day of their birth by Brother G. Neisser. Sp. Heinrich and Johanna Leinbach and Johannes and Catharina Leinbach.
17. Samuel, born in Oley at 10 a.m. 25 July 1762, bp. 8 Aug. 1762 by Brother C. Gottfried Rundt. Sp. Johan Wolfgang and Maria Barbara Michler and Johannes and Catharina Leinbach.

Johan Henrich Leinbach was born at Hochstadt in Germany 26 Nov. 1705, and baptized there right after his birth by Pastor Bender of the place, in the Reformed religion. His parents were Johannes Leinbach and Elisabeth, nee Kleiss, with whom he emigrated in 1723, becoming a farmer and remaining with them until 2 Nov. 1739, when he married Salome, later renamed Johanna, nee Herrmann. In 1748 he was received into the congregation.

Johanna Leinbach, nee Herrmann, was born in Conestoga in Pennsylvania [i.e. Lancaster County] 16 Mar. 1718. She was of the Reformed religion, but remained unbaptized until 6 May 1742, when she was baptized by Brother Ludwig with the name Johanna and lost her original name Salome. Her parents were Daniel Herrmann and Maria Catharina Elisabeth, nee Obermüller. She was received into the congregation in 1743. Children [surname Leinbach]:

1. Anna, born in Bethlehem 25 Sept. 1740, baptized in Bethlehem at the Synod in 1748 by Johannes; moved to Bethlehem in 1752.
2. Elisabeth, born in Oley 17 Feb. 1742, bp. in Bethlehem in 1748 by Brother Cammerhoff. Sp. Mrs. Cammerhoff. Moved to Bethlehem in 1752.
3. Anna Catharina, born in Oley 8 Feb. 1744, and bp. right away by Brother Kohn. Died Jan. 1748 in the institute in Oley, buried by Michler.
4. Daniel, born in Oley 8 Jan. 1746, bp. not long thereafter by Leonhard Schnell. Sp: Johannes Leinbach Sr., Daniel Herrmann.
5. Maria, born in Oley 14 Jan. 1748, bp. not long thereafter by Philipp Meurer.
6. Christina, born in Oley 13 Feb. 1750, bp. not long thereafter by Brother Cammerhoff.
7. Henrich, born in Oley 11 Mar. 1752, bp. right thereafter by Brother Uthley. Sp. the father.
8. Salome, born in Oley 10 Feb. 1755, bp. 16 Feb. 1755 in the *Gemeinhaus* by Brother Soelle. Sp. Mrs. Johannes Leinbach, Catharina Börstler, Mrs. Neukirch, Rosina Müller. Died 18 ___ 1757, buried by Johannes Müller.
9. Christian, born in Oley 16 Mar. 1757, bp. the 23rd by Brother Soelle in the *Gemeinhaus*. Sp.: Johannes and Friedrich Leinbach, Henrich Neukirch, Johannes Müller.
10. Johannes, born in Oley 25 May 1759, bp. 27 May 1759 by Johan Heinrich Moeller. Sp.: the father, Johann Leinbach, Friedrich Leinbach, and Heinrich Neukirch.

Bethlehem Moravian Records, Northampton County, PA:
Barbara Nitschmann, maiden name Leinbach, b. 1722 Hochstadt, Wetterau.

Nazareth Moravian Cemetery Records, Northampton County, PA:
Anna Elisabeth Leinbach, maiden name Kleiz, born 1680, married 1700 John Leinbach. Came to Pennsylvania in 1723.

Lancaster County Release, estate of Johannes Leinbach, Sr.:
Abraham Riehm of Cocallico in the County of Lancaster, PA, Yeoman and Anna Maria, his wife, one of the daughters of John Leinbach late of Oley in the County of Berks, Yeoman deceased; whereas the said John Leinbach

died intestate leaving issue: three sons Frederick, Henry and John; and two daughters, Anna Maria, wife of Abraham Riehm; and Maria Barbara, wife of David Nitchman. Abraham Riehm and wife Anna Maria release their claims for £84 to the three sons. Dated 5 Apr. 1755. Wit. by Eberhard Rihm, Tobias Rihm. Recorded 2 May 1755.

56. LERCH, ANDREAS age 50
   LERCH, PETER age 20
   LERCH, ANTHON age 18
Queen Elizabeth, 1738
S-H, I: 216, 218, 220

EUROPEAN RECORDS

Langenselbold Reformed KB:
Conrad Lerch, son of Stoffel Lerch, m. 6 Nov. 1673 Gertraut, daughter of Johannis Bien from Wittgenborn. Their son:
   Andreas Lerch, bp. 12 June 1687
   Sp.: Andreas Schneider, the shepherd here.

Married 3 Sept. 1710, Andreas Lerch, son of Conrad Lerch, *Mitnachbar* here, and Elisabeth, widow of the late Johan Henrich Henckel. The marriage was necessary. The widow Elisabeth Henckel was b. 5 Apr. 1686, daughter of Johan Faust and Kunigunda. (Kunigunda, widow of Johan Faust, died 1721, age 74 years.)
[See 1733 immigrants Joh. Peter and Joh. Philip Faust for additional data on the family of Johannes and Kunigunda Faust.]

The first marriage of Elisabeth Faust is recorded in the KB on 27 Jan. 1707: Johann Henrich Henckel, a carpenter, son of the late Henrich Henckel, former *Inwohner* and linenweaver at *?Berauerswein in Oberfürstenthum Hess* married Elisabeth, daughter of Johan Faust. They had one child, born after the father's death:
   1. Anna Catharina Henckel, bp. 30 Oct. 1707
      Sp.: a daughter of Jost Henrich Weber.

The children of Andreas and Elisabeth (nee Faust) Lerch were:
   1. Anna Sabina, bp. 7 Dec. 1710; [she married 1737 Joh.
      Georg Freyman [q.v.] and emigrated 1739.]
      Sp.: single daughter of Adolff Roth.
   2. Johanna Gertrud, bp. 26 Mar. 1712
      Sp.: the wife of Tönges Lerch, the child's father's brother.

3. Anna Maria, bp. 1 Sept. 1715; buried 26 May 1718.
   Sp.: single daughter of Peter Schehrer
4. **Johann Peter**, bp. 10 Apr. 1718
   Sp.: single son of Otto Caspar Roth
5. **Antonius**, bp. 29 Sept. 1720; Sp.: Tönges Fuchs
6. Pancratius, bp. 30 May 1723 [surname Lörch]
   Sp.: Pancrat. Buchhold, here.
7. Johannes, bp. 9 Sept. 1725 [surname Lörch]
   Sp.: Johannes Rudel, *Herrschafftl. Hoffmann* here.

AMERICAN RECORDS

Lower Saucon Reformed KB, Lower Saucon Twp., Northampton County, PA:
Anthony Lerch and Anna Margaretha [nee Lauer] had children:
1. John, b. 6 Nov. 1747; Sp.: Gratius Lerch
2. Anthony, b. 18 Mar. 1750
   Sp.: Theobald Machelin and wife
3. Catharina, b. 8 Mar. 1752
   Sp.: Catharina Freymann
4. Anna Margaret, b. 31 Dec. 1754
   Sp.: Margaretha Oberlin
5. Nicholas, b. 30 Mar. 1757
   Sp.: Nicholas Michel
6. John Friedrich, b. 17 Apr. 1759, bp. 13 May 1759
   Sp.: Frederick Frutschy and wife
   [Above six baptisms entered by Rev. John Egidius Hecker.]
7. Anna Maria, b. 4 Feb. 1762; no sp. given
8. Peter, b. 7 Mar. 1764; no sp. given
9. Elisabeth, b. 2 Aug. 1768; no sp. given
10. Susanna, b. 31 Jan. 1773; bp. 3 Apr. 1773
    Sp.: Georg Freyman [q.v.] and wife Anna Sabina

Peter Lerch had a daughter:
    Anna Maria, b. 9 July 1757, bp. 24 July
    Sp.: Gratius Lerch and wife

Tohickon Reformed KB, Bucks County, PA:
Peter Lerch and Anna Eva had a daughter:
    Anna Maria b. 2 July 1759, bp. 24 July 1759
    Sp.: Cratias Lerch and wife

Frieden's Union Church, Friedensville, Upper Saucon, Lehigh County, PA:
Gratius Lerch and wife Anna Maria had a daughter:
    Abbolona b. ca 1763 (no other date recorded).

Lower Saucon Cemetery Records, Northampton County, PA:
Anthon Lerch, son of Andreas Lerch, b. in Germany 20 Sept. 1720;
emigrated 1738; d. 29 Aug. 1793.
(Church burial record: Died 29 Aug. 1793: Anthony Lerch, aged 72 years, 11
months, 8 days.)

Anna Margaretta Lerch, nee Lauer, wife of Anton Lerch, b. 7 May. 1728, d.
14 Feb. 1796.

Gratius Lerch died 1794; had 6 children, no marker in cemetery.

Anna Maria Lerch, nee Bahl, wife of Gratius Lerch, b. 11 Sept. 1727, d. 11
Dec. 1796. (Church burial record: d. 11 Dec. 1795: Anna Maria, widow of
Gratius Lerch, aged 68 years, 2 months.)

Williams Township congregation records, Northampton County, PA:
Peter Lerch and wife Anna Maria had a daughter:
    Susanna b, 13 Oct. 1747, bp. 15 Nov. 1747

Peter Lerch, widower m. 2 Jan. 1748 Eva, widow of Johannes Faaser.

Tohickon Reformed KB, Bedminster Twp., Bucks County, PA:
Anthony Lerch and wife Margaret had:
    1. Anthony bp. 15 Apr. 1750; (no Sp. listed)
    2. Nicholas, b. 30 Mar. 1757, bp. 11 Apr. 1757
       Sp.: Nicholas Michel & Maria Melcher
    3. Frederick, b. 17 Apr. 1759, bp. 13 May 1759
       Sp.: Frederick Frutschy and wife.

Pancratius Lerch and Anna Maria had:
    Eva Barbara, b. 16 Jan. 1759, bp. 15 Mar. 1759
    Sp.: Eva Barbara Neukommer
    Tobias, b. 15 Mar. 1761, bp. 10 May 1761
    Sp.: Philip Baal & Elisabeth Freyman

A Peter Lerch died 2 Jan. 1759 buried 4 Jan. 1759.

Nicholas Scull Notebook 5, Historical Society of PA Collections:
Survey of a tract for George "Gorman" [Kerman, German] under date of 10
Dec. 1737. Kerman had abandoned this land by 1749, and a new warrant was
then issued to Gratzius Lergh [Pancratius Lerch]. See Patent Book A-17 &
PA Archives, Third Series, Vol. XXIV, pg. 138.

Will Abstracts of Northampton County, PA. 1752-1802, by John Eyerman: Gratus LERCH, L. Saucon. 5/6/1794-9/10/1794. Anna Maria, wife. Sons Jacob and Tobias, exrs. Daughters Maria, Appolona, Elizabeth, Catharine. Mentions 2 children of son Philip, dec'd: John and Henry. Wit: Henry Ohl and Chas. Hartman.

Antony LERCH, the elder, L. Saucon, yeoman. Margaret, wife. Children: John (eldest), exr; Andrew, exr.(read Anthony); Frederich; Peter; Margaret (wife of Geo. Emrich); Elizabeth (wife of John Leidy); Susanna. Mentions John Shymer, son of daughter Anna Maria, dec'd. Mentions John, Anthony, Frederick, Peter, John, Margaret, Adam, Esther, and Samuel Beidelman, children of daughter Catharine, late wife of Adam Beidelman. Wit: Frederick Laubach, Andreas Heller, Robert Traill. [No dates given in abstract; the index of Northampton County Wills indicates probate in 1793, Will # 1548.]

Philadelphia Will Book F: 533; dated 7 Jan. 1754; prob. 26 Mar. 1754. John Peter Lauer of Upper Hanover Twp., Philadelphia Co., yeoman. Estate to wife Anna Margreth and seven (7) children: Peter Lauer, John George Lauer; Anna Elisabeth Mechlin; Anna Mary Morner(in); Mary Eva Holdeman(in); Anna Margreth Lerch(in); Catharina Schell(in). Adm. to **Anthony Lark and Margaret, his wife,** daughter of John Peter Lauer.

As noted above, the first daughter of Andreas Lerch married Georg Freyman and they emigrated in 1739. Additional data will be found under Freyman. The second daughter, Johanna Gertrud, also may have emigrated with her first husband _____ Michel. [He is possibly Paul Michel who also arrived on the ship *Samuel* in 1739 with the Freymans.] They had a son Nicholas Michel. The father of this child died soon after arrival, and Gertrud Lerch Michel m. (2) ca. 1741 in PA Johannes Nowlane (Naulin, Nohlen etc.) For more detail, see article by David Green, C.G., F.A.S.G., "The Parents of Nicholas Michel of Northampton County, Pennsylvania: Using Circumstantial Evidence in Pennsylvania German Research" in *The Pennsylvania Genealogical Magazine,* Volume XXXVIII, No. 4, Fall/Winter 1994. On 1 Feb. 1754, John Nowlan of Bethlehem Township, Northampton County, mortgaged 250 acres for £ 18 to Anthony Lereck [Lerch] of Lower Saucon. Also, Johannes Nohlen and wife Gertraud had a son Johann George, b. 18 June 1742, bp. 27 June 1742; the sponsors at the baptism were Johann Georg Freymann and his wife Anna Sophia [sic: should read Sabina].

Naturalized 24 Sept. 1757, Antony Lerch [no residence stated.]

57. LERCH, CASPAR age 44
Queen Elizabeth, 1738
S-H, I: 217, 218, 220

EUROPEAN RECORDS

Langenselbold Reformed KB:
Johannes Lerch, son of Johannes Lerch, married 9 Feb. 1688 Catharina,
daughter of Christian Fuchs. They had children:
 1. Anna Barbara, bp. 16 Dec. 1688
    Sp.: Henrich Leimbach, schoolmaster at Hochstatt
 2. Johannes [q.v.], bp. 8 Nov. 1691
    Sp.: Johannes Döll, *Mitnachbar* here.
 3. **Caspar**, bp. 28 Oct. 1694
    Sp.: the father's brother, Caspar Lerch, single
 4. Helena, bp. 25 May 1697
    Sp.: the wife of Conrad Grauel
 5. Anna Elisabeth, bp. 13 Jan. 1701; she m. (1) 6 Dec. 1724 Johann
    Henrich Fischer [q.v.] and came to PA with him in 1733; she m.
    (2) Stephan Brecht in Berks County, PA.
 6. Johan Henrich, bp. 31 Jan. 1704
    Sp.: the child's father's brother.

Caspar Lörch, son of the late Johan Lörch, m. (1) 19 Jan. 1724 Anna
Margretha Fuchs, daughter of the late Niclaus Fuchs. They had children:
 1. Johann Wilhelm, bp. 11 Feb. 1725
    Sp.: the single son of Weychel Fischer
 2. Anna Christina, bp. 15 Sept. 1726
    Sp.: Georg Fuchs' daughter
 3. Niclaus, bp. 28 Nov. 1728
    Sp.: Niclaus Wacker, the young *Burgmüller*
 4. Johannes, bp. 29 Aug. 1731
    Sp.: Joh. Conrad Adam's youngest son

Caspar Lörch, widower, m. (2) 10 Dec. 1732 Anna Margretha, daughter of
Joh. Henrich Ströder at Wernings. They had:
 5. Joh. Christoph, bp. 31 Jan. 1734
    Sp.: Joh. Christoph Ströder, son of Joh. Henrich Ströder
    at Wernings, the child's mother's brother.

Eckhartshausen Reformed KB:
Caspar Lerch, H. Doctor Bock's *Hofmann* here, and wife Anna Margretha
had a son:

6. Johannes Balthasar, b. 24 May 1737; bp. 30 May 1737
Sp.: Joh. Balthasar Kaÿser from Wernings, Hochgräff
Birstein.

AMERICAN RECORDS

1754 Berks County tax list, Heidelberg Township: Casper Lerg

Hain's (St. John's) Reformed KB, Wernersville, Berks County, PA:
Casper Lerch and wife had:
A daughter [Rachel], bp. 11 Jan. 1747
Sp.: John Adams and his wife Rahel

Christ "Little Tulpehocken" Lutheran KB, Berks County, PA:
Caspar Lerch (and wife) had:
A daughter Anna Eliesabetha, b. 6 June 1741, bp. 2 Aug. 1741
Sp.: Anna Eliesabetha Ermantraut [q.v.]

Bern Reformed KB, Bern Township, Berks County, PA:
Balthasar Lerch's widow had a son:
John, bp.24 July 1774
Sp.: John Staut and wife.

Christopher Lerch and wife had:
Daniel, bp. 25 Dec. 1776; sp.: Daniel Albrecht

John William, b. 7 Jan. 1785, bp. 6 Feb. 1785
Sp.: John William Lerch and Maria Margaret.

Bern Reformed Church Cemetery: Tombstone inscription:
Balthaser Lerch
b. 18 May 1737, d. 24 Apr. 1774; had 7 children.

Abstracts of Berks County Wills and Administrations:
Casper Lark, Heidelberg, 8 Sept. 1766, prob. 18 Oct. 1766. Provides for wife
Margaret; to sons William, Nicholas, Balser, Jacob and Jost £25 each. To
daughters Elizabeth Lark, alias Fox, £25 To dau. Margaret Lark, alias
Lowery, £25. To dau. Caterina Lark, alias Feb, £25. To dau. Rachel Lark
£25. To my son Christopher all my land, tenements, etc. and he is also
executor. Witness: Ulrich Ritschart, Thomas Jones and Casper Lörch.

Baltzer Lerch, Bern, 1 Jan. 1774 - 16 May 1774. Provides for wife Barbara
and refers to children who are under 14 but does not name them. Friends

William Lerch and Johannes Staut, executors. Witness: Conrad Schneider and John George Staudt. Translation.

Nicholas Lerch, Heidelberg, 4 June 1787. Adm. to Margretha Elisabetha Lerch, the widow.

Yost Lerch, Heidelberg, 21 Jan. 1806. Adm. to Rosina, the widow.

Rev. Boos' Pastoral Records, Scrwartzwald, Berks Co., burials:
Johann Jost Lerch, b. 30 Jan. 1752; d. 10 Dec. 1805

Naturalized 10 Apr. 1761, Caspar Lerk, Heidleburg Twp., Berks Co., PA.

58. LERCH, JOHANNES age ~~44~~ 47
Queen Elizabeth, 1738
S-H, I: 217, 218, 220

EUROPEAN RECORDS

Langenselbold Reformed KB:
Johannes Lerch, son of Johannes Lerch, married 9 Feb. 1688 Catharina, daughter of Christian Fuchs. They had children:

     1. Anna Barbara, bp. 16 Dec. 1688
        Sp.: Henrich Leimbach, schoolmaster at Hochstatt
     2. **Johannes**, bp. 8 Nov. 1691
        Sp.: Johannes Döll, *Mitnachbar* here.
     3. Caspar, bp. 28 Oct. 1694
        Sp.: the father's brother, Caspar Lerch, single
     4. Helena, bp. 25 May 1697
        Sp.: the wife of Conrad Grauel
     5. Anna Elisabeth, bp. 13 Jan. 1701; she m. (1) 6 Dec. 1724 Johann Henrich Fischer [q.v.] and came to PA with him in 1733; she m. (2) Stephan Brecht in Berks County, PA.
     6. Johan Henrich, bp. 31 Jan. 1704
        Sp.: the child's father's brother.

AMERICAN RECORDS

This Johannes Lerch was a brother of the Caspar Lerch, above, who arrived on the same ship; if he is the immigrant, his age is wrong in the ship's list.

There are several other members of the Lerch family who appear in the Rev. Boos' burial records at Schwartzwald Church in Berks Co., PA; they are possibly related to the above family.

  Jost Lerch, b. 13 Mar. 1733, d. 23 Oct. 1783.
  Andreas Lerch, b. 25 Jan. 1737, d. 6 Aug. 1793.
  Jacob Lerch, b. 26 Aug. 1739, bp. 16 Jan. 1802.

Another Lörch [Lerich] immigrant named Johannes also arrived on the ship *Samuel* in 1733. He was age 26, and came with a wife Anna Maria, age 28 and a son Hans Jerich [Johann Georg], age 3. There were several other Langenselbold emigrant families on this ship, also. This 1733 immigrant may be the Johannes Lerch at Williams Twp. congregation in Northampton County, PA, who, with wife Anna Maria, had a child bp. 10 Feb. 1740.

Half-timbered structure near the church in Langenselbold.

59. MELL, MELCHIOR
Ann Galley, 1746
S-H, I: 360, 362

EUROPEAN RECORDS

Langenselbold Reformed KB:
Johannes Mell, son of the late Conrad Mell, m. 22 Jan. 1705 Anna, daughter
of Matthes Bock from Eichenzell, Fürst. Fuldischer jurisdiction, (Eichenzell
near Fulda). Johannes Mell and Anna had a son:
  Johan Melchior, bp. 26 May 1709 at Selbold
  Sp.: Johan Melchior Mell, the child's father's brother

Died 26 Dec. 1737: Johannes Mell, age 60 years and 3 months.
Died 26 Apr. 1750: Anna, widow of the late Johannes Mell, age ca. 60 years.

Johann **Melchior Mell**, son of the late Johannes Mell, m. 8 Jan. 1742
Elisabetha, daughter of Carl Hedderich, inhabitant here. Johann Melchior
Mell and wife Elisabetha had:
  1. Carl Johann Henrich, bp. 21 Feb. 1742
     Sp.: Carl Hedderich, the child's grandfather on the mother's side
     "das Kind aber ist aus unehel. beyschlaff"
  2. Carl Henrich, bp. 7 June 1744
     Sp.: Carl Hedderig, the child's grandfather on the mother's side.

AMERICAN RECORDS

1754 Berks Co. Tax List, Heidelberg Twp.: Melchor Mehl.

Hain's (St. John's) Reformed KB, Berks County, PA:
John Melchior Mell and wife Elisabeth had:
  a son, bp. 19 Nov. 1749
  Sp.: John Traut.

**Pennsylvania Archives, Sixth Series, Vol. 6, Rev. John Waldschmidt's
records (baptisms also recorded in Hain's KB):**
Carl Mell and wife Anna Maria had children:
  1. Elisabeth b. 8 Dec. 1774, bp. 26 Dec. 1774
     Sp.: Melchior Mell and wife Elisabeth
  2. Johannes b. 15 Apr. 1776, bp. 30 Apr. 1776
     Sp.: Johannes Mell and wife Susanna
  3. Johann Heinrich b. 1 Feb. 1778, bp. 4 Apr. 1778
     Sp.: Heinrich Fischer and wife Christina

 4. Joh. Wilhelm b. 5 Oct. 1779, bp. 11 Oct. 1779
    Sp.: Joh. Wilhelm Michael and wife Elisabeth.

Conf. 30 Mar. 1766 at Cacusy:
Johann, son of <u>Michael</u> Mell [presumably Melchior intended].

Conf. 15 Apr. 1770 at Cacusy:
Elisabeth daughter of Melchior Mell

First Reformed KB, Reading, Berks County, Burials:
Carl Mell buried at Haehns (Hain's church)
14 May 1807, age 62 y. 10 mo. 6 days.

Charles Mell, 3rd Class, Capt. Conrad Kershner's Co., Militia, return 23 Oct.
1788.

60. MELLHAUSEN, CASPAR age 28
Samuel, 1733
S-H, I: 107, 111, 112

EUROPEAN RECORDS

Langenselbold Reformed KB:
Married (1) 21 Dec. 1690 Johan Wilhelm Mellhausen, born *aus Hessen vom Hayngen--fen von Cassel*, and Engel, daughter of Hans Faust the elder, whom he had impregnated. They had children:
 1. Christina Margretha, bp. 10 Oct. 1692, sick and bapt. at home
 2. Johannes, bp. 17 Feb. 1695
    Sp.: Hans Faust's son Johannes, single

Engel, wife of Johan Wilhelm Mellhausen, died 26 Feb. 1695 age about 30 years.

Married (2) 22 Aug. 1695 at Selbold, Johan Wilhelm Mellhausen, widower, and Susanna, daughter of Caspar Rauch. Children of second marriage:
 1. Johan Peter, bp. 16 Aug. 1696 [Em. 1739, q.v.]
    Sp.: Burckhard Koch's single son
 2. Joh. Jacob, bp. 4 May 1698
    Sp.: The child's father's brother
 3. Catharina, bp. 4 Aug. 1700
    Sp.: Catharina, single dau. of Caspar Rauch

    4. Anna Ursula, bp. 30 July 1702
       Sp.: Caspar Rauch's wife
    5. Anna Catharina, bp. 8 Mar. 1705
       Sp.: the child's father's sister, from
       Langendibach, widow of Jörg Hempel.
    6. **Johan Caspar**, bp. 5 June 1707
       Sp.: Caspar Rauch, the child's grandfather

AMERICAN RECORDS

1754 Berks County tax list, Alsace Twp: Casper Millhouse.

61. MELLHAUSEN, PETER age 42
Samuel, 1739
S-H, I: 256, 259, 261
  (signed Peder Meelhus) A list: Peter Mill house

EUROPEAN RECORDS

Langenselbold Reformed KB:
Johan Wilhelm Mellhausen and his second wife Susanna nee Rauch had a
son:
      Johan Peter, bp. 16 Aug. 1696
      (see Caspar Mellhausen for complete list of family)

Joh. Conrad Fuchs, son of Peter Fuchs, *Mitnachbahr* here, married 24 Nov.
1698 Anna Maria, daughter of Johann Höyn, also *Mitnachbahr*.

Mstr. Joh. Peter Mellhausen, mason, son of the late Wilhelm Mellhausen,
m. 4 Dec. 1726 Anna Rosina Fuchs, daughter of the late Johan Conrad
Fuchs. They had children:
    1. Anna Catharina, bp. 26 Oct. 1727, d. 2 Nov. 1727
       Sp.: The child's father's single sister
    2. Johann Henrich, bp. 30 Dec. 1728
       Sp.: David Ehl's single son
    3. Anna Maria, bp. 3 Oct. 1731
       Sp.: Johannes Wolff's daughter
    4. Maria Elisabetha, bp. 6 May 1734
       Sp.: a daughter of Wörner Leyss

AMERICAN RECORDS

Augustus Lutheran KB, Trappe, Montgomery County, PA:
Jacob Joachim m. 30 Dec. 1755 at Providence Maria Christina Mühlhaus, daughter of the late Peter Mühlhaus.

Lower Bermudian Lutheran and Reformed KB, Adams County, PA:
Married 16 Nov. 1760, Henrich Mühlhaus and Margaret, daughter of George Schnauffer.
Communicants list, dated 11 May. 1761:
Margaretha Mühlhaus, wife of Henrich.

62. MOHN, JOHANNES age 33
Elizabeth, 1733
S-H, I: 113, 114, 115, 765, 766
  [with Margret Moon age 44, Maria Moon age 10, Matiles Moon age 8, Vernor Moon age 6, Conen Lutwick Moon 3½]

EUROPEAN RECORDS

Langenselbold Reformed KB:
Peter Mohn, son of the late Hans Mohn, m. 14 Apr. 1681 Margretha, daughter of Hans Rack, the *Kloster Wirth*.

Peter Mohn and Margreth had a son:
        Johannes, bp. 2 Nov. 1701
        Sp.: Johannes Hübener, single son of Henrich Hübener

Johannes Mohn, son of Peter Mohn, m. 4 Mar. 1722 Margretha, daughter of the deceased Melchior Hack of Lichenroth. Children:
    1. Anna Maria, bp. 27 Feb. 1723
        Sp.: single daughter of David Ehl
    2. Johanna Magdalena, bp. 14 Mar. 1725
        Sp.: the daughter of Joh. Conrad Hix
    3. Wörner, bp. 18 Dec. 1726
        Sp.: Wörner Mohn, here.
    4. Johann Ludwig, bp. 5 Jan. 1729
        Sp.: Joh. Ludwig Ermold, tailor.

AMERICAN RECORDS

1754 Berks Co. Tax List, Cumru Twp.:
Lodwick Moon, Werner Moon, John Moon.

Berks Co. Deed Book 1: 290:
John Moon of Cumru Twp., Berks Co.(previously Lancaster Co.), yeoman,
and wife Margaret deeded a 59 acre tract in Cumru Twp., to Lodowick
Moon of the same place, yeoman, their son.

Hain's (St. John's) Reformed KB, Berks Co., PA:
John Mohn and wife were sp. in 1747 for Anna Margaret, dau. of Georg
Hep (or Hen?) and wife.

Ludwig Mohn and wife (Anna Odilia) had children:
      1. Magdalena bp. 14 Aug, 1748
         Sp.: Michel Kleber [q.v., Gleber] and wife.
      2. a son bp. 3 Sept. 1749
         Sp.: Johannes ?Bautz, the mother's brother.
      3. Susanna (mother recorded as *Andilla*) b. 12 Sept. 1762
         Sp.: Catharina Schaarman.   bp. 26 Sept. 1762
      4. Daniel b. 25 Dec. 1771, bp. 19 Jan. 1772
         Sp.: Werner Weizel.

Abstracts of Berks County Wills:
John Mohn, Cumru, dated 2 June 1764, prob. 2 Oct. 1764. To son Ludwig
the plantation whereon I now live in Cumru containing 245 acres, he paying
legacies as follows: To son Werner Mohn £100, to dau. Magdalena, wife of
George Hean £50, to dau. Maria, wife of Jacob Ledy, £50. Remainder to
son Ludwig. Friends Henry Christ and Samuel Weiser, executors. Witnesses
Valentine Kerber, Geo. Geisler, George Wunder.

Ludwig Mohn, Brecknock, 26 Feb. 1791 - 2 Feb. 1796 (trans.) To son
Daniel all my land containing about 170 acres in Brecknock, with stock and
farming utensils, subject to provisions for wife Ottilia. To eldest son John
200 pounds. To son Ludwig 50 pounds, to son Henry 50 pounds, to dau.
Susanna and Elisabeth 50 pounds each. Son Peter has had his share, gets
no more. Eldest son John and son Ludwig executors. Witnesses John Heyll
and Balzer Fritz.

Records of Deaths from Berks Newspapers:
On Sunday the 12th inst. in Brecknock twp., Berks Co.: Peter Mohn in the
67th year of his age (Chronicle of the Times, 29 Jan. 1823).

Rev. Boos' Pastoral Record, Schwartzwald, Berks Co., burials:
Anna Ottilia Mohn, b. 13 Nov. 1729, d. 18 Nov. 1802.

John Mohn, Cumru Township, Berks County, nat. 10 (11) Apr. 1761.
Ludwick Mohn, Cumru Township, Berks County, nat. 24-25 Sept. 1761.

63. REBER, CONRAD
Ann Galley, 1746
S-H, I: 359, 361
                    EUROPEAN RECORDS

Langenselbold Reformed KB:
Daniel Reber, son of the late Herman Reber, m. 14 Oct. 1655 Maria,
daughter of Conrad ?Ronpel.

Daniel Reber [also Räber] and wife Maria had children:
1. Michael, bp. 29 Oct. 1657
   Sp.: Michael Pharo, linenweaver.
2. Conrad, bp. 2 Oct. 1659; sp.: Conrad Gerhardt
3. Johannes, bp. 20 Mar. 1661; sp.: Hans Gerth
4. Johann Conrad, bp. 25 Dec. 1662
   Sp.: Conradt Henckhel from Neuenhassel [Neuenhasslau].
5. Anna Maria, bp. 11 June 1665; sp.: his sister Anna.
6. Johann Peter, bp. 1 July 1666
   Sp.: brother-in-law Peter Ring.
7. Catharina, bp. 13 Sept. 1668
   Sp.: Catharina, dau. of Conradt Hinckel.
   She m. Peter Lamb [q.v. Lamm]
8. Hans Bernhard, bp. 15 Jan. 1671; Sp.: Hans Ebernaw's son

Bernhard Reber, son of Daniel Reber, m. 5 Jan. 1702 Anna Maria, daughter
of Valentin Ähl. They had children:
1. Anna Maria, bp. 28 Mar. 1703; sp.: Henrich Lofinck's wife
2. Johannes [q.v.] bp. 22 Feb. 1705
   Sp.: Johannes Ähl, single son of Johan Ähl.
3. Johan Paul, bp. 7 Dec. 1712
   Sp.: Johan Paul Dauber at Hanau.
4. Anna Elisabetha, twin dau. bp. 17 July 1716
   Sp.: the wife of Conrad Mohn.

    5. Eleonora Amalia, twin dau. bp. 17 July 1716
       Johannes Ehl's eldest, single daughter.
    6. Anna Magdalena, bp. 3 June 1720
       Sp.: the child's mother's sister, Johanes Schäffer's wife.
       She m. 1740 Joh. Conrad Bloss [q.v.]
    7. Joh. Conrad, bp. 21 Mar. 1723
       Sp.: the single son of the late Michael Reber.

Died 16 Dec. 1743 - Johann Bernhard Reber, age 72 y. 11 mo.

Died 27 Apr. 1730 - Bernhard Reber's wife Anna Maria, age 47 y. 4 mo. and some days.

AMERICAN RECORDS

Blue Mountain (Zion) Union KB, North Tulpehocken Twp., Berks Co., PA:
Conrad Räber and wife had:
    1. Conrad, bp. 10 Dec. 1751
       Sp.: Conrad Werth and wife
    2. Anna Catharina, bp. 10 Apr.1753
       Sp.: John Dückert and wife
    3. Elisabeth, b. 18 Mar. 1766, bp. 31 Mar. 1766
       Sp.: Jacob Loos and wife

1754 Berks Co Tax list, Tulpehocken twp: Conrad Reber

Abstracts of Berks County Wills & Adm:
Conrad Reber, Bethel 24 Sept. 1796. Adm. to Conrad, eldest son, Margaret, the widow, renouncing.

Conrad Reber, Bern, 12 June 1817. Adm. Adam Reber, brother, father renouncing.

Valentine Reber, Bern, 14 Dec. 1818. Adm. Adam, son, widow renouncing.

Thomas Reber, Bern, 2 Oct. 1821 - 30 Sept. 1823, to son Conrad the farm at £3750, to sons John, Peter, Valentine and Conrad the farm in Ohio as tenants in common. To dau. Catharine personal property and 1/2 proceeds . . . and the benefit of dwelling house during life and interest of £1000 yearly. Also mentions daughters Magdalena, Anna Maria, Elizabeth and Susanna. Executors sons John and Conrad and son-in-law Henry vanReed. Witnesses John Spayd and John Witman.

Jacob Reber, Bethel, 30 Sept. 1822, Adm. Peter, brother, widow renouncing.

Hain's (St. John's) Reformed KB, Berks Co., Tombstone Inscriptions:

Magdalena Werner, nee Reber   William Werner
Wife of William Werner   b. 16 July 1769
b. 10 Oct. 1775   d. 7 Nov. 1834
d. 27 Oct. 1823   (son of Henry Werner & Margaret,
(Daughter of Thomas Reber &   nee Meyer.)
wife Elisabeth, nee Kerschner)

Conrad Raber, Tulpehoccon Twp., Berks County, nat. Autumn, 1765.

64. REBER, JOHANNES
possibly on *Francis and Elizabeth*, 1742, with others
[Emigration document dated 23 Apr. 1742]

EUROPEAN RECORDS

Langenselbold Reformed KB:
Bernhard Reber, son of Daniel Reber, m. 5 Jan. 1702 Anna Maria, daughter
of Valentin Ähl. Joh. Bernhard Reber and Anna Maria had a son:
>   **Johannes**, bp. 22 Feb. 1705
>   Sp.: Johannes Ähl, single, son of Johan Ähl
>   [See immigrant Conrad Reber for complete family record.]

Johannes Reber, son of Joh. Bernhard Reber, "*Mitnachbar*" m. 8 Feb. 1736
Johanna Magdalena, daughter of Conrad Hahn, "*auch Einwohner*" [See
immigrant Joh. Thomas Hahn for her bp. and more detail on the family.]
They had children:
>   1. Johannes, bp. 16 Dec. 1736
>   Sp.: The child's mother's brother, son of Conrad Hahn
>   2. Ludwig Friederich August bp. 11 Sept. 1740

AMERICAN RECORDS

Rev. Boos' Pastoral Records, Schwartzwald, Berks County, PA, burials:
Johannes Räber, b. 22 Feb. 1705, d. 14 Nov. 1784

Bern Reformed Church, Bern Twp., Berks County, PA:
John Reber and wife had:
>   Anna Margaret, bp. 28 Oct. 1750

Thomas Raeber [Räber], and wife had:
1. Peter, bp. 1 Nov. 1772; sp.: Peter Kerschner.
2. Catharine, bp. 22 May 1774
3. Joh. Valentin, bp. 19 May 1777
   Sp.: Valentin Raeber and wife.
4. Anna Maria, bp. 25 Dec. 1778
   Sp.: Peter Ebler and wife.
5. Elizabeth, b. 25 Dec. 1783, bp. 12 Apr. 1784
   Sp.: Elizabeth Lerch.
6. Susanna, b. 5 July 1785, bp. 7 Aug. 1785
   Sp.: Valentin Raeber and wife Susanna.
   (She d. 15 Oct. 1834; date of death from tombstone at Bern
   Church Cemetery).

John Raeber [Räber], and wife had:
1. Anna Maria, bp. 1 Aug. 1773; sp.: Cath. Räber, single.
2. Abraham, bp. 10 Sept. 1775; sp.: Abraham Haas, widower.
3. Joh. Michael, bp. 10 Nov. 1777; sp.: Michael Lauer and wife
4. John Nicholas, bp. 26 Mar. 1780; sp.: John Nicholas Haas & w.
5. Maria Susanna, b. 4 July 1782, bp. 4 July 1782
   Sp.: Valentin Raeber and wife.

Valentin Raeber and wife had:
John, bp. 30 July 1775; sp.: John Raeber and wife.

Bernville, Berks County, Cemetery Records: Tombstone Inscriptions:
Valentin Reber, b. __ Dec. 1742, d. 12 Mar.? or May? 1818
m. Susanna Haas, b. 28 Sept. 1744, d. 11 Apr. 1823;
they had 5 sons and 2 daughters.

Conrad Reber, son of Valentin Reber
b. 12 Oct. 1778, d. 16 Feb. 1817

Tombstone Inscriptions, Bern Reformed Church, Berks County, PA:
Thomas Reber, b. 1746, d. 27 Aug. 1823, age 77 years;
husband of Elizabeth Kerschner; had 5 sons and 6 daughters.

Susanna Reber, nee Lasch, wife of Nicolaus Reber
b. 15 Sept. 1783, d. 4 Sept. 1822

Catharine Reber, nee Fleischer; second wife of Nicolaus Reber
b. 21 Aug. 1787, d. 28 Sept. 1857

Nicolaus Reber, b. 23 Jan. 1780, d. 23 Jan. 1844

Elizabeth Reber, wife of Johannes (?Thomas) Reber
b. 1 Nov. 1747; d. 27 Dec. 1817

Magdalena Reber, wife of Johannes Reber, b. 1750, d. 8 Oct. 1818.

Johannes Reber, b. 16 Dec. 1736, d. 27 Aug. 1821.

Rev. Daniel Schumacher's Pastoral Records:
Johannes Rebber and wife Elisabeth had a son:
    Daniel, b. __ Jan. 1763 in Heidelberg
        bp. 13 Feb. 1763, 3 weeks old
        Sp.: Conrad Bloss [q.v.] and wife Magdalena [nee Reber,
    daughter of Bernhard Reber].

Pennsylvania Patent Book AA-5: 211:
Warrant dated 30 Nov, 1744, surveyed to *John Reibert*, 135 A. of land in
Heidleburg Twp. in the county then Lancaster, now Berks, adjoining land
of Peter Tressler [q.v.- Dressler], John Morris, Philip Hause [Haas ?].
The said John Reibert by Deed Poll dated 3 Jan. 1749 sold to Andrew
Reiger; Andrew Reiger on 17 Apr. 1752 sold to Conrad Fink; Fink sold to
Johannes ?Keoler or ?Kesler on 18 Mar. 1762. Patent to Johannes Kesler,
19 Sept. 1763.
On page 568 of the same Patent Book, Hans *Rever,* of Bern Twp., patented
a tract of 209 A. on 9 June 1764, on the Tulpehocken Creek.

Abstracts of Berks County Wills & Adm.:
John Reber, Heidelberg, 28 Sept. 1821, Adm. to John and Nicholas, sons.

Johannes Reber, 1742 emigrant, brought an emigration permit with him to
America. This document has survived, and is pictured on page 111 of Kathy
M. Scogna's History of Lower Heidelberg Twp., Berks County, titled *Now
and Then,* published by the township as part of its 150th anniversary
celebration in 1992. Johannes Reber also appears on the list of 1742
Langenselbold emigrants that was located by Rolf Kirschner in the archive
at Marburg. See introduction for more information about this document.

One John Reber, Heidleberg Township, Berks County, nat. 13 May 1768.
[There were other immigrants with this name: one Johannes Räber arrived
on the ship *Ranier* in 1749, and a Johannes Reber on the *Phoenix* in 1749.]

65. REICHERT (RIGERD) LUDWIG age 28
Richard and Elizabeth, 1733
S-H, I: 127, sick

EUROPEAN RECORDS

Langenselbold Reformed KB:
Friedrich Richard, son of Henrich Richerd, deceased *Einwohner* at Allendorff, *Frühlinger Grunds*, m. 15 Apr. 1686 Catharina, daughter of Tönges Troid. They had children, surname Reichard in some records:
  1. Christoffel, bp. 29 June 1687
  2. Anna Margretha, bp. 11 May 1690
     Sp.: Nicklas Keller's wife
  3. Kunigunda, bp. 20 Aug. 1696; Sp.: Hans Wetzel's daughter.
     [Kunigunda was the first wife of Jacob Freÿman, q.v.].
  4. Joh. Philipps (Reichard), bp. 21 Dec. 1698
     Sp.: single son of Conrad Geibel.
  5. Elisabeth, bp. 16 Oct. 1701; sp.: dau. of Christian Lerch.
     [Elisabeth was the first wife of Joh. Henrich Fischer, q.v.]

Fritz Reichard and Catharina, his wife, had:
  6. **Johann Ludwig**, bp. 2 Dec. 1703
     Sp.: Ludwig, single son of David Troyd

AMERICAN RECORDS

Weisenburg Township (now Lehigh County) tax list 1762: Ludwig Reichard

Ziegel Reformed KB, Weisenburg Twp., Lehigh County, PA:
Ludwig Reicher sp. ch. of Georg Schäffer in 1752.

Charles Roberts et al, *History of Lehigh County, Pennsylvania*, Vol. III:
Ludwig Reichard, a pioneer of Weisenburg Township, paid a federal tax of seventeen pounds in 1762. The tax list of 1781 does not contain his name any more, but that of his son George already appears in 1762 and also in 1781. In 1812 Michael and Henry Reichard, sons of George, were residents in Weisenburg, Michael removed from that district to South Whitehall township.

Abstracts of Northampton County, PA Wills, 1752-1802: by John Eyerman:
REICHERD: Ludwig, Weissenberg Twp. 24 July 1777-(?) ch: George, exr., Margareth (issue), Catherine (issue), and ch. of dau. Catherine Elizabeth dec'd.   Son in law John Gackenbach, co-exr.   Michael Brobst, Joseph Seefried Jr., Mathias Probst, Wit.

REICHERT: George, Lower Saucon, yeoman; 5 April 1787-2 Oct. 1787. Eve Sellomy wife. Ch: Michael, Andrew, John, George (exr), Jacob, George William, Magdalena (wf. of Andrew Zegenfuse) issue), Mary Barbara, Elizabeth, Catherine. Wit: T. Cally, Peter Sean, Math. Schneider.

Ludwick Ricart, Weisenberg Twp., Northampton Co., nat. Fall 1765.

66. RÖHRIG, NICLAUS
Francis and Elisabeth, 1742
S-H, I: 329
                              EUROPEAN RECORDS

Langenselbold Reformed KB:
Johann Jörg Röhrich, son of Hans Conrad Röhrich from *Freyenstein in Ried-Eselischen Jurisdiction*, m. 17 Nov. 1701 Anna Sabina Brüning, daughter of the late Peter Brüning. They had:
1. Severinus, bp. 4 Feb. 1703
   Severin Röhrich, the child's father's brother here.
2. Anna Maria, bp. 22 Sept. 1704
   Sp.: Anna Maria, dau. of the late Johan Jörg Ermold.
3. Johan Michael, bp. 2 Feb. 1707; sp.: Michael Spindler.
4. Christina, bp. 19 Aug. 1708
   Sp.: a daughter of Severin Röhrich.
5. Johanna Esther, bp. 8 Jan. 1710
   Sp.: a dau. of Peter Brünig, the child's mother's sister,
   Joh. Wilhelm Euler, single son of Thomas Euler, *Beysass.*
6. Anna Margretha, bp. 1 Feb. 1713
   Sp.: a single daughter of Michael Rörig, here.
7. Johann Caspar, bp. 3 July 1715
   Sp.: a son of the old carpenter Johann Ehrlich.
8. Johannes, bp. 28 Feb. 1717
   Sp.: Hans Freÿmann, master linenweaver.
9. Anna Maria, bp. 23 Aug. 1720
   Sp.: a servant of the *Oberschultheis* Lörey.

Severin Röhrig and wife Juliana had a son:
   Johan Niclaus, bp. 7 Feb. 1725; died 24 Nov. 1726.
   Sp.: Michael Röhrig's single son here.

An emigration record for the year 1742 lists Nicolaus Röhrig as a emigrant from Langenselbold. The immigrant is possibly the single son of Michael

Röhrig who sponsored this Johann Niclaus, b. 1725, d. 1726. The list of emigrants also includes Georg Röhrig's daughter Eva Catharina. Her baptism has not been located in the Langenselbold records.

AMERICAN RECORDS

St. Michaelis and Zion Lutheran KB, Philadelphia, PA:
Married 5 May 1747 in Philadelphia: Niclas Röhrig (Reformed) and Anna Maria Johnson, Lutheran, widow; married in presence of relatives of Schippach Mennonites.

Nichs. Rehrig, nat. Fall 1765, Salford Twp., Philadelphia Co., PA

67. ROTH, ANNA SABINA
Elizabeth, 1733
S-H, I: 766 (name on list: Savena Cowell)
[She appears to be listed in S-H as Sabina Crowl, arriving with her brother-in-law and sister, Michael Grauel and his wife Elisabetha.]

EUROPEAN RECORDS

Langenselbold Reformed KB:
Immanuel Roth m. 15 Jan. 1705 Elisabeth, daughter of the late Christian Lerch. They had an illegitimate child bp. 22 Dec. 1704, no name recorded. It is mentioned in the record that Roth was away on military service, *ein Churpfältzischen Reuter.*

Immanuel (also given as Emanuel) Roth and Elisabetha had children:
1. **Sabina,** bp. 10 Mar 1707
   Sp.: Peter Blum's wife
2. Anna Elisabetha, bp. 18 Dec. 1708;
   [she m. 1729 Michael Grauel, q.v.]
   Sp.: Conrad Geibel's wife
3. Johann Peter, bp. 10 June 1713, twin
   Sp.: Joh. Peter Troid
4. Henrich, bp. 10 June 1713, twin
   Sp.: son of Conrad Lerch, the younger.

AMERICAN RECORDS

Christ "Little" Tulpehocken Church:
Married 7 Jan. 1735: Johan Georg Petry and Sabina Roth, Cumru (also recorded in Rev. Stoever's personal record).

Johan Georg Petry and wife Sabina had children:
1. Anna Eliesabetha, b. 17 May 1735, bp. 23 July 1735
   Sp.: Joh. Michael Krauel [q.v.-Grauel] and his wife
2. Johann Michael, b. 4 July 1736, bp. 23 Aug. 1736
   Sp.: Joh. Michael Krauel
3. Joh. Georg, b. 5 Apr. 1741, bp. 2 Aug. 1741
   Sp.: Joh. Georg Ermentraut [q.v.]

68. SCHADT, ANTON
Two Brothers, 1752
S-H, I: 479.   [Anthon X Sheyed on list]

EUROPEAN RECORDS

Langenselbold Reformed KB:
Johannes Schad m. 4 Oct. 1677 Anna Maria, daughter of Peter Lohefinck.
They had children:
1. Johan Caspar, bp. 18 Apr. 1679
   Sp.: The father's brother
2. Johan Henrich, bp. 25 Sept. 1681
   Sp.: Johan Henrich Lerch
3. A daughter, bp. 11 Mar. 1683
   Sp.: The child's mother's sister
4. Antonius, bp. 6 Oct. 1686
   Sp.: The son of Johannes Lerch here
5. Johan Peter, bp. 1 Sept. 1688
   Sp.: Peter Lohfinck.

Johan Caspar Schad, son of Johan Schad, *Almosenpfleger* and inhabitant
here, m. 6 Jan. 1701 Margretha Adam, daughter of Conrad Adam.

Hans Caspar Schadt and Anna Margretha had a son:
     Anton, bp. 22 Mar. 1716
     Sp.: Tönges Schad, the child's father's brother

AMERICAN RECORDS

One Anthon Schadt signed a 1727 petition for a road from the Lutheran
Meeting House in Tulpehocken to George Boone's mill in Oley. This,
however, is said by some historians to be the 1709er Anthon Schadt who
came to NY, then into the Tulpehocken region ca. 1723/25. Information

located by Hank Jones indicates that the Anthon Scheidt of the 1709 migration may have come briefly into the Tulpehocken region of Pennsylvania and then returned to New York or he may have remained in New York, and possibly never came into the Tulpehocken region. The New York Anthon Scheidt has been identified in Henry Z Jones, Jr., *The Palatine Families of New York, 1710* (1985) in the Mensfelden records. The burial records of this Anthony Schaidt and his wife Dorothea are found in the Schoharie Lutheran KB in New York. One Anton Schadt appears on early Tulpehocken tax lists (1726/27) and a land warrant for 86¾ was granted in Lower Heidelberg Twp. (now Berks Co.) in 1736 to an *Adam* Schad. Another possibility for researchers to keep in mind is that the sponsor listed above at this child's baptism, Tönges (Antonius) Schad could be a prelist immigrant; he disappears from the Langenselbold records.

69. SCHAD, CONRAD age 50
Elizabeth, 1733
S-H, I: 113, 114, 115, 765, 766
 with Anna Catrina Shott age 49, Anna Clara Shott age 16, (Johannes) Conhenas Shott age 9. The immigrant did not sign; appears on B list as Shodt, and on C list as Shoot. A Johann Henrich Schötte also arrived on this ship, but he does not appear in the Langenselbold records; since he signed his name Schötte, he is probably not a member of this Schad family.

EUROPEAN RECORDS

Langenselbold Reformed KB:
Hans Wolff, the *Jäger*, and Engel had a daughter:
　　　Johanna Catharina, bp. 27 Sept. 1684 at Roneburg.

Conrad Schad, son of Jost Schad, *des Gerichts Freyenstein*, m. 16 May 1715 Anna Catharina, daughter of the late Hans Wolff. Children:
　　　1.　Anna Clara, bp. 14 Nov. 1717
　　　　　Sp.: Stoffel Fuchs and wife
　　　2.　Johannes, bp. 16 Feb. 1724
　　　　　Sp.: Mstr. Christian Neidert's (the baker)
　　　　　single son.
　　　3.　Anna Kunigunda, bp. 17 May 1726
　　　　　Sp.: a servant girl from Marienborn

AMERICAN RECORDS

Charles Roberts et al, *History of Lehigh County, Pennsylvania,* **Vol. III:**
"The pioneer of the family, settling in this vicinity, was Conrad Schad. He arrived at Philadelphia, August 27, 1733, on the ship *Elizabeth,* of London, Edward Lee, master, from Rotterdam, last from Dover. He was fifty years of age and was accompanied by his wife, Anna Catherin, aged forty-nine; his daughter, Anna Clara, sixteen, and his son, Johannes, nine years of age. His name is written Conrad "Shott," as subscribed to the oath of allegiance, to which he made his mark. The name, no doubt, was so written by a clerk accustomed to English sounds and to whose English ears Shott had the sound of Schad, as pronounced by its owner. He took out a warrant Oct. 28, 1737, for a tract of land called "The Seine", containing 220 & 1/8 acres, situated about a mile west of Egypt and bounded by lands of Nicholas Saeger, Peter Good and Casper Wistar, and by vacant ground on the north. This tract Conrad Schad conveyed to his son, Johannes, Oct. 15, 1747, when 60 years of age. Conrad Schad was born 1683 and died in 1747. His wife, Anna Catharine, was born in 1684. Of the daughter, Anna Clara, nothing is known beyond the fact of her sailing with her father to this country."
"Johannes Schad, born 1724, died 1777, took out a warrant for 185 acres on Coplay creek, adjoining the above tract, on Jan. 24, 1754. He was a consistent member of the Reformed church at Egypt and appears in the account book of 1767 to have contributed to the erection of the parsonage."
[The biographical sketch continues with data on later generations.]

Rev. Daniel Schumacher's Pastoral Records:
Johannes Schad and wife Magdalena Elisabeth had:
     Johannes, b. 4 Oct. 1760, Egypt; bp. 19 Oct. 1760
     Sp.: Johannes Rever, Magdalena Balliets, Paul Bohe's wife.

Anna Margaretha Schad(in) conf. 1760 at Egypt, Whitehall twp.
Catharina Elis. Schad(in) conf. 1765 in Egypt.

70. SCHAD, PETER
Townsend, 1737
S-H, I: 184, 185, 187

EUROPEAN RECORDS

Langenselbold Reformed KB:
Hans Bernhard Schad, son of Hans Schad, m. 9 Jan. 1690 at Selbold [Langenselbold] Maria, daughter of Caspar Kniess.

Hans Bernhard Schad, deceased, and Maria, his widow, had a son:
Johan Peter, bp. 18 Feb. 1691

Johann Peter Schad, son of the late Johan Bernhard Schad, m. 12 Jan. 1713 Sabina, daughter of Johan Conrad Adam.
Johann Peter Schad was a half brother of Johannes Kirschner, 1733 immigrant [q.v.] and Johan Georg Kirschner, 1731 immigrant [q.v.].

AMERICAN RECORDS

Pennsylvania Land Warrants:
Penn Twp., (now Berks Co.) Peter Shad 203½ A, warrant dated 21 Dec. 1737. Surveyed 28 Dec. 1737.

Hain's (St. John's) Reformed KB, Berks Co., PA:
Anna Margreta, daughter of Peter *Schott*, was a sp. in 1749 for a child of Johan Peter Dresler [q.v.].

Other Schad, Schäd, Shade families appear in Berks County records at Northkill, Altalaha, Schwartzwald, and in the records of Rev. Johann Caspar Stoever; however, no firm connection has been made with the above Schad families.

71. SCHUFFARD, GEORG age 44
Richard and Elizabeth, 1733
S-H, I: 127, 129, 130
[with Schuffard, Gertrud age 32, and Schuffard, Johannes age 10].

EUROPEAN RECORDS

Langenselbold Reformed KB:
Joh. Henrich Hübener from Rückging, son of the late Reinhard Hübener, *Schreiner* there, m. 26 Nov. 1696 Elisabetha Straub, daughter of Johan Straub, *Hoffmann* at Bruderdibach. They had children:
    1. Gertrudis bp. 1 Mar. 1699 at Bruderdibach
        Sp.: the wife of M. Peter Eÿring, miller there.
    2. Johan Henrich bp. 3 Sept. 1700
        Sp.: J. Henrich Straub, the mother's single brother.

Michael Schuffert, son of Caspar Schuffert, m. 19 Feb. 1685 Catharina, daughter of Paul Gerhard. They had a son:
  Johan Jörg, bp. 18 Oct. 1691 at Selbold
  Sp.: Jörg, son of Hans Schad

Joh. Jörg Schuffert, son of the late Michael Schuffert, m. 5 Nov. 1721 Gertraud, daughter of Hans Henrich Hübener at Baumwiessen [Baumwieserhof, near Hüttengesäss]. They had:
  1. Johan Jörg Conrad, bp. 15 Apr. 1722
     Sp.: Conrad Schneider *des Herrn Ampts verwesers Knecht*
  2. Johannes, bp. 1 Jan. 1724
     Sp.: Stoffel Strud *des Schäffers* son, single
  3. Anna Elisabetha, bp. 7 July 1726
     Sp.: The child's mother's sister, single
  4. Johanna Maria, bp. 26 May 1729
     Sp.: The child's mother's sister, single, servant here
  5. Niclaus, bp. 13 Jan. 1732
     Sp.: Mstr. Niclaus Fress, the joiner

AMERICAN RECORDS

Jordan Lutheran KB, Lehigh County, PA:
Johannes Schuffert and Maria Clara had:
  1. Anna Maria, b. 30 Mar. 1748, bp. 24 Apr. 1748
     Sp.: Johannes Küchler and Maria Magdalena

Christ Lutheran (Mertz') KB, Bieber Creek, Berks County, PA:
Michael Klein, single son of Moritz Klein[1], m. 17 June 1750 Catharina Schufert, single daughter of Joh. Georg Schufert. They had:
  1. Christina Magdalena, b. 13 Apr. 1751, bp. 12 May 1751
     Sp.: Michael Biber, Jacob Biber, Christian Klein, and Anna Mar. Schufert.

Reading, Berks County, PA tax list 1754: Nichlas Shofart.

Anson County, NC, Deed Book C-1, 19/20 Sept. 1755:
Georg Shuford purchased 500 A from Samuel Wilkins on the south side of the South fork of the Catawba River.

---

[1] For additional information on the immigrant Moritz Klein, see family # 289 in Annette K. Burgert, *Eighteenth Century Emigrants from the Northern Alsace to America*. 1992. Pg. 297-299.

Mecklenburg County, NC Wills, dated 16 Aug. 1762:
George Shuford. Names wife Rodey [shortened version of Gertrude?] to have all estate during her life; then to be equally divided between all children. Eldest son John to have all lands and pay £10 to each of the other children.

[Johannes Schuffert, son of Georg Schuffert, m. Maria Clara before 1748. Was she possibly Maria Clara, dau. of Conrad Schad, bp. 14 Nov. 1717?].

Lincoln County, NC Wills:
Johannes Schuffert. Will dated 3 June 1788, probated July 1790. Names wife Mary Clara; sons: George, Daniel, David and deceased son John's children; daughters: Mary Ichard's children; dau. Catreena, wife of John Bost; dau. Mautlena; dau. Catrout Conrad's children; son Jacob.
Exrs: sons Daniel and David Shuford.
Wit: Reinhart Brunner, Jacob Summey and Robert Blackburn.

72. STAMM, ANNA BARBARA age 26
Richard and Elizabeth, 1733
S-H, I: 127
                              EUROPEAN RECORDS

Langenselbold Reformed KB:
David Stamm, son of *Meister* Hans Stamm, *Wagner,* m. 15 Feb. 1688 Elisabeth, daughter of Christian Fuchs.
David Stam and wife Elisabeth had:
1. Wörner, bp. 23 Feb. 1689
2. Anna Margretha, bp. 13 Mar. 1692; she m. 1728 Philip Filtzmeyer [q.v.].
3. Anna Maria, bp. 9 May 1697
4. Joh. Adam [q.v.] bp. 23 Apr. 1702; he m. 1726 Rachel Filtzmeyer
   Sp.: M. Adam Schad, *der Schlosser* here
5. **Anna Barbara,** bp. 4 Mar. 1706
   Sp.: Johan Lerch's single daughter

73. STAMM, JOHANN ADAM
Francis and Elizabeth, 1742
S-H, I; 329

EUROPEAN RECORDS

Langenselbold Reformed KB:
David Stamm, son of *Meister* Hans Stamm, *Wagner*, m. 15 Feb. 1688
Elisabeth, daughter of Christian Fuchs. [See daughter Anna Barbara Stamm,
1733 immigrant, for a list of their children].

David Stam, *Wagner*, and Elisabeth, his wife had:
    Johan Adam, bp. 23 Apr. 1702
    Sp.: M. Adam Schad, *der Schlosser* here
[See his sister Barbara, above, for additional data.]

Mstr. Johann Adam Stamm, *Wagner*, son of the late *Mstr.* David Stamm,
Mitnachbar, also *Wagner* here, m. 30 Jan. 1726 Rachel, daughter of Mstr.
Dieterich Filtzmeyer, smith and *Unterthanen.* Children:
    1. Wörner bp. 13 Nov. 1726
       Sp.: Mstr. Wörner Stamm, the father's brother.
    2. Johan Henrich bp. 20 Mar. 1735; died 25 Sept. 1735.
       Sp.: the son of Mstr. Michael Spindler, *Binder.*

AMERICAN RECORDS

Land Warrants, Penn Township, Berks County, PA:
Hans Adam Stam, 110 acres. Surveyed 16 Dec. 1737. Pat. 24 Feb. 1763 to
Werner Stam on warrant to accept dated 21 Feb. 1745.

Berks County, PA, Orphans Court Records:
Yost Stamm, Heidelberg, 18 Dec. 1777. Adm. to Werner Stamm, only
brother.

Bern Reformed KB, Bern Twp., Berks County, PA:
Werner (Winer) Stamm and wife had:
    1. Joh., bp. 11 Mar. 1750
       Sp. Joh. Conrath
    2. Nicholas, bp. 3 May 1752
       Sp.: Nicholas Seysinger and wife

Nicholas Stamm and wife had:
    1. Anna Cath., bp. 10 Sept. 1775
    2. Nicholas, bp. 28 Mar. 1777
    3. Joh., bp. 4 Sept. 1778
    4. Joh. Adam, bp. 17 Sept. 1780
    5. Philip, 13 Nov. 1785
       (TS Bern: b. 4 Oct. 1785, d. 12 Sept. 1875; m. Christina)

Bern Reformed Church Cemetery, Tombstone inscriptions:
Werner Stam, b. 13 Nov. 1726; d. 16 May 1795
Catharina, wife of [m. 26 May 1748] Werner Stamm; b. 1728, d. 4 Oct. or
Nov. 1812, age 84 y.

Catharine Stamm, nee Lerch, wife of Nicolaus Stamm, b. 21 Apr. 1754, d.
16 May 1844.

Nicholas Stamm, b. 22 Apr. 1752, d. 6 Oct. 1818.

Frederick Stamm, b. 18 Sept. 1759, d. 9 Dec. 1827.

Margaretha Stamm, nee Lerch, wife of Fred, b. 8 Mar?May? 1762, d. 5 Oct.
1844.
[Many later Stamm burials here.]

PA Archives, Sixth Series, Vol.6: Rev. John Waldschmidt's records:
Johan Jost Stam, son of Adam Stam, m. 2 Nov. 1768 Elisabeth, daughter of
Anthon Faust [q.v.].

Hain's (St. John's) Reformed KB, Berks County, PA:
Johann Jost Stamm and wife had children:
      1. Gertraut bp. 26 July 1772
         Sp.: Nickolas Stamm and Gertraut Faust
      2. Anna Maria bp. 17 Apr. 1774
         Sp.: Anna Maria Faust
      3. Johannes bp. 19 Jan. 1777
         Sp.: Antoni Faust [q.v.] and Elisabetha.

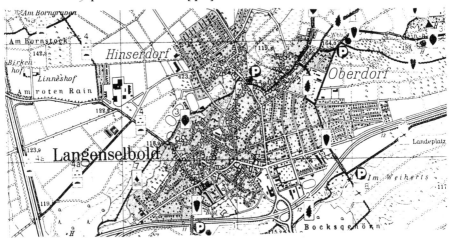

Detailed map of Langenselbold

APPENDIX A

1709 Emigrants to England from the Langenselbold Area
1710 immigrants to New York

The eight families presented here were first documented by my colleague Henry Z. Jones, Jr. in his two volume work *The Palatine Families of New York 1710* published in 1985. They are included in the study of emigration from Langenselbold and vicinity with his gracious consent, in order that the study may be as complete as possible. For the most part, only those records that actually appear in the Langenselbold KB are included here, with a few additions from the Hüttengesäss records; the reader is advised to consult the Jones' work for additional lineage before their appearance in the Langenselbold records and after their arrival in America.

Since many of the immigrants in the main text came directly into the Tulpehocken region of Berks County, Pennsylvania, an area originally settled by transplanted 1710 New York Palatines, the study of the overall emigration is essential for a full understanding of the emigration process and the relationships of the families involved in it.

Sources Used for Appendix A

Hüttengesäss Reformed Church Records, typed copy provided by Patricia Gunderson; translated by Patricia Gunderson and Trudy Schenck, Salt Lake City, Utah.

Henry Z. Jones, Jr., *The Palatine Families of New York, 1710*, 2 volumes. Universal City, CA: 1985.

Henry Z. Jones, Jr., *More Palatine Families*. Universal City, CA: 1991.

Explanation of Short Citations
used by Mr. Jones

(Albany Nats.) *Albany Common Council Minutes* in Manuscript Division, N.Y. State Library, Albany, N.Y.

(Burnetsfield Patent) "Misc. Data On The Burnetsfield Patent, 1722" in *Calendar of N.Y. Land Papers*, 120, 138, 195, & 196.

(Hunter Lists) *N.Y. Palatine Subsistence Lists of Governor Robert Hunter 1710 - 1712* (C.O. 5/1230 and C.O. 5/1231 in the Public Record Office, London, England).

(Livingston Papers) *The Livingston Papers,* microfilmed at the Franklin Delano Roosevelt Library, Hyde Park, N.Y.

(Livingston Debt Lists) "Palatine Debotrs Lists" in *The Livingston Papers,* microfilmed at the Franklin Delano Roosevelt Library, Hyde Park, N.Y.

(Palatine Volunteers To Canada) "Palatine Volunteers In The Canadian Expedition of 1711" in *New York Colonial Manuscripts*, Vol. LV, pp. 144 - 146.

(Settlers And Residents) *Settlers And Residents*, by Arthur M. Kelly (Rhinebeck, N.Y., 1973) Vol. I: Palatine Debt Book 1712/13.

(Simmendinger Register) "*Warhoffte Und Glaubwürdige Verzeichnüss Jeniger Personen, Welche Sich Anno 1709 Unter Des Herren Wunderbarer Führung Aus Teutschland In Americam Oder Neue Welt Begeben...*", by Ulrich Simmemdinger (Reutlingen, Germany, ca. 1717).

(Stone Arabia Patent) "Misc. Data On The Stone Arabia Patent" in *Calendar Of New York Land Papers*, p. 120.

BELLINGER, JOHANNES
to NY 1710

EUROPEAN RECORDS

Langenselbold Reformed KB:
Johannes Bellinger, son of Dietrich Bellinger at Niderrodenbach, m. 24 Apr. 1690 Anna Margretha, daughter of Hans Kuhn. Children:
1. Johann Friederich, bp. 13 Sept. 1691, *Hüttengesäss*
   Sp.: Friederich Bellinger, the father's brother from Niederrodenbach
2. Philipp, bp. 16 Dec. 1694, *Hüttengesäss*
   Sp.: Philipps Schmied, son of the late Bernhard Schmied
3. Johann Peter, bp. 30 Apr. 1697
   Sp.: Johann Peter Frantz of Rodenbach
4. Johann Adam, bp. 15 Jan.1699
   Sp.: Adam Schröder

See Henry Z Jones, Jr., *The Palatine Families of New York, 1710*, Vol. 1: 47-49 for additional Bellinger lineage before their appearance in the Langenselbold vicinity. Anna Margaretha, wife of Johannes Bellinger, was a sister of Samuel Kuhn [q.v.].

AMERICAN RECORDS

See Henry Z Jones, Jr., *The Palatine Families of New York, 1710*, Vol. 1: 49: "Johannes Bellinger made his first appearance on the Hunter Lists 4 Aug. 1710 with 4 persons over 10 years of age in the family; the household increased to 5 over 10 years 4 Oct. 1710. He was listed among some carpenters with Frederik Bellinger in a Palatine Debt Book dated 1712/13 (Livingston Papers). Johannes Bellinger and his wife Anna Maria Margretha with 2 children were at Neu-Quunsberg ca. 1716/17 (Simmendinger Register). Johannes Pellinger was a patentee on the north side, and Margaret Pellinger his wife was a patentee on the south side of the Mohawk 30 April 1725 (Burnetsfield Patent). Fred Bellinger of Queensbury was a soldier in 1711 (Palatine Volunteers to Canada) and was nat. 22 Nov. 1715 (Albany Nats.). Johann Friederich Bellinger, his wife Anna Elisabetha and 3 children were at Neu-Heessberg ca. 1716/17 (Simmendinger Register). Ffrederick Pellinger was a patentee on the south side of the Mohawk 30 April 1725 (Burnetsfield Patent). Peter Bellinger was nat. 31 Jan. 1715/16 (Albany Nats.). Peter Pellinger and Margaret his wife each were patentees on the north side of the Mohawk 30 April 1725 (Burnetsfield Patent)."

BELLINGER, NICOLAUS
to NY 1710
EUROPEAN RECORDS

Langenselbold Reformed KB:
Nicolaus Bellinger and Anna, daughter of Hans Kuhn, were m. 25 Nov. 1685 as per the order of the noble government. She had married some years ago (11 June 1674) Jörg Brüning at Hüttengesäss; but she was not compatable with him, so Brüning went from her and she from him. She went away with this Nicolaus Bellinger and had an illegitimate child - a little son, so that the aforementioned Jörg Brüning has contracted another marriage. After all this, however, the above-mentioned Bellinger has remained as a stranger... She sent a request to the honourable government to let them stay in the country, and this finally has been permitted by the aforementioned honourable government which ordered me to marry them with prior-published penitence and to avoid further trouble and also to legitimize the rearing of this blameless child. Children:
1. Marcus, (bp. not recorded at Langenselbold)
2. Henrich, twin, bp. 16 Jan. 1687 at Hüttengesäss
   Sp.: Henrich Philipps Feuerstein, an apprentice
   carpenter born in Helbrig
3. Anna Barbara, twin, bp. 16 Jan. 1687, d.1691
   Sp.: the surviving daughter of Samuel Neidert
4. Johannes, bp. 19 Dec. 1688
   Sp.: Johannes, son of Dietrich Bellinger at Nieder Rodenbach
5. Dieterich, twin, bp. 18 Feb. 1694
   Sp.: Dietrich Bellinger of Nieder Rodenbach
6. Barbara Elisabetha, twin, bp. 18 Feb. 1694
   Sp.: Barbara, wife of H. Niklas Ziegen, *Schultheisen*
   at Hüttengesäss
7. Margaretha Elisabetha, bp. 14 Jan. 1698
   Sp.: the daughter of Johannes Jeckel at Nieder Rodenbach

AMERICAN RECORDS

See Henry Z Jones, Jr., *The Palatine Families of New York, 1710*, Vol. 1: 50-51: "Nicolaus Bellinger made his first appearance on the Hunter Lists 4 Aug. 1710 with 6 persons over 10 years of age; on 4 Oct. 1710 the family decreased to 4 over 10 years. After several fluctuations, the household had 3 persons over 10 years through the year 1712. Nicolaus Bellinger, widower with 1 child, was at Neu-Ansberg ca. 1716/17 (Simmendinger Register). Marcus Bellinger first appeared on the Hunter Lists as #38 4 Oct. 1710, recorded next to Niclaus Bellinger; as Nicolaus's family decreased, Marcus began his entries. On 24 June 1711 Marcus was registered next to Niclaus

and Henrich Bellinger; on 24 Dec. 1711 he had 4 persons over 10 years of age and 1 under 10 in his family. He sp. his uncle Samuel Kuhn in 1714 (West Camp Luth. KB). Marcus Bellenger of Annsberg was a Palatine soldier to Canada in 1711 (Palatine Volunteers To Canada) and was recorded with his wife Anna and 5 children next to his brother Heinrich Bellinger at Neu-Ansberg ca. 1716/17 (Simmendinger Register).
Henrich Bellinger appeared with his father as Niclaus and Henrich Bellinger on the Hunter Lists 24 June 1711; his entries alone began 24 Dec. 1711 next to Nicolaus and Marcus Bellinger. On 24 June 1711 he was noted with 2 persons over 10 and 1 person under 10 years. He sp. Hartmann Windecker in 1711 (West Camp Luth. KB) and was a Palatine soldier that year. (Palatine Volunteers To Canada). Heinrich Bellinger, his wife Anna Maria and 2 children were at Neu-Ansberg ca. 1716/17 (Simmendinger Register). He settled in the Schoharie region."

See Henry Z Jones, Jr., *The Palatine Families of New York, 1710*, Vol. 1: 50-51 for additional family data.

BENDER, GEORG
to NY 1710
EUROPEAN RECORDS

Langenselbold Reformed KB:
Velten Bender died at Hüttengesäss, buried 19 Mar. 1679, age 75 years.

Lorentz Benner, son of Velthen Bender, of Hüttengesäss, m. (1) 28 Jan. 1664 Magdalena, daughter of Johann Koch. They had:
1. Maria, bp. 17 Dec. 1665
2. Adam, bp. 14 June 1668
3. **Geörg,** bp. 26 Jan. 1670. Sp.: Geörg Stromb
4. Anna Christina, bp. 11 May 1673
5. Philips, bp. 19 Oct. 1678

Lorentz Bender, widower, m. (2) 17 Mar. 1681 Anna, daughter of Hans Jörg Zimmermann, *Wagner*, of Michelstadt in the Odenwald.

Jörg Bender of Hüttengesäss, son of Lorentz Bender, m. 1 Oct. 1696 Anna Maria, daughter of Johannes Becker of Rommelshausen, Friedberg Jurisdiction. [For additional Becker data, See Henry Z Jones, Jr., *The Palatine Families of New York, 1710*, Vol. 1: 52.] Children:
1. Anna Maria, bp. 6 Aug. 1697 at Hüttengesäss
   Sp.: wife of Johan Caspar Müller from Marckköbel

Hüttengesäss Reformed KB:
Georg Bender had:
    2. Engel Catharina, bp. 4 Feb. 1702
        Sp. Lips Bender's daughter Engel
    3. Johann Philips, bp. 7 Feb. 1706 at Hüttengesäss;
        Sp.: Philips Geibel

AMERICAN RECORDS

See Henry Z Jones, Jr., *The Palatine Families of New York, 1710*, Vol. 1: 52:
"Georg Bender first was entered on the Hunger Lists 4 Aug. 1710 with 2
persons over 10 years of age and 1 under 10 years; the family increased to
2 over 10 years and 2 under 10 on 4 Oct. 1710. The last notation was for
3 persons over 10 years and 1 under 10 on 13 Sept. 1712. George Bender
of Hunterstown was a soldier in 1711 (Palatine Volunteers To Canada).
Jurry Beenner was nat. 11 Oct. 1715 (Albany Nats.). Anna Maria Bender
sp. Adam Klein and Johann Peter Kneskern in the Schoharie Valley in 1716
(West Camp Luth. KB); she may have d. shortly thereafter (HJ) as the
Simmendinger Register ca. 1716/17 recorded Georg Bender and his wife
Maria Dorothea with 2 children at Neu-Heidelberg. Jurch Bender received
land in the Staley Patent (34,000 acres on the south side of the Mohawk
River) 24 Sept. 1724."

DEICHERT, WERNER
to NY 1710
EUROPEAN RECORDS

Langenselbold Reformed KB:
Buried 8 Apr. 1700: Hans Deichert, age 63 years.
Buried at Hüttengesäss 26 June 1721: Gerdraut Deichert, widow of Hans
Deichert, aged 81 years.

Wörner Deichert, son of Hans Deichert from Hüttengesäss, m. 16 Jan. 1690
at Selbold Anna Catharina, daughter of Valentin Ähl. They had:
    1. Anna Magdalena, bp. 25 Feb. 1691, d. 30 June 1691
        Sp.: The mother's sister.
    2. Elisabetha, bp. 11 Jan. 1694, at Selbold
        Sp.: Henrich Zuber's wife

3. Johann Peter, bp. 8 Aug. 1696, at Selbold
   Sp.: Johan Friedrich Steuel, the *Bierbrauer*, his son.
4. Sabina, bp. 5 Jan. 1698
   Sp.: Sabina, wife of Peter Blum
5. Severinus, bp. 3 Oct. 1700
   Sp.: Severin Röhrich
6. Anna Margaretha, bp. 1 Nov. 1702
   Sp.: The wife of Johann Caspar Schad
7. Ottilia, bp. 18 Feb. 1705
   Sp.: The daughter of H. Lieut. Schäfer
8. Johann Conrad, bp. 4 Dec. 1707, d. Aug. 1708
   Sp.: A single apprentice, son of Henrich Schuffert

See Henry Z Jones, Jr., *The Palatine Families of New York, 1710*, Vol. 1: 163: "Wörner Deichert of Hüttengesäss was listed 3 March 1701 with 2 oxen and 1 cart in a mss. found at the Birstein archives; on the same roll were members of the Kuhn, Bellinger, and Bender families who later emigrated to colonial N.Y."

AMERICAN RECORDS

Henry Z Jones, Jr., *The Palatine Families of New York, 1710*, Vol. 1: 162-164: "Werner Deuchert made his first appearance on the Hunter Lists 4 July 1710 with 5 persons over 10 years of age and 2 persons under 10 years; the family size increased to 5 persons over 10 years and 3 under 10 on 4 Aug. 1710, and to 6 persons over 10 years and 3 persons under 10, 24 June 1711. Warner Dyker, mayer, was on a list from a Palatine Debt Book dated March 1712/13 (*Settlers & Residents*, Vol. I, p. 16). Werner Reichert of Queensbury was a Palatine soldier in the Canadian expedition (Palatine Volunteers To Canada). Warnaer Deygert was nat. 11 Oct. 1715 (Albany Nats.). Warner Deickert, his wife Anna Catharina, and 6 children were at Neu-Quunsberg ca. 1716/17 (Simmendinger Register). He was a patentee at Stone Arabia in 1723 (Stone Arabia Patent)."

Albany Naturalizations:
Johann Peter Deichert was nat. 31 Jan. 1715/16 as Johan Pieter Diegert.
Severinus Deichert was nat. 31 Jan. 1715/16 as Sefreen Devgert.

KUHN, SAMUEL
to NY 1710
                          EUROPEAN RECORDS

Langenselbold Reformed KB:
Hans Kuhn and wife Catharina had a son Samuel bp. 11 Apr. 1664 at
Hüttengesäss. Conrad Gerth and wife Elisabeth had a daughter Magdalena
bp. 18 June 1671 at Hüttengesäss.
Samuel Kuhn, son of Hans Kuhn of Hüttengesäss, m. 1 Nov. 1688
Magdalena, daughter of Conrad Gerth [Gereth, Gerhart?]. Children:
   1. Johann Valentin, bp. 4 June 1690 at Hüttengesäss
      Sp.: Valentin, surviving son of Samuel Neidert
   2. Johann Conrad, bp. 9 July 1693
      Sp.: The son of Conrad Gerth
   3. Anna Barbara, bp. 4 Dec. 1696
      Sp.: The daughter of Johannes Köhler
   4. Barbara Elisabetha, bp. 18 Sept. 1700
      Sp.: Elisab. daughter of *H. Schultheiss* Clos Zieg.
Hüttengesäss Reformed KB:
   5. Anna Catharina, bp. 19 Aug. 1703 at Hüttengesäss
      Sp.: Anna Catharina, daughter of Georg Horr.

                          AMERICAN RECORDS

See Henry Z Jones, Jr., *The Palatine Families of New York, 1710*, Vol. 1: 497:
Samuel Kuhn m. (2) Elisabetha (possibly Rosenzweig). They had issue:
   6. Johann Herman
   7. Marcus, b. 30 July 1714 (West Camp Luth. KB)
      Sp.: Marcus Bellinger

[Ann Kuhn, sister of Samuel Kuhn, was the wife of Nicolaus Bellinger [q.v.]

Henry Z Jones, Jr., *The Palatine Families of New York, 1710*, Vol. 1: 495:
"Samuel Kuhn made his initial appearance on the Hunger Lists 4 Aug. 1710
with 6 persons over 10 years and 1 person under 10; he was enrolled directly
next to Niclaus Bellinger, his brother-in-law, on this entry (HJ). He was
registered with 5 over 10 years on 24 March 1711, with 4 over 10 and 1
under 10 years on 24 June 1711, with 3 over 10 and 1 under 10 on 24 Dec.
1711, with 3 over 10 years and 2 under 10 on 25 March 1712, and finally
with 4 over 10 and 2 under 10 years on 24 June 1712. Samuel Kuhn and
Rosenzweigin were noted on 24 June 1711 on the Hunter Lists. Samuel
Kuhn of Annsberg was a soldier in 1711 (Palatine Volunteers To Canada).
Samuel Kun and Elisabetha with 5 children were at Wormsdorff ca. 1716/17

(Simmendinger Register). Samuel Koen was a Palatine Debtor in 1718, 1721, and 1726 (Livingston Debt Lists)."
"Valentin Kuhn was entered next to Samuel Kuhn and Rosenzweigin on 24 June 1711 on the Hunter Lists. Valtin Kuhn of Annsberg was a soldier in 1711 (Palatine Volunteers To Canada). Valentin Kuhn and Anna Catharina with 3 children were living next to Marx and Heinrich Bellinger at Neu-Ansberg in 1716/17 (Simmendinger Register). " See Henry Z Jones, Jr., *The Palatine Families of New York, 1710*, Vol. 1, p. 495-8 for additional data. See also Henry Z Jones, Jr., *More Palatine Families* p. 351.

LOHMEYER (LAHMEYER), JOHANNES
to NY 1710
EUROPEAN RECORDS

Langenselbold Reformed KB:
Georg Lahmeyer, teacher at Hüttengesäss and widower, m. 12 Aug. 1700 (2) Gertraud Schad, widow.

Marcus Lohmeyer, son of the teacher Jörg Lahmeyer at Hüttengesäss, m. (1) 16 Nov. 1681 Magdalena, daughter of Clos Jacobs, also inhabitant there. She died in 1687.   Children of first marriage:
  1. Anna Elisabetha, bp. 19 Sept. 1682
     She m. 12 Jan. 1702 Johannes Schneider [q.v.] at Hüttengesäss
  2. **Johannes,** bp. 6 Jan. 1684
     Sp.: Johannes Köhler
  3. Anna Catharina, bp. 14 Oct. 1686
     Sp.: The dau. of Clos Jacobs, the mother's sister

[See Henry Z Jones, Jr., *The Palatine Families of New York, 1710*, Vol. 1: 512 for further data.]

Marcus Lohmeyer, widower of linenweaver, m. (2) 19 Nov. 1691 Engel, daughter of Hans Deichert. [She was a sister of Werner Deichert, q.v.]. Children of second marriage:
  4. Anna Barbara, bp. 13 Nov. 1692
     Sp.: The child's father's sister Anna Ursula
  5. Johann Gregorius, bp. 18 Mar. 1694
     Sp.: Jörg Lohmeyer, the grandfather, a
     schoolmaster from the Palatinate.

6. Anna Magdalena, bp. 19 July 1696 at Hüttengesäss
   Sp.: The daughter of Jost Raidel
7. Johann Henrich, bp. 4 May 1697, d. 1699
   Sp.: Joh. Henrich Euler from Berckheim
8. Johann Henrich, bp. 30 Apr. 1699 at Hüttengesäss
   Sp.: Joh. Henr. Reichart, single, from Eckartshausen

Hüttengesäss Reformed KB:
Marcus Lohmeyer and Engel had:
   9. Anna Catharina, bp. 12 Sept. 1702
   10. Henrich, bp. 1 Feb. 1705
       Sp.: Heinrich Lörch from Selbold
   11. Georg, bp. __ __ 1707
       Sp.: Georg Heussel and wife from Rüdigheim

Died 27 Apr. 1714, Marcus Lohmeyer, aged 58 years.

AMERICAN RECORDS

Henry Z Jones, Jr., *The Palatine Families of New York, 1710*, Vol. 1: 512-13:
"Johannes Lahmeyer made his initial appearance on the Hunter Lists 4 July
1710 with 1 pers. over 10 yrs. On 4 Oct. 1710, Johannes Lahmeyer was but
a few names from Werner Deuchert and others from Hüttengesäss (HJ).
Hance Lemire was recorded near Necoshehopin in 1734 ("Landholders of
Philadelphia Co., 1734" in *Genealogical Society of Pa. Publications*, Vol. I,
1895 - 99)."

See also Hank Z Jones, Jr., *More Palatine Families*, (1991), p. 351-52.

SCHNEIDER, JOHANNES
to NY 1710
EUROPEAN RECORDS

Langenselbold Reformed KB:
Marcus Lahmeyer, son of the teacher Jörg Lahmeyer m. (1) 16 Nov. 1681
Magdalena, dau. of Clos Jacobs. Their first child was:
       Anna Elisabetha, bp. 10 Sept. 1682
       [She was a sister of Johannes Lohmeyer (Lahmeyer), q.v.]

Hüttengesäss Reformed KB:
Johannes Schneider (parentage not given) m. 12 Jan. 1702 Anna Elisabetha,
daughter of Marcus Lohmyer. Children:
1. Johannes, bp. 8 Aug. 1703
   Sp.: Johannes, son of ___Scheucher
2. Johann Jost, bp. 8 Aug. 1703
   Sp.: Jost Krum of Nieder Grundau
3. Johann Jost, bp. 6 Jan. 1706
   Sp.: Joh. Jost son of Hans Kuhn
4. Balthasar, bp. 19 Feb. 1708
   Sp.: Balthasar Eisenach, carpenter

AMERICAN RECORDS

Henry Z Jones, Jr., *The Palatine Families of New York, 1710*, Vol. 2: 903:
"Johannes Schneider made his initial appearance on the Hunter Lists 4 July
1710 with 2 persons over 10 years and 3 persons under 10. The household
showed 3 over 10 and 2 under 10 on 31 Dec. 1710, 2 over 10 years and 3
under 10 on 24 June 1711, 2 over 10 and 2 under 10 on 24 Dec. 1711, 2 over
10 and 3 under 10 years on 25 March 1712, and 3 over 10 and 2 under 10
on 24 June 1712. Johan Joest Sneyder was nat. 14 Feb. 1715/16 (Albany
Nats.).

See also Hank Z Jones, Jr., *More Palatine Families,* (1991), p. 371-372.

SCHÜTZ, CONRAD
to NY 1710
to Tulpehocken 1723
EUROPEAN RECORDS

Langenselbold Reformed KB:
Closs Eichelbörner and Margaretha had a daughter:
   Anna, bp. 15 Aug. 1661 at Rottenbach
   Sp.: Anna, wife of Peter Kirschner

Conrad Schütz, (linen) weaver, son of Hermann Schütz of Altenburschla in
Hesse, m. 19 May 1687 Anna, dau. of Clos Eichelbörner, citizen here.
Children:
1. Johan Michael, bp. 9 Feb. 1688
   Sp.: Michael May, son of Johan May, formerly from Diebach;
   now servant for the innkeeper *am Marckt*

2. Henrich, bp. 3 Aug. 1690
   Sp.: Henrich Lohfinck, son of the late Peter Lohfinck
3. Anna Margretha, bp. 3 Nov. 1693
   Sp.: Margretha, dau. of Wörner Repp, the *Burckmüller*
4. Anna Catharina, bp. 29 Apr. 1696
   Sp.: the wife of Philips Adam

Niedergründau Reformed KB:
Conrad Schütz was a linenweaver at Lieblos (1705). One child bp. here:
   Anna Elisabetha, bp. 12 July 1705.

AMERICAN RECORDS

St. Paul's Ev. Lutheran KB, West Camp, Ulster Co., NY:
Anna Catharina Schütz, legitimate daughter of Conrad Schütz, former
inhabitant of Langensellwelt in the earldom of Isenberg, m. 1 Nov. 1715
Leonhard Feg of Schoharie, son of Johann Feg of Oberstein, Nassau-Sigen
jurisdiction.

Henry Z Jones, Jr., *The Palatine Families of New York, 1710*, Vol. 2: 948:
"Conrad Schutz made his initial appearance on the Hunter Lists 4 Aug.1710
with 5 persons over 10 years of age. The family was recorded with 4 over
10 on 31 Dec. 1710. On 24 June 1711, Conrad Schutz and Zimmermännin
were registered together with 5 persons over 10 years and 1 person under 10.
The household showed 5 persons over 10 on 29 Sept. 1711, 3 persons over
10 years on 24 June 1712, and 4 persons over 10 years of age on 13 Sept.
1712. Conrad Schutz and his wife Anna Maria Margretha were at Neu-
Heessberg ca. 1716/17 (Simmendinger Register); they were noted next to the
family of Jacob Zimmermann and his wife Anna Margretha (Schutz) on this
roll, a double-tie as the Hunter Lists strongly suggest that the second wife
of Conrad Schutz was the widow of Jacob Zimmermann (HJ). Conrad
Schutz sp. Henrich Jung in 1716 and Georg Mattheus in 1717, both at
Schoharie (West Camp Luth. KB). Conrad Sheetz lived in the Tulpehocken
region before 13 May 1723 *(1723-1973 Anniversary Magazine of the
Tulpehocken).*"

APPENDIX B

Presented in this appendix are several families who appear in the Langenselbold records, and then disappear, but there is not sufficient evidence to state that they are the immigrants who appear on the cited ship's lists; rather than loose the clues to origin that they provide they are included here, but the researcher should remember that they are not proven. Confirming evidence was simply not available, but may surface later. At the end of the appendix, there are presented several possible clues to other immigrant origins that were found in the Langenselbold records.

****

DIEL, WILHELM age 19
Glasgow, 1738
S-H, I: 204, 206, 208

EUROPEAN RECORDS

Langenselbold Reformed KB:
Johann Henrich Diehl, *Hoffman* at Bruderdiebacher Hoff, son of the late Johann Diel at Altstat, m. 18 Feb. 1717 Anna Barbara Roth, dau. of Adam Roth of Ravoltshausen. They had children:
1. Anna Barbara, bp. 28 Nov. 1717
2. **Johann Wilhelm,** bp. 4 Mar. 1719
   Sp.: The child's father's youngest and single brother.
3. Johanna Magdalena, bp. 15 Dec. 1720
4. Johannes, bp. 23 Jan. 1724
   Sp.: Johannes Haas from Oberdorfelden

AMERICAN RECORDS

Hain's (St. John's) Reformed KB, Berks Co., PA:
One Johannes Diehl and wife appear in the KB in 1774, 1778, and subsequent years. One Johannes Diehl with wife Catharina were sp. in 1785 for a child of Wilhelm Freymeurer.

A Peter Diehl and wife (n.n.) had a son:
     Antoni, b. 15 June 1786; bp. 13 Aug. 1786
     Sp.: Antoni Faust [q.v.].

ERMANTROUD, JOHANNES age 22
Samuel, 1739
S-H, I: 256
with Philipus, age 18; Johan Fredrick, age 16

EUROPEAN RECORDS

Langenselbold Reformed KB:
Johannes Ermenträud, *Schäfer uff dem hoff* and his wife Catharina had a son:
Johann Henrich, bp. 8 Aug. 1714 at Brud(er)diebach
Sp.: *Frembd mann,* named Johan Henrich Müller

[It is likely this couple had more children, but they are not recorded in the Langenselbold KB. The Ermentrouds in PA settled with other families from Langenselbold, and appear in the same church records, closely connected to other families in this volume. Further research is needed in the area records to verify their emigration.]

A Friederich Ermendraut, a shepherd from Baumwiesen, appears as a sponsor at a baptism in 1701.

Eckartshausen Reformed KB:
Johannes Ermentraut, widower and shepherd at Wiedermus, m. 8 Nov. 1736 Anna Maria, daughter of the late Johannes Eürich former *Bestandmüller* at Kettenbach. Several children to this second marriage.

AMERICAN RECORDS

Christ "Little Tulpehocken" Lutheran KB, Berks Co., PA:
Johannes Ermentraut m. 22 May 1743 Anna Eliesabetha Hedderich [q.v., she was a daughter of Joh. Adam Hedderich, 1742 immigrant].

Hain's (St. John's) Reformed KB, Berks Co., PA:
John Ermentrout had a son:
John Henry, b. 22 Nov. 1747, bp. __ ___ 1747
Sp.: John Henry Ermentrout

Frederick Ermentrout had children:
Anna Magdalena, b. __ ___ 1748
Sp: Jost Hetrich [q.v.] and wife

a son (n.n.), bp. 26 Nov. 1751
Sp.: John Peter Lamm

Chalkley's Chronicles, Vol. 3, pg. 141:
Augusta County, VA, Will Book V, pg. 351: dated 5 June 1774.
Elizabeth Armentrout's will, widow. (Legacies) to son, Philip; to children living, being six in number; to grandsons, Henry Armentrout and John Armentrout, sons of her son John, deceased. Exrs: son Philip and friend Charles Rush. Son Henry Armentrout and Frederick Harris are indebted to her. Wit: Gabriel Jones, John Rush and (a German). Proved 20 June 1775 by Jones and Rush. Charles Rush refuses to execute. Philip qualifies (bond signed Elizabeth Armentrout) with Valentine Cloninger, Frederick Armentrout.

FREYMAN, HENRICH age 30
Patience & Margaret, 1748
S-H, I: 387
EUROPEAN RECORDS

Langenselbold Reformed KB:
Johann Peter Freÿman, son of the late Lenhard Freÿman, linenweaver here, m. 18 Feb. 1697 Anna Catharina, daughter of the late Hans Caspar Scherp, citizen at Wächtersbach. [See immigrant Georg Freyman for more data on the children of Lenhard Freÿman].
Peter Freyman and wife Anna Catharina had a son:
    Johan Henrich, bp. 26 Dec. 1705
    Sp.: the young *Jäger* here Joh. Henrich Ermold

Joh. Henrich Freymann, linenweaver, son of *Meister* Peter Freymann, linenweaver, m. 18 Mar. 1734 Maria Barbara, daughter of Andreas Schad, at Roth, *Hochgraffl. Ÿsenb.-Meerholtzischen Jurisdiction.* They had children:
    1. Maria Magdalena, bp. 9 Feb. 1735
       Sp.: The child's mother's sister from Roth
    2. Anna Rosina, bp. 2 July 1736
       Sp.: daughter of *Meister* Dieterich Filtzmeyer here

AMERICAN RECORDS

Note: the immigrant appears only on the A ship list, and did not sign either of the oath lists for the passengers on this ship; he may have died aboard ship or soon after arrival. One Henrich Freymann appears in Berks county records, but he may be a son of a prelist immigrant; one Jacob Freyman appears on the 1725/26 tax list for Tulpehocken Township. The following records may apply to that family:

Records in Berks County reveal that Maria Elisabetha Freyman married Joh. Christian Berger, Bern Twp., Berks Co. before 1765. Brother: Heinrich Freyman, had nephew Casper Freyman.

PA Archives, Sixth Series, Vol. 6, Rev. Waldschmidt's Records:
Johann Christian Berger and wife Maria Elisabetha had a son:
Johann Henrich b. 3 Apr. 1765, bp. 27 Apr.
Sp.: Henrich Freymann and wife Catharina.

Note also: the 1748 immigrant Henrich Freyman was age 30 on arrival. This would place his birth ca. 1718, rather than 1705.

One Henry Frieman, Bern Twp., Berks Co., nat. Sept. 1765.

HÜBENER, HENRICH
Lydia, 1749
S-H, I: 421

EUROPEAN RECORDS

Langenselbold Reformed KB:
Joh. Henrich Hübener from Rückging, son of the late Reinhard Hübener, *Schreiner* there, m. 26 Nov. 1696 Elisabetha Straub, daughter of Johan Straub, *Hoffmann* at Bruderdibach. They had children:
1. Gertrudis bp. 1 Mar. 1699 at Bruderdibach
   Sp.: the wife of M. Peter Eÿring, miller there.
   [She m. Georg Schuffert and they emigrated 1733.]
2. Johan Henrich bp. 3 Sept. 1700
   Sp.: J. Henrich Straub, the mother's single brother.

There were other children of this name in the Langenselbold records:
1. Anton Hübener and wife Anna had a son:
   Johann Henrich, bp. 21 June 1731
   Sp.: Joh. Henrich Lofinck

2. Caspar Hübener and wife Anna Catharina had a son:
   Johan Henrich, bp. 28 Oct. 1706
   Sp.: Henrich Kürschner

The 1749 immigrant arrived on the ship *Lydia* with several other men with surnames that appear in the Langenselbold records: Bloss, Arnolt [Ermold], Kniess, Koch, and Kirschner. More information is needed to determine if the 1749 immigrant is one of these Hübeners born in Langenselbold.

KALCKLÖSER, JOHANN HENRICH
Allen, 1729
S-H, I: 27, 29, 30

EUROPEAN RECORDS

Langenselbold Reformed KB:
Johann Henrich Kalcklöser from Windecken, *Beysass* here and his wife Maria Magdalena had a son:
> Johann Henrich, bp. 9 July 1695
> Sp.: Johann Kürschner, *Gerichtschöff* here

AMERICAN RECORDS

Philadelphia Will Book G: 91:
Catharina Weidner, Cocalico, Lancaster Co.
22 Sept. 1742- 18 Feb. 1743. Names children: John Henry Calckgleaser and Trivena Weidner.

This information from the Langenselbold KB is included here to make it available on this very unusual name. There was an early immigrant with this name, who became prominent in the Brethren denomination. A few records are to be found in the *Brethren Encyclopedia* and also in the Ephrata records on the Johann Henrich Kalcklöser of Pennsylvania; there is no confirming evidence that he is the child b. 1695 in Langenselbold. However, the data is published here to provide the Windecken clue to other researchers.

A Christian Kalcklöser settled in Lower Heidelberg Twp., (now Berks Co.) with other Langenselbold immigrants. He appears on the connected land warrantee map on tract C-107-131 with 226 A. in 1738, adjacent to Ermantrout and Hettrich land.

Johann Heinrich Kalckgläser originally settled in Germantown, and eventually went to Ephrata in Lancaster County where he became a member of the Cloister. His burial record at Ephrata: Brother Joel fell asleep in the Lord in 1748, his age 52 years.

KIRSCHNER, CONRAD
Possibly 1722-23 to New York

EUROPEAN RECORDS

Langenselbold Reformed KB:
Johan Kirchner, the herdsman at Baumwiesen, born at Bissheim an der Röhn, and wife Anna Catharina had a son:
    Conrad, bp. 1 Sept. 1687
    Sp.: Conrad Lang, born *aus dem Hessischen Ambt Mellsung*,
    a day laborer at Hüttengesäss

AMERICAN RECORDS

Montgomery, History of Berks Co., PA, p. 1118:
"The heads of the Kershner families in Berks Co. emigrated from Amsterdam and arrived at New York during the winter of 1722-23."

Scott T. Swank, in his book titled *Arts of the Pennsylvania Germans*, published by the Winterthur Museum in 1983 devotes several pages to the Hehn-Kershner house at Wernersville, Berks County, Pa. On page 98, of Swank's book, he gives the following information:
"The first Conrad Kershner (1687-1771) and his wife Marie, arrived in New York in 1722 and eventually settled in Bern Township, Berks County. The Conrad Kershner who bought George Hehn's house, probably a grandson of the first Conrad Kershner, owned the house from 1772 to 1803."

There is at least one unidentified Kirschner in Berks County:
Joh. Philipp Strauss had a daughter Anna Eliesabetha, bp. 28 Sept. 1746 and recorded in Christ Little Tulpehocken Lutheran KB. Sp. at this baptism were Dinnes Kürschner and his wife. [This given name Dinnes might be Tönges, Antonius.]

KNISS, JOHANNES
Edinburgh, 1750
S-H, I: 430
EUROPEAN RECORDS

Langenselbold Reformed KB:
Johann Bernhard Kniess and wife Catharina had a son:
    Johannes, bp. 9 Nov. 1721

Johannes Kniess, son of Joh. Bernhard Kniess, m. 25 Feb. 1749 Elisabetha, daughter of Johannes Keÿser. They continued to have children born in Langenselbold after the emigration year 1750.

Conrad Kniess and wife Magdalena Elisabeth had a son:
      Johannes, bp. 22 Nov. 1705
      Sp.: Hans Reber, single son of Michael Reber.

[One Johannes Kniss arrived on this ship with several other immigrants from Langenselbold: Kassler, Feuerstein, Dippel, Hamburger, and Kirschner all appear on this list.]

KOLB, CONRAD age 34
Pleasant, 1732
S-H, I: 99, 100, 101

EUROPEAN RECORDS

Langenselbold Reformed KB:
Johan Jost Kolb, master smith, born *"am Marck von Herborn"* and his wife Anna Barbara had children:
      1. Joh. Barthel, bp. 22 Mar. 1696
      2. Johan **Conrad**, bp. 3 Apr. 1698
         Sp.: Johan Conrad Adam, here
      3. Antonius, bp. 30 July 1699
      4. Joh. Peter, bp. 12 Mar. 1702

(No later records found; no supporting PA data found.)

ROTH, VALENTIN age 35
Lydia, 1743
S-H, I: 341, 342, 343

EUROPEAN RECORDS

Langenselbold Reformed KB:
Johann Jacob Roth and Juliana had a son:
      Johann Valentin, bp. 8 Feb. 1708
      Sp.: the son of M. Henrich Hix, the *Gemeineschmied*
(No later records found; no supporting PA data found.)

WOLFF, JOHANN HENRICH
Francis and Elizabeth, 1742
S-H, I: 329

EUROPEAN RECORDS

Langenselbold Reformed KB:
Hans Wolff, *Jäger,* and wife Engel had:
    Isaac, bp. 20 Dec. 1699
    Sp.: Isaac Müller, *Ziegler* here

Mstr. Isaac Wolff, tailor, son of the late Hans Wolff, former hunter *(Jäger)* at Ronnenburg, m. 7 Mar. 1725 Anna Maria Wacker, daughter of Mstr. Johannes Wacker, *Riedmüller.* They had a son:
    1. **Johan Henrich**, bp. 8 Sept. 1726
        Sp.: the son of *Mstr.* Michael Spindler, *Binder*

AMERICAN RECORDS

St. Michael's and Zion KB, Philadelphia:
Married 13 July 1746: Johann Heinrich Wolf (Reformed) and Juliana Maria Fellendser. Wit: Jacob Fister and Joh. Adam Fuchs.

OTHER CLUES TO VILLAGES OF ORIGIN IN THE
LANGENSELBOLD RECORDS

Johann Jost Heck from Rüdigheim, now shepherd at Baumwiesen, and his wife Anna Margretha had children bp. in 1706 and 1708. One Jost Heck with wife Anna Eva arrived on a ship with other Langenselbold families and then appear in the Hain's (St. John's) Reformed KB with others from the area.

Frantz Krick also appears in the Hain's records; he was not located, but a Joh. Henrich Krick, son of Peter Krick at Udenhaÿn in Graffschaft Isenburg, Wachtersbach, m. 21 Apr. 1718 Anna Rosina, daughter of Johannes Klingenstein.

APPENDIX C

Presented in this appendix are a few other immigrant families who appear in the records of certain adjacent villages. They were researched and included here to help clarify certain family relationships, and to help the researcher distinguish between the various Johannes Fischers, and Philip Fausts.

****

FAUST, PHILIP age 30   Ravoltshausen
Elizabeth, 1733
S-H, I: 113, 114, 115, 765, 766, 767
   other passengers on ship: Anna Catrina Faust, age 21; John Jacob Faust, age 4; John Adam Faust, age 2: John Hendrick, age ½ year.

EUROPEAN RECORDS

Langenselbold Reformed KB:
Hans Faust, son of Johannes Faust, m. (1) 2 Mar. 1640 Elisabetha, daughter of Antonius Fischer. They had:
   1. Maria Elisabetha, bp. 15 Feb. 1641
   2. Johann, b. 3 weeks before Easter 1643, twin
      Sp.: Johan Ermuth
   3. Wörner, b. 3 weeks before Easter, 1643 twin
      Sp.: Wörner Moon
   4. Giel (Julianna), bp. (no day given) 1645
      Sp.: Giel, daughter of Peter Lerch
   5. Endres, bp. 16 Jan. 1648; d. 21 Apr. 1697
      Endres Hartman, *Baumeister* at Selbold
   6. Johannes, bp. 29 Apr. 1649; sp.: Hans Gerard.

Hans Faust m. (2) Tuesday after Easter 1654 Kunigunda, daughter of Hans Gaul from Ravoltshausen. Children of second marriage:
   7. Anna, bp. 21 Jan. 1655; sp.: wife of Conrad Lerch
   8. Engel, bp. 15 Mar. 1657; sp.: Engel, wife of Tönges Mohn
   9. Johann Caspar, bp. 17 Apr. 1659; sp.: Caspar Wohl
   10. Elisabetha, bp. 31 Mar. 1662
      Sp.: Elisabetha, daughter of Peter Kirschner
   11. Johann Görg, bp. 23 Dec. 1666. [Lived in Ravolzhausen.]
      Sp.: Wörner Ermold's son Joh. Görg.

12. Johann, bp. 25 Oct. 1669; sp.: Johann Wörner, *Mitnachbar.*
He m. 23 June 1701 Anna Elisabetha, daughter of Johann
Keÿser. He was a soldier and died near Landau in the Palatinate
14 Dec. 1704. His widow m. (2) Wilhelm Gerhart and was the
mother of 1739 immigrant Fredrich Gerhart [q.v.].

Ravolzhausen Reformed KB:
Johann Georg Faust and wife (name unknown) had a son:
Johann Philipp, b. 23 Jan.1702 in Ravolzhausen.

Johann **Philipp Faust** m. 18 Feb. 1726 Anna Catharina Ruth. They had:
1. Jacob, b. 18 Nov. 1728
2. Adam, b. __ ___ 1731
3. Heinrich, b. 3 June 1733

Ravolzhausen Faust data from the *Ringer Genealogy*, by Dorothy Ringer Paul, privately
published, Oklahoma City, OK (1987). Researchers are urged to consult this book for American
data on the family.

FISCHER, JOHANNES age 48   Eckartshausen
Samuel, 1739
S-H, I: 256, 258, 261
                        EUROPEAN RECORDS

Eckartshausen Reformed KB:
Johannes Fischer m. 8 Mar. 1688 Joh. Scheid's daughter. [Her given names
not recorded; however a later record names Johannes Fischer's wife Susanna
Maria.] They had children:
1. **Johannes**, bp. 3 Jan. 1690
   [NOTE by compiler: Moravian records in PA give his birth as
   December 1693; the record probably should read Dec. 1689].
2. A son [Werner?] bp. 24 Sept. 1691
   Sp.: Werner Möller
3. A daughter, bp. 17 Sept. 1694
4. Catharina, bp. 11 Feb. 1698

Johannes Fischer, son of Johannes Fischer, inhabitant at Eckartshausen, m.
27 Mar. 1721   Eva Maria, daughter of Thomas Kiltau(en), citizen at
Wächtersbach. They had:
1. Susanna Maria, bp. 3 June 1721
   Sp.: Susanna Maria, wife of Johannes Fischer, the grandmother

AMERICAN RECORDS

Heidelberg Moravian Catalog, 1746, Berks Co., PA:
(Johannes Fischer, Sr.) Children:
1. Barbara Elisabetha, b. Aug. 1733
2. Catharina, b. Sept. 1740
3. Anna Maria, b. circa end of Jan. 1743

Heidelberg Moravian Catalog, 1780, Berks Co., PA:
Anna Sybilla Fischerin, widow, b. 1701 in Creutznach, m. 1737. Child:
1. Anna Maria, b. Jan. 1743

Heidelberg Moravian KB, Berks Co.:
Johannes Fischer, Sr., from Eckartshausen, Amt Marienborn, Graffschaft
Isenberg, born in December in the year 1693 and baptized at the same place
in the beginning of January 1694, by Pastor Friedrich Grim. His sponsors
were Johann Pielman and his wife Anna Maria. He was married at the same
place in Feb. 1721 by Pastor Rost of Eckartshausen, to Eva _____.
Johannes Fischer died on 22 July 1759 and was buried in our God's acre.
They had one child: [Note: his will names 3 children to his first marriage.]
1. Barbara Elisabeth, born in Hanau not far from Frankfurt, in
   August 1733. She was baptized by Pastor Jüngst at that place.
   Sp.: Barbara Elisabeth, daughter of..... of Hanau.

Eva, first wife of Johannes Fischer, died in October 1737 and he was
remarried by Inspector Grimm in Hanau to Anna Sybillen born in
Creusenach in 1701. In this marriage they had two children:
1. Catharina, born in the middle of Sept. 1740 in Heidelberg,
   bp. by Caspar Stöver in the old Lutheran church in Tulpehocken.
   Sp.: Johannes Kirschner and his wife.
2. Anna Maria, born in Heidelberg at the end of Jan. 1743,
   bp. by Jacob Lischy in the Reformed church in Bern.
   Sp.: Heinrich _____ and daughter Anna Maria.

Burial record # 26: Johannes Fischer, born 31 Dec. 1693 in Eckartshausen
in the Wetterau. Married the first time in 1721, and the second time in 1738
to Anna Sibilla nee Hag. He came to Pennsylvania in 1739 and lived here
since 1742. He died 22 July 1759, buried by Anton Wagner.

Burial record # 72: Anna Sybilla Fischer, widow, nee Haag, was born 7 Jan.
1700 in Kreuznau. She lived with her parents until 18 years old when she
moved to Hanau. In 1738 she married Johannes Fischer who was a widower.
Johannes died in 1759. She had two daughters: one married Jacob Schmidt,
with whom she lived after she was a widow, and the other married James

Hall of Bethlehem. She had 7 grandchildren and died 16 Dec. 1780, age 80
years less 3 weeks and 18 days.

Burial record # 61: Catharina Schmid, nee Fischer, born in Heidelberg in
September 1740. She was bp. by a Lutheran minister. She was married on
27 Sept. 1759 to Jacob Schmidt, by Brother Anton Wagner. They had 3 sons
and two daughters. She died 17 Aug. 1775.

Bern Reformed KB, Bern Twp., Berks Co., PA;
John Fischer and wife Anna Sibylla had a child:
>   Anna Maria, bp. 1 May 1745
>   Sp.: Henry Schuckert and Catharina.

Abstracts of Berks County Wills and Adm.:
Johannes Fischer, Heidelberg, 18 July 1759, prob. 18 Aug. 1759. All estate
to be sold. My 3 children by first wife, to wit: Susanna, Charles and
Barbara shall have 10 s. each. Wife Sybilla to have 1/3 of estate and
remainder to 2 children by her, viz: Catharina and Anna Maria Fischer,
John Mayer and Frederick Gerhard, executors. Witness Henrich Stöhr,
Nicholas Glaude [Glad]. Translation.

SCHUCHARDT, HEINRICH   Eckartshausen
Probably prelist;
Last appears in Eckartshausen KB in 1715; married in PA ca. 1726/7 and (2)
in 1728.
(not in S-H)
                          EUROPEAN RECORDS

Eckartshausen Reformed KB:
Johan Schuckert (wife not named) had children:
>   1. Maria Elisabetha, bp. 18 Apr. 1682
>   2. Catharina, bp. 7 Sept. 1684
>   3. A son (N.N.), bp. 12 Apr. 1688
>   Sp.: Möller's son at Marienborn

One Joh. Wilhelm Schuckert married in 1714 Anna Maria Sprenger. They
had a son Johann Henrich b. 4 Dec. 1715. The sponsor at this child's
baptism was Joh. Henrich Schuchert, son of Johannes Schuchert. It is the
opinion of this researcher that this baptismal sponsor is the Heinrich
Schuchart who emigrated to PA. There are no further entries for him in the
Eckartshausen KB.

AMERICAN RECORDS

Heidelberg Moravian KB, Berks Co., PA:
Heinrich Schuchardt, born in Eckartshausen, district of Marienborn, County Ysenburg in the year 1695 and was baptized by the pastor at the same place, Inspector Friedrich Grimm in Hanau. When 32 years old, he married Miss Catharina Baus. They had one daughter, Anna Maria.

His first wife, Catharina, died, and in 1728 he married Miss Anna Catharina Klapp, daughter of Jost Klapp of Iste, Hesse. They were married by Georg _____ a justice in Oley. Anna Catharina was born in 1707. They had children:

1. Johann Jost, b. 7 Feb. 1731, old style, bp. by Caspar Stöver
2. Johannes, b. Aug. 1733, bp. by Johannes Müller
3. Anna Maria, b. 9 Mar. 1735, bp. by Philip Boehm
4. Maria Catharina, b. 9 May 1736, bp. by Philip Boehm
5. Maria Christina, b. 1737, bp. by Philip Boehm
6. Johann Heinrich, b. 8 Sept. 1741, old style, bp. by Philip Boehm
7. Carl, b. in the year 1743, bp. the same year in the Bern Church by Jacob Lischy
8. Tobias, b. 8 Feb. 1747, old style, bp. the same day in the parents' house, by Brother Pyrlaeo. The sponsors were Stephen Brecht, Tobias Böckel, Nicol Glat, Friedrich Gerhardt and Johannes Meyer.
9. Anna Elisabeth, b. 4 Dec. 1749, bp. on the 11th in the parents' house by Brother Christian Rauch. The sponsors were Christina Böckel, Maria Catharina Conrad, Anna Rauch and Hanna Neubert.

In 1749, Mrs. Catharina Schuchart had communion with us for the first time.

Heinrich Dock and his wife Maria nee Schuchard had a son:
1. Jacob Heinrich, b. 4 Apr. 1756; bp. 11 Apr. 1756.
   Sp.: Heinrich Schuchart, Henrich Stöhr, Tobias Böckel and Jacob Müller.

Pennsylvania Archives, Sixth Series, Vol. 6, Rev. Waldschmidt's records:
Confirmed at Cacusy, 30 Mar. 1766:
Joh. Heinrich, Wilhelm Carl, and Tobias, sons of Heinrich Schucker.
Anna Elisabeth, daughter of Heinrich Schuckert.

Berks County Wills:
Henry Shuckert, Heidelberg Twp., 24 Apr. 1772; 13 Aug. 1773:
Provides for wife Catharine. To son John Jost 5 shillings, he having received

his share. All the rest of children, to wit: John; Henry; Charles [Carl]; Tobias; the children of daughter Johanna Maria, dec'd; Anna Maria, wife of Henry Dock; Maria Christina, wife of John Hahn [q.v.]; and Anna Elisabeth; to have equal shares. Ex: Friends John & Jonas Eckert [q.v.]. Wit: Nicholas Eckert, Samuel Weiser.

[Note by AKB: it is possible that the maiden name of Heinrich Schuchardt's first wife was Gans, Gantz. **Philadelphia Will Book F: 18:** contains the will of John Gantz of Lancaster, probated 8 Nov. 1734, in which he names his wife Gurtrad Gantz as his executrix, and mentions his grandchild Anna Maria Schucker(in). The will was witnessed by John Artz and Michael Blattner.]

-A-

Allen, 1729: 143
Ann Galley, 1746:
 50, 60, 64, 69,
 71(2), 89, 111
Ann Galley, 1764: 106

-C-

Chance, 1766: 6, 27
Charming Molly, 1773:
 23, 52

-E-

Edinburgh, 1750: 8, 12,
 39, 66, 82, 144
Edinburgh, 1753: 10
Elizabeth, 1733: 11, 34,
 62, 72, 84, 109,
 118, 120, 121, 147

-F-

Francis and Elizabeth,
 1742: 5, 15, 17, 32,
 33, 37, 54, 55, 68,
 86, 91, 113, 117,
 124, 146

-G-

Glasgow, 1738: 139
Good Hope, 1753: 13

-K-

King George, 1761: 10

-L-

Lydia, 1743: 145
 1749: 142

-M-

Minerva, 1769: 51

-P-

Patience and Margaret,
 1748: 141
Phoenix, 1749: 115
Pleasant, 1732: 145
prelist: 93, 144, 150

-Q-

Queen Elizabeth, 1738:
 2, 29, 75, 98, 102, 104

-R-

Ranier, 1749: 115
Richard and Elizabeth,
 1733: 3, 40, 116,
 122, 124

-S-

Samuel, 1731: 47, 61, 80
 1733: 1, 42, 45, 46,
 47, 105, 107
 1739: 7, 16, 49, 56,
 108, 140, 148

-T-

Townsend, 1737: 121
Two Brothers, 1752: 119

154

St. John's (Hain's) Reformed Church, Lower Heidelberg Twp.,
Berks Co., PA, established in 1735.

The following place name index transcribes the place names as they are given in the seventeenth and eighteenth century records. These entries in the original records often reflect older and obsolete spellings of the village names, including Selbold, the name used for Langenselbold in the earlier records. Since Langenselbold appears on every page of the text, it is not included in this index, but the earlier version, Selbold, is indexed. Several unusual spellings of this place name that were located in American records also appear in the index. Added to each index entry is the modern spelling, along with the current five-digit zip code designation to assist the researcher with location of the place on today's maps. Only a few places have defied exact identification, usually when there are several places with the same name, and no locality clue is given in the original record.

-A-

ALLENDORFF, Frühlinger Grunds, 116 (10 Allendorfs in Hessen)
ALTEN HASEL, (Altenhasslau = 63589 Linsengericht), 45
ALTEN HASELAU, (Altenhasslau = 63589 Linsengericht), 45
ALTENBURSCHLA, Hesse, (=37281 Wanfried) 137
ALTENHASSLAU (= 63589 Linsengericht), 77
ALTSTAT (= ? 63674 Altenstadt), 139
AMBT MELLSUNG, Hessen, (= 34212 Melsungen) 144

-B-

BAUMWIESEN, (Baumwieserhof = 63776 Hüttengesäss) 140, 144, 146
BAUMWIESSEN, (Baumwieserhof = 63776 Huttengesass), 123
BENKEN, Canton Baselland, Switzerland, (CH-4105 Benken, BL) 58
BERAUERSWEIN?, Oberfurstenthum Hess, 98
BERCKHEIM, (Bergheim = 63683 Ortenberg, Hessen) 136
BERGHEIM, (= 63683 Ortenberg, Hessen) 12, 13
BICKEN, (= 35756 Mittenaar) Furstenthumb Dillenburg, 43, 47
BINKEN [SEE BENKEN], Canton Baselland, Switzerland, 59
BIRSTEIN, (= 63633 Birstein) 32
BISSHEIM (? Bischheim) AN DER RÖHN, 144
BRANDE?, Bischthum Auchspurg, 33
BRESSANONE, Italy, 11
BRIEG in Schlesien, (= ?18556 Breege) 15, 16
BRIXEN, Tyrol, 11
BRUD(ER)DIEBACH, (Bruderdiebacherhof = 63505 Langenselbold) 140
BRUDERDIBACH, (Bruderdiebacherhof = 63505 Langenselbold) 122, 142
BRUDERDIEBACHER HOFF, (Bruderdiebacherhof=63505 Langenselbold) 139
BÜDINGEN, (= 63654 Büdingen, Hessen) 51, 69

-C-

CLOSTERBERG, (= 63505 Langenselbold), 70, 77
COBURG, (= 96450 Coburg) 70
CREUSENACH, (= 55543 Bad Kreuznach) 149
CREUTZNACH, (= 55543 Bad Kreuznach) 149

-D-

DIEBACH, (Diebach am Haag = 63654 Büdingen, Hessen) 137
DORFELDEN, (Oberdorfelden = 61137 Schöneck, Hessen), 93, 94

-E-

ECKARTSHAUSEN, 136, 140, 148, 149, 150
    Amt Marienborn, Graffschaft Isenberg, 149
    District of Marienborn, County Ysenburg, 151
    Wetterau, 149   (all = Eckartshausen = 63654 Büdingen, Hessen)
ECKHARTSHAUSEN, (= 63654 Büdingen, Hessen) 102
EICHENZELL, near Fulda, (= 36124 Eichenzell) 106
EIDENGESÄSS, Wetterau, (= 63589 Linsengericht) 94
EYSENBERGISCHE HOFF, 8, 10 (Estate of the Count of Isenberg)

-F-

FISCHBORN, (= 63633 Birstein) 54
FRANCE, 49
FRANCKFURT, (= 60324 Frankfurt am Main) 15, 16
FRANCKFURTH, (= 60324 Frankfurt am Main) 15, 16
FRANKFURT, (= 60324 Frankfurt am Main) 149
FREYENSTEIN, Ried-Eselischen Jurisdiction, 117
    (most likely 36399 Freiensteinau)
FROHNHAUSEN, 12 (several in Germany, 3 in Hessen)

-G-

GELNHAUSEN, (= 63571 Gelnhausen) 76
GERTERODE, (= 37355 Gerterode) 93
GERTHENROTH, Ried-Eselischen, (= 37355 Gerterode) 93
GONNSCHROD?, (Gondsroth = 63594 Hasselroth) 43
GRAFFSCHAFT YSENBURG-MERHOLS, 57
    (County of Isenberg-Meerholz)

-H-

HANAU, (= 63450 Hanau) 48, 111, 149, 151
    Bavaria, 91 (Bavaria is an error; 63450 Hanau, Hessen)
HAYNGEN--FEN, Hessen-Cassel, 107

HELBRIG, (Hilbringen = 66663 Merzig) 130
HELDENBERG, (Heldenbergen = 61130 Nidderau, Hessen) 39
HERBORN, (= 35745 Herborn, Hessen) 145
HERRNHAAG, Wetteravia, (Diebach am Haag=63654 Büdingen, Hessen) 61
HOCHSTADT, Hessen, (= 63477 Maintal) 93
  Wetterau, 94, 95, 96, 97
HOCHSTATT, (Hochstadt= 63477 Maintal), 102, 104
HOINGEN, (Höingen, Hessen = 35315 Homberg), 8, 10
HUNGEN, (= 35410 Hungen) 8, 10
HÜTTENGESÄSS, (= 63776 Hüttengesäss) 25, 129, 130, 131, 132, 133, 134,
  135, 136, 137, 144

-I-

ISENBERG, 90 (County of Isenberg, Ysenberg)
ISTE, Hesse, (Istha = 34466 Wolfhagen) 151

-K-

KETTENBACH, (= 65326 Aarbergen) 140
KLEINDORFELDEN, (= 61138 Niederdorfelden)
  Graffschaft Hanau, 68
  Hanau, 48
KREUZNAU(CH), (= 55543 Bad Kreuznach) 149
KÜNZELSAU, Graffschafft Hohenloh, (= 74653 Künzelsau) 27

-L-

LANDAU, Palatinate, (= 76829 Landau in der Pfalz) 148
LANGEN SELBOLT, Wetterau, (= 63505 Langenselbold) 94
LANGEN-SELBOT (sic), County Ysenberg in the Wetterau, 58
LANGEN-SELBURG (sic), (= 63505 Langenselbold) 66
LANGENDIBACH, (Langendiebach = 63526 Erlensee), 108
LANGENDIEBACH, (= 63526 Erlensee) 2, 5, 30, 34
LANGENSELBOLD, County of Ronnenburg, (= 63505 Langenselbold) 46
LANGENSELBOT (sic), (= 63505 Langenselbold)
  Amt Ronnerburg, Graffschaft Ysenburg, 57
  Isenburg, 44
  Ysenberg, 90
LANGENSELLWELT (sic), (= 63505 Langenselbold) 138
  Isenberg, 138
LEIMEN, near Heidelberg, (= 69181 Leimen, Baden) 95
LICHENROTH, (= 63633 Birstein) 109
LIEBLOS, (= 63584 Gründau) 138
LONGASALZA, (= 63505 Langenselbold) 22, 23

-M-

MARBURG, (= 35039 Marburg) 115
MARCKKÖBEL, (Marköbel= 63546 Hammersbach, Hessen) 131
MARIENBORN, (Eckartshausen = 63654 Büdingen, Hessen) 1, 150
   Wetteravia, 61
MARKOEBEL, Hanau, (Marköbel= 63546 Hammersbach, Hessen) 18
MEERHOLTZ, (= 63571 Gelnhausen) 2
MENSFELDEN, (= 65597 Hünfelden) 120
MERCKENBACH, Nassau-Dillenburg, (= 35745 Herborn, Hessen) 27
MICHELSTADT, Odenwald, (=64720 Michelstadt) 131
MITTELGRÜNDAU, (Mittel Gründau = 63584 Gründau) 64
MITTLAU, (Niedermittlau = 63594 Hasselroth) 56

-N-

NEU HANAU, (= 63450 Hanau) 39
NEUEN HASSLAU, (Neuenhasslau = 63594 Hasselroth) 70
NEUENHASSEL, (Neuenhasslau = 63594 Hasselroth) 57, 111
NEUENHASSLAU, (Neuenhasslau = 63594 Hasselroth) 57
NEUHASSEL, (Neuenhasslau = 63594 Hasselroth) 55
NIDERRODENBACH, (Niederrodenbach = 63517 Rodenbach b. Hanau) 129
NIED(ER) MITLAU, (Niedermittlau = 63594 Hasselroth) 56
NIED(ER) MITTLAU, (Niedermittlau = 63594 Hasselroth) 57
NIEDER GRÜNDAU, (Niedergründau = 63584 Gründau) 137
NIEDER MITTL(AU), (Niedermittlau = 63594 Hasselroth) 56
NIEDER MITTLAU, (Niedermittlau = 63594 Hasselroth) 56
NIEDER RODENBACH, (Niederrodenbach = 63517 Rodenbach b. Hanau) 130
NIEDERGRÜNDAU, (Niedergründau = 63584 Gründau) 138
NIEDERLISINGEN, Unterhessen Ampts Zierenberg, (= 34479 Breuna) 11
NIEDERLISTINGEN, Unterhessen Ampts Zierenberg, (= 34479 Breuna) 11
NIEDERRODENBACH, (Niederrodenbach = 63517 Rodenbach b. Hanau) 129

-O-

OBERDORFELDEN, (= 61137 Schöneck, Hessen) 93
   Kreis Hanau, 93
OBERDORFELDEN, (= 61137 Schöneck, Hessen) 139
OBERDORFF, (= 63505 Langenselbold) 32, 85
OBERSTEIN, Nassau-Sigen, (= 55743 Idar-Oberstein) 138
OFFENBACH, (= 63071 Offenbach am Main) 2
OKRIFTEL, (= 65795 Hattersheim am Main) 8, 10

-P-

PALATINATE, (Pfalz) 135

-R-

RAEDGEN?, in Busecker Thal, (Röthges = 35321 Laubach, Hessen) 2
RAVOLTSHAUSEN, (= 63543 Neuberg, Hessen) 139, 147
RAVOLTZHAUSEN, (= 63543 Neuberg, Hessen) 61, 148
RAVOLZHAUSEN, (= 63543 Neuberg, Hessen) 148
RODENBACH, (= 63517 Rodenbach b. Hanau) 129
ROHRBACH, Eckartshausen, (= 63654 Büdingen, Hessen) 78
ROMMELSHAUSEN, Friedberg Jurisdiction, (Rommelhausen = 63694 Limeshain) 131
RONNEBURG CASTLE, Wetteravia, 61 (= 63549 Ronneburg, Hessen)
RONNENBURG, (= 63549 Ronneburg, Hessen) 146
ROTENBERG, (? Rothenbergen = 63584 Hasselroth) 76
ROTH, Ysenb.-Meerholtz, (= 63571 Gelnhausen) 141
ROTTENBACH, (= 63517 Rodenbach b. Hanau) 137
RÜCKGING, (Rückingen = 63526 Erlensee) 122, 142
RÜDIGHEIM, (= 63543 Neuberg, Hessen) 136, 146

-S-

SAXONY, 70, 73
SCHLICHTERN, (= 36381 Schlüchtern) 30
SCHLIERBACH, (by Wächtersbach = 63636 Brachttal) 56
SCHLÜCHTERN, (= 36381 Schlüchtern) 62
SELBOLD, 3, 34, 62, 78, 106, 107, 121, 122, 132, 133, 136, 147
  County Isenberg, 90 (17th & 18th century name for = 63505 Langenselbold)
  Principality of Isenberg, 90
SELIGEN, Rhenish Bavaria, (possibly 63500 Seligenstadt) 9
STEINAU AN DER STRASSE, (= 36396 Steinau) 66
STREITBERG, (Streitberg by Wächtersbach = 63636 Brachttal) 18, 79
SWITZERLAND, 39

-U-

UDENHAYN, Graffschaft Isenburg, (Udenhain = 63636 Brachttal) 146

-V-

VILBEL, (= 61118 Bad Vilbel) 5, 6

-W-

WÄCHTERSBACH, (= 63607 Wächtersbach) 64, 141, 146, 148
WALLROTH, Esslischer jurisdiction, (= 36381 Schlüchtern) 64
WALTERSBACH, Lower Alsace, (= F-67130 Schirmeck) 44
WERNINGS, (Wenings = 63688 Gedern) 102
  Hochgraff Birstein, 103
WETTERAVIA, Germany, 91 (Wetterau, jurisdiction in Hessen)

WIEDERMUS, (Altwiedermus = 63549 Ronneburg, Hessen) 140
WINDECKEN, (= 61130 Nidderau, Hessen) 143
WITTGENBORN, (= 63607 Wächtersbach) 1, 24, 51, 98

-Z-

ZIEGENHAIN, Hessen, (= 34613 Schwalmstadt) 7, 72
ZITTAU, Saxony, (= 02763 Zittau) 90

-A-

Adam,
  "Lips", 1
  Anna Catharina,
    1(2), 138
  Anton, 1
  Catharina, 1(2)
  Conrad, 1,
    45(2), 119
  Conrad Sr., 45
  Hennerich, 40
  Joh. Conrad, 1,
    102
  Joh. Heinrich,
    1, 48
  Joh. Henrich, 1
  Johan Conrad,
    122, 145
  Johann Conrad,
    35
  Johann Henrich,
    1(2)
  Johann Wilhelm,
    1
  Johannes, 1(2),
    45, 89, 102
  Johannes Conrad,
    1
  John George, 2
  Künigunda, 45
  Magdalena, 1, 35
  Magdalena
    Elisabeth, 1
  Margretha, 119
  Michael, 2
  Philipps, 35, 45
  Philips, 1, 138
  Sabina, 122
Adams,
  John, 103
  Peter, 19
  Rahel, 103
Ähl,
  Anna Catharina,
    132
  Anna Maria, 111,
    113
  Johan, 111, 113
  Johannes, 111,
    113
  Valentin, 111,
    113, 132
Albert,
  John, 65
Albrech,
  Barbara, 37

Jacob, 36
Albrecht,
  Christian, 36
  Daniel, 103
Albright,
  Barbara, 37
Alt,
  Anna Elisabetha,
    2
  Anna Margreha, 2
  Anna Maria, 2
  Elisabeth
    Catharine, 2
  Joh. Adam, 2
  Johann Martin, 2
  Johannes, 2, 87
  John, 2
Altbrech,
  Christian, 36
Altstatt,
  Martin, 36
Armentrout,
  Elizabeth, 141
  Frederick, 141
  Henry, 141
  John, 69, 141
  Philip, 141
Armold,
  Martin, 25
  William, 26
Armolt,
  Martin, 25
Arnolt, 143
Artz,
  John, 152

-B-

Baal,
  Philip, 100
Bahl,
  Anna Maria, 100
Baker,
  Catharine, 50
  William, 50
Balliets,
  Magdalena, 121
Barthel,
  (Anna
    Catharina), 77
  Anna Margreth,
    15, 16
  Johannes, 77
  Jörg, 15, 16
  Susanna
    Elisabetha, 15,
    16
Bast,

John, 27
  Margretha, 27
Baum,
  John, 82
  Joseph, 82
  Martin, 82
Baus,
  Catharina, 151
Bautz,
  Johannes, 110
Baver,
  Adam, 74
Beak,
  George, 82
Beck,
  Anna Catharina,
    3(3), 4
  Anna Elisabetha,
    3
  Anna Engel, 3
  Anna Maria, 3
  Anthony, 4
  Antony, 3(2)
  Catharina, 4(2),
    86(2)
  Catharine, 4
  Christoff
    Herman, 3
  Elisabeth, 4
  Elisabetha, 3
  Elizabeth, 4
  Engel, 3, 4
  Engelina, 3
  Herman, 3
  Herman
    Christoph, 3
  Hermann, 3
  Ingel, 4
  Joh. Conrad, 3
  Joh. Henrich,
    3(2)
  Joh. Peter, 3
  Johan Peter, 3
  Magdalena, 3
  Matheas, 4
  Mathias, 4
  Matthias, 3
  Susanna, 4
Beckel,
  Christina, 58
  Tobias, 58
Becker,
  Anna Maria, 131
  Christofel, 39
  Johannes, 131
  William, 50
Beenner,
  Jurry, 132

Beidelman,
  Adam, 101(2)
  Anthony, 101
  Catharine, 101
  Esther, 101
  Frederick, 101
  John, 101
  Margaret, 101
  Peter, 101
  Samuel, 101
Bekel,
  Anna Elisabeth,
    58
  Friedrich, 58
  Tobias, 58
Bellenger,
  Anna, 131
  Marcus, 131
Bellinger, 133
  Ann, 134
  Anna, 130
  Anna Barbara,
    130
  Anna Elisabetha,
    129
  Anna Margretha,
    129
  Anna Maria, 131
  Anna Maria
    Margretha, 129
  Barbara
    Elisabetha, 130
  Dietrich, 129,
    130
  Fred, 129
  Frederik, 129
  Friederich, 129
  Heinrich, 131,
    135
  Henrich, 130,
    131
  Johann Adam,
    129
  Johann
    Friederich,
    129
  Johann Peter,
    129
  Johannes, 129,
    130
  Marcus, 130,
    131, 134
  Margaretha
    Elisabetha, 130
  Marx, 135
  Niclaus, 130,
    134
  Nicolaus, 130,
    131, 134
  Peter, 129

  Philipp, 129
Belser,
  Joh. Caspar, 48
  Johann Henrich,
    48
Bender, 133
  Adam, 131
  Anna, 131
  Anna Christina,
    131
  Anna Maria,
    131(2), 132
  Engel, 132
  Engel Catharina,
    132
  Georg, 131(2),
    132
  George, 132
  Johann Philips,
    132
  Jörg, 131
  Jurch, 132
  Lips, 132
  Lorentz, 131
  Magdalena, 131
  Maria, 131
  Maria Dorothea,
    132
  Maria Elisabeth,
    8, 10
  Pastor, 95
  Philips, 131
  Velten, 131
  Velthen, 131
Benner,
  Lorentz, 131
Bercker,
  Christofel, 39
  Salome, 39
Berger,
  Anna Maria, 65
  Joh. Christian,
    142
  Johann
    Christian, 142
  Johann Henrich,
    142
  Maria
    Elisabetha,
    142(2)
  William, 65
Berlet,
  Bastian, 38
Bernges,
  Andrew, 24
  Peter, 24
Betz,
  Anna Maria, 80
  Conrad, 80
Beyer,

  Christoph, 36
  Margaret, 50
  Michael, 50
Biber,
  Jacob, 123
  Michael, 123
Bien,
  Gertraut, 98
  Johannis, 98
Blackburn,
  Robert, 124
Blattner,
  Michael, 152
Blecker,
  Barbara
    Christina, 14
  Henry, 14
Blos,
  Anna Elizabeth,
    5
  Anna Margaret, 5
  Catharina, 23
  Hans, 23
Blose,
  Conrad, 5
  Magdalena, 5
Bloss, 143
  Anna Catharina,
    50
  Anna Magdalena,
    5, 112
  Anna Margretha,
    5(2), 6
  Conrad, 5, 6,
    115
  George, 6
  Hans, 50
  Henrich, 5, 6
  Joh. Conrad, 112
  Johan Daniel, 5,
    6
  Johann Conrad,
    5, 6
  Johann Georg, 5
  Johann Henrich,
    6
  Johann Peter,
    5(2), 6(2), 24
  Johannes, 5, 6,
    24
  Magdalena, 115
  Maria Barbara,
    5(2), 6
  Maria Dorothea,
    6
  Maria Margretha,
    6
  Peter, 6
Blotz,
  Conrad, 6

Blum,
  Johann Conrad,
  45
  Peter, 45, 118,
  133
  Sabina, 118, 133
Bock,
  Anna, 106
  Matthes, 106
Böckel,
  Christina, 58,
  151
  Friderich, 85
  Tobias, 58, 151
Boeckel,
  Tobias, 58
Boehm,
  John Philip Jr.,
  62
  Philip, 151
Bohe,
  Paul, 121
Böhl,
  Anna Elisabetha,
  11
  Caspar, 11
Böhler,
  Peter, 96
Böhm,
  Johann Philipp,
  58
Bökel,
  Christina, 58
Bollman,
  Catharina, 46
Bombgardner,
  John, 70, 72, 75
Boone,
  George, 119
Boos,
  Rev., 105
Börstler,
  Catharina, 95,
  97
Bost,
  Catreena, 124
  John, 124
Boyer,
  Andrew, 45
Brandel,
  Eva Catharina,
  58
Brandmüller,
  Brother, 96
Braumüller,
  Anna Maria,
  7(2), 72
  Joh. Henrich,
  36, 66
  Johan Henrich,

72
Johan Nicklas,
  7, 72
Johann Henrich,
  7
Johannes, 7
Johannes
  Henrich, 72
Magdalena, 7,
  72(2)
Braun,
  Michael, 67
Bräuning,
  Casper, 41
  Maria Elisabeth,
  41
Braunmiller,
  Johannes, 7
  Luttwick, 7
Braunmüller,
  Anna Maria, 35,
  36
  Joh. Heinrich,
  35
  Joh. Henrich, 36
Brecht,
  Adam, 45
  Anna Elisabeth,
  102, 104
  Catharine, 45
  David, 45
  Elisabeth, 44
  Elizabeth, 44,
  45
  George, 45
  Magdalena, 45
  Margaret, 45
  Maria Magdalena,
  44
  Mary, 45
  Peter, 88
  Stephan, 44, 45,
  58, 102, 104
  Stephen, 45, 151
  Wendell, 45
Brendle,
  George, 59
Bright,
  David, 42
Briselie,
  Paul Daniel, 58
Britsch,
  Anna, 39
  Jacob, 39
Brobst,
  Michael, 116
Brosius,
  Abraham, 54
Brownmiller,
  Ludwig, 7

Luttwick, 7
  Nicholas, 7
Brucker,
  Johannes, 58
Brüning,
  Anna, 49, 130
  Anna Sabina, 117
  Elisabeth, 49(2)
  Elisabetha, 49,
  66
  Johanna Esther,
  117
  Jörg, 130
  Peter, 49(2),
  117
Brunner,
  Reinhart, 124
Buchhold,
  Pancrat., 99
Buchs,
  John, 53
Bulman,
  John, 42

  -C-

Cake,
  Jacob, 25
Calkgleaser,
  John Henry, 143
Cally,
  T., 117
Cammerhoff,
  Brother, 97
  Mrs., 97
Carpenter,
  Emanuel, 44
Caslar,
  Lewis, 9
Casler,
  Ludwig, 9
Casner,
  John, 82
Casseler,
  Henrich Wilhelm,
  8, 10
  Joh. Ludwig, 8
  Johann Ludwig,
  8, 10
  Johannes, 8, 10
  Maria Elisabeth,
  8, 10
  Philip Henrich,
  8, 10
  Wilhelm
  Christian, 8, 10

Cassler,
  Anna C., 9
  Anna Christina,

Cassler (continued)
    9
    Anna Elisabetha,
    9
    Anna Maria, 9
    Catharina, 8
    Christina, 9
    Elisabetha, 9
    Lewis, 9
    Louis, 9
    Ludiwig, 10
    Ludwick, 9
    Ludwig, 8, 9, 10
    Rosina, 9
    William, 9(2)
    William
        Christian, 10
Christ,
    Henry, 110
Cleim,
    John Michael, 62
Cleverin,
    Maria Elizabeth,
    61
Cloam,
    Maria, 44
Cloninger,
    Valentine, 141
Conrad,
    Catrout, 124
    Henry W., 78
    Jacob, 58
    Maria Catharina,
    151
Conrath,
    Joh., 125
Copeheaver,
    Catharine, 19
    Thomas, 19
Copenhaven,
    Catharine, 23
    Henry, 23
Counts,
    Elizabeth, 69
    John, 69
Coutts,
    Elisabeth, 69
Cowell,
    Savena, 118
Coxley,
    Anna, 82
Creter,
    Barbara, 58
    Jacob, 58
Crowl,
    Michael, 63
    Sabina, 118

        -D-

Daenig,
    Anna Margaret,
    12(2)
    Anna Maria, 12
    Jacob, 12
Dänig,
    Anna Barbara, 11
    Anna Margaret,
    11
    Anna Margret, 11
    Henry, 11
    Johan Henrich,
    11
    Michael, 11
Daubenspeck,
    Jacob, 6
    Juliana, 6
Dauber,
    Johan Paul, 111
    Johannes, 63
Daubert,
    Anna Mary, 14
    Catharine, 14
    John, 14
    Maria Magdalena,
    14
    Peter, 14
Dautrich,
    John, 18
Decker, 19
    Henrich, 20
    John Henry, 18
    Magdalena
        Elisabeth, 18
Deckert,
    Elizabeth, 19
    Henrich, 22
    Henry, 19
Deichert,
    Anna Catharina,
    132
    Anna Magdalena,
    132
    Anna Margaretha,
    133
    Elisabetha, 132
    Engel, 135
    Gerdraut, 132
    Hans, 132, 135
    Johann Conrad,
    133
    Johann Peter,
    133
    Ottilia, 133
    Sabina, 133
    Severinus, 133
    Werner, 132, 135
    Wörner, 132, 133
Deickert,
    Anna Catharina,

    133
    Warner, 133
Dein,
    Anna Margretha,
    2
    Johannes, 2, 34
Denich,
    Johannes, 11
Denig,
    Anna Elisabetha,
    11
    Balthasar, 11
    Henry, 12
    Jacob, 11
    Johan Henrich,
    11
Deuchert,
    Werner, 133, 136
Devgert,
    Sefreen, 133
Deygert,
    Warnaer, 133
Diegert,
    Johan Pieter,
    133
Diehl,
    Anna Barbara,
    139
    Antoni, 139
    Catharina, 139
    Daniel, 19
    Johann Gasper,
    54
    Johann Henrich,
    139
    Johann Wilhelm,
    139
    Johanna
        Magdalena, 139
    Johannes, 139
    Peter, 139
Diel,
    Anna Barbara,
    139
    Johann, 139
    Wilhelm, 139
Dieterich, 85
    Anna Catharina,
    83
    Anna Rosina, 32,
    38
    Caspar, 32
    Cathar., 32
    Gertraud, 32,
    84, 87
    Helena, 32, 62
    Henrich, 32, 62
    Johann, 32, 84
    Stoffel, 32
Dingee,

Captain, 10
Dippel, 145
  Anna Elisabetha,
    13
  Anna Maria, 13
  Anna Mary, 14
  Anna Philippina,
    12, 13
  Catharina, 12,
    13, 14
  Christina
    Philippina, 12,
    13
  Elisabetha
    Cathar. Judith,
    16
  Henry, 13
  Herman, 12, 13
  Joh. Henrich,
    11, 12, 13, 14
  Joh. Herman, 13,
    16
  Joh. Matthias,
    12, 14
  Johan Herman, 14
  Johann Henrich,
    12, 14, 16
  Johann Hermann,
    12(2), 14
  Johann Peter,
    12, 13(2)
  Johann Philips,
    12, 13
  John Herman, 13,
    14
  John Peter, 13,
    14
  Magdalena, 13,
    14(2)
  Margaret, 13
  Maria Loysa, 12,
    13
  Maria Magdalena,
    14
  Martin, 12, 13
  Mary Magdalena,
    14
  Peter, 14(2)
  Philippina, 12,
    14, 16
Dock,
  Anna Maria, 152
  Heinrich, 151
  Henry, 152
  Jacob Heinrich,
    151
Doenig,
  Jacob, 12
Döll,
  Anna, 43, 48

Anna Catharina,
  78
Catharina, 79
Johan Conrad, 83
Johann Philips,
  52, 53
Johannes, 83(2),
  102, 104
Johannis, 43, 48
Nickel, 78, 79
Peter, 57
Domig,
  Henry, 11
Dönig,
  Anna Elisabetha,
    11
  Anna Margaretha,
    11
  Anna Margretha,
    11
  Anna Philippina,
    11
  Balthasar, 11
  Johann Heinrich,
    11
  Johann Jörg, 11
  Maria Barbara,
    11
  Michael, 11
Drechsler,
  Melchior, 2
Drechssler,
  Anna Elisabetha,
    57
  Melchior, 15,
    16, 57
  Susanna, 15, 16
Dresler,
  a daughter, 17
  Elisabet
    Gertrut, 17
  Elisabeth, 17
  Johan Peter, 122
  John Peter, 17
Dressler,
  Anna Elisabeth,
    15
  Charlotta
    Eleonora, 15,
    16, 17
  Joh. Henrich,
    12, 13, 15, 17
  Johan Henrich,
    15
  Johann Henrich,
    16
  Johann Peter,
    15, 17
  Johannes, 15(2),
    16(2), 17

Melchior, 15,
  16, 17
Peter, 16, 17,
  25, 70, 72, 75,
  115
Dreut,
  Elisabeth
    Catharina, 2
  Joh. Peter, 2
Droit,
  Anna Elisabeth,
    79
  Tönges, 79
Duckert,
  John, 112
Dueppel,
  Catharine, 13
Dunkel,
  Elisabeth, 4
  Michael, 4
Düppell,
  Catharina, 13
  Herman, 13
  Susan Louisa, 13
Durst,
  Casper, 46
  Christina, 46
Dyker,
  Warner, 133

              -E-

Ebernaw,
  Hans, 111
  Hans Bernhard,
    111
Ebler,
  Peter, 114
Echard,
  Captain, 23
Eckert,
  a daughter, 18
  a son, 18
  Abraham, 19
  Angel, 19
  Angelica, 18(2),
    19
  Anna Maria, 18,
    19
  Barbara, 19, 23
  Catharina, 19
  Catharine, 19,
    23
  Christina, 19
  Conrad, 18,
    19(2), 23(2)
  Daniel, 19, 23
  David, 19, 23
  Elisabeth, 18,
    19

Eckert (continued)
  Elizabeth,
    19(2), 23
  Engel, 18
  George, 19, 23
  Johann, 20
  Johann Conrad,
    18, 19
  Johann Henrich,
    60, 71
  Johann Valentin,
    18
  Johannes, 17,
    18(2), 19(2), 20

  John, 18, 19(3),
    23(2), 63, 152
  John Nicholas,
    19
  Jonas, 18,
    19(2), 20, 21,
    22, 152
  Magdalena
    Elisabeth, 18

  Margaret, 19
  Nicholas, 19(2),
    152
  Nicolas, 19, 20
  Peter, 18, 19,
    23
  Sarah, 19
  Solomon, 19, 23
  Valentin, 19
  Valentine, 19,
    22, 23
Ehl,
  Anna Maria, 109
  David, 108, 109
  Eleonora Amalia,
    112
  Johann Henrich,
    108
  Johannes, 112
Ehrlich,
  Johann, 117
  Johann Caspar,
    117
Eichelberger,
  Elisabetha, 31
  Gottfried, 31
  Juliana, 31
Eichelberner,
  Catharina,
    30(2), 31
  Elisabetha, 30
  Godfried, 30
  Jacob, 30(2), 31
  Joh. Jacob, 31
  Juliana, 30

  Margaretha, 31
  Peter, 31
Eichelbörner,
  Anna, 137
  Clos, 137
  Margaretha, 137
Eichelbrenner,
  Daniel, 30
  Gottfried, 30
  Juliana, 30
Eichelbronner,
  Jacob, 30
  Maria, 30
Eichelburner,
  Clos, 30
  Johann Caspar,
    30
  Magdalena, 30
Eigereicher,
  Conrad, 28
Eirich,
  Catharine, 29
  Daniel, 29
  Elizabeth, 29
  Georg, 25
  George, 29(2)
  John, 29
  Magdalena, 29
  Margaret, 29
  Margareth, 25
  Mary, 29
  Rebecca, 29
Eisenach,
  Balthasar, 137
Emrich,
  Geo., 101
  Margaret, 101
Enders,
  Philip, 9
Enders Sr.,
  Philip, 9
Engel,
  Andreas, 14
Ermantraud,
  Catharina, 140
  Johann Henrich,
    140
  Johannes, 140
Ermantraut,
  Anna
    Eliesabetha, 103

Ermantroudt,
  Johan Fredrick,
    140
  Johannes, 140
  Philipus, 140
Ermantrout, 143
Ermel,
  Daniel, 27

  Elizabeth, 26
  Isaac, 26, 27
  Jacob, 27
  Margaret, 27
  Sarah, 27
  Susann, 27
  William, 26, 27
Ermendraut,
  Friederich, 140
Ermentraut,
  Anna
    Eliesabetha, 140

  Anna Maria, 140
  Fritrich, 92
  Joh. Georg, 119
  Johannes, 140
Ermentrout,
  Anna Elizabetha,
    68
  Anna Magdalena,
    140
  Elizabeth, 69
  Frederich, 74
  Frederick, 140
  John, 68, 69,
    140
  John Henry, 140
Ermold, 143
  Anna Catharina,
    25, 68
  Anna Elisabeth,
    24, 25
  Anna Elisabetha,
    24
  Anna Margareth,
    25(2)
  Anna Maria, 25,
    27, 29, 117
  Anton, 25
  Antonius, 25
  Carl, 51
  Carl Johan
    Heinrich, 24
  Carl Johann
    Heinrich, 26
  Carl Johann
    Henrich, 24
  Catharina, 24
  Catharine, 23,
    24, 25, 26, 27
  Daniel, 25, 28
  daughter, 73
  Elisabetha, 25,
    72
  Ernst, 23, 26,
    68, 73
  Georg, 27, 29
  George, 24, 25,
    27

Gertrud, 24
Hans, 25(2)
Joh. Georg, 27
Joh. Görg, 147
Joh. Henrich,
   141
Joh. Peter, 23
Johan Jörg, 117
Johan Wilhelm,
   26
Johann, 27
Johann Adam,
   24(2)
Johann Ludwig,
   109
Johann Martin,
   25, 26
Johann Peter, 24
Johanna Maria,
   24
Johannes, 25
John, 25
John George, 24
John Peter, 24
Judith, 28
Magdalena, 29
Magdalena
   Elisabeth, 24
Margareth, 25
Margretha, 26,
   27
Maria, 27
Maria Elisabeth,
   24
Maria Judith,
   24(2), 29
Martin, 25(3),
   26, 29
Mary, 25
Mrs., 73
Niclaus, 24
Peter, 24, 25,
   27
Rosina, 24
Susanna, 27
Wilhelm, 23, 24,
   26, 73
Ermoldt,
   An Els (Anna
      Elisabeth), 81,
      84, 87
   Catharine, 24
   Ernst, 50
   Hans, 81, 84, 87
   Maria, 24
   Wörner, 50
Ermolt,
   Cahtarine, 24
   Daniel, 24
   Peter, 24

Ermontrout,
   George, 69
   Henry, 69
   John, 69
Ermuth,
   Johann, 34
   John, 147
Eschenbach, 96
Euler,
   Adam, 54
   Joh. Wilhelm,
      117
   Johann Henrich,
      136
   Johann Michael,
      54
   Sybilla, 54
   Thomas, 117
Eürich,
   Anna Clara
      Elisabetha, 28
   Anna Maria, 28,
      29, 140
   Anna Sabina, 27
   Bastian, 28
   Conrad, 27,
      28(2)
   Elisabetha, 27
   Georg, 29
   Hans Georg, 27
   Henrich, 27
   Joh. Conrad, 28
   Joh. Georg, 27
   Johan Georg,
      28(2)
   Johan Jörg, 27
   Johann Georg,
      27, 28
   Johannes, 28,
      29, 140
   Magdalena, 29
   Margaretha, 29
   Maria Catharina,
      28(2)
   Maria Gerdraut,
      27
   Maria Gertraud,
      28
   Maria Judith, 28
   Michael, 28
   Sebastian, 28
   Susanna, 29
   Susanna
      Elisabetha, 28
Eürig,
   Conrad, 29
   Juliana, 29
Eÿchelbörner,
   Clos, 67
   Johann Caspar,

   30
   Magdalena, 30
   Margretha, 67
Eyerich,
   Conrad, 28
   Judith, 28
   Juliana, 28
Eÿgelbörner,
   Anna Catharina,
      30
   Caspar, 5, 6
   Hans Caspar, 30
   Joh. Daniel, 29
   Johann Conrad,
      30
   Johann Daniel,
      30
   Johann
      Gottfried, 30
   Johann Henrich,
      30
   Johann Jacob, 30
   Maria Barbara,
      5, 6
   Maria Margretha,
      30
Eyrich,
   Conrad, 27
   John Jörg, 27
Eÿring,
   Gertrudis, 142
   Peter, 122, 142
Eyrricker,
   Judith, 28

          -F-

Faaser,
   Eva, 100
   Johannes, 100
Faust,
   (Jo)Hannes, 37
   Adam, 148
   Anna, 147
   Anna Barbara,
      35, 38, 60, 71
   Anna Catharina,
      76, 148(2)
   Anna Catrina,
      147
   Anna Elisabeth,
      35, 38, 57, 62
   Anna Elisabetha,
      36, 38, 148
   Anna Gertraud,
      32, 38
   Anna Maria, 7,
      33, 35, 36,
      38(2), 72, 126
   Anna Rosina, 32,

Faust (continued)
    38
  Anthon, 33, 126
  Anthony, 33(2),
    38
  Anton, 32, 38,
    62, 85
  Antoni, 33, 126,
    139
  Antonius, 32(2),
    38, 63
  Antony, 32
  Barbara, 37
  Caspar, 35, 76
  Catharina, 38
  Catharine
    Elisabeth, 36
  Christina, 38
  Elisab. Cathar.,
    34
  Elisabeth, 32,
    33(2), 34, 38,
    98, 126
  Elisabetha, 32,
    35, 38, 126,
    147(2)
  Elisabetha
    Catharina, 33,
    34
  Elizabeth, 33
  Endres, 147
  Engel, 107, 147
  Georg, 34
  George, 34
  Gertraut, 126
  Gertrude, 46, 87
  Giel (Julianna),
    147
  Hans, 1, 32, 34,
    35, 37, 38, 40,
    71, 85, 107, 147

  Heinrich, 38,
    148
  Helena, 32(2),
    35, 38, 62
  Henry, 38
  Jacob, 148
  Joh., 36, 43, 48
  Joh. Georg, 33
  Joh. Henrich,
    32, 36, 38
  Joh. Jörg, 33
  Joh. Michael, 33
  Joh. Peter, 1,
    32, 33, 34, 35,
    38, 62(2), 85,
    98
  Joh. Philip, 34,
    98

Johan, 60, 62,
    71, 72, 98
  Johan Peter, 38
  Johann, 1, 7,
    32, 33, 34, 35,
    37, 57, 62, 147,
    148
  Johann Caspar,
    147
  Johann Georg,
    33, 34, 148
  Johann Görg, 147
  Johann Henrich,
    35
  Johann Martin,
    25
  Johann Peter,
    33, 35, 36
  Johann Philipp,
    148
  Johannes, 1,
    33(2), 34,
    35(3), 36, 98,
    107, 147(2)
  John, 36, 37(2),
    38, 55
  John Adam, 147
  John Christian,
    36
  John George, 2,
    34
  John Hendrick,
    147
  John Jacob, 147
  John Philip, 34
  Kunigunda, 7,
    33, 35, 36, 98,
    147
  Lips, 33, 36
  Ludwig, 25
  Magdalen
    Elisabeth, 33
  Magdalena,
    35(2), 37, 38(3)

  Magdalena
    Elisab., 16
  Magdalena
    Elisabeth, 34,
    36
  Magdalena
    Elisabetha, 36
  Maria, 38
  Maria Elisabeth,
    33
  Maria
    Elisabetha, 147
  Maria Kunigunda,
    33
  Maria Margretha,

    33
  Michael, 35(2),
    36, 37, 62, 67
  Peter, 37, 38
  Philip, 34, 36,
    37, 38, 147
  Philipp, 33, 35
  Philippus, 40
  Philips, 16, 33,
    35
  Weigel, 35
  Wörner, 35, 147
Feather,
  Jacob, 9
Feb,
  Caterina, 103
Feg,
  Anna Catharina,
    138
  Johann, 138
  Leonhard, 138
Fegely,
  George, 4
Fellendser,
  Juliana Maria,
    146
Fellsmeyer,
  Catharina, 41,
    73
Felsmaÿer,
  Anna Rosina, 40
  Dieterich, 40
  Hieronymus, 40
  Joh. Caspar, 40
  Joh. Michael, 40
  Johanna Maria,
    40
  Margretha, 40
  Philippus, 40
  Rachel, 40
Fetter,
  Barbara, 9
  Jacob, 9
Feuerstein, 145
  Anna, 39(2)
  Augusta Maria,
    39
  Daniel, 39
  Görg, 39
  Henrich
    Philipps, 130
  Johan Jacob, 39
  Johannes, 39(2)
  Justina Maria,
    39
  Magdalena, 39
  Maria Catharina,
    39
  Salome, 39
Fewerstein,

Anna, 39
Conrad, 39
Philipps
Henrich, 39
Ffaust,
Johannes, 36
Michel, 36
Peter, 36
Filbert,
Philip, 88
Filchmir,
Philip, 42
Filsmayer,
Anna Maria, 41
Filsmeyer,
Jost, 41(2)
Philip, 41
Filtsmeyer,
Johann Jost, 41
Filtzmeier, 78
Filtzmeior,
Johan Adam, 78
Filtzmeyer,
Anna Catharina,
40
Anna Margretha,
40(2), 124
Anna Margrethaa,
40
Anna Maria, 40,
41, 42
Anna Rosina, 141
Catharina, 40
Catharine, 42(2)
Dieterich, 40,
125, 141
Elizabeth, 42
Johanna Maria,
40
John Jost, 41
Jost, 41, 42
Margaret, 42
Margaretha, 40
Maria Elisabeth,
41
Philip, 40, 41,
124
Philips, 40
Rachel, 124, 125
Yost, 42
Filzmeyer,
Catharine, 42
Elisabeth, 42
Magaret, 42
Mary, 42
Yost, 42
Fink,
Conrad, 115
Firestone,
see Feuerstein,

40
Fischer,
Anna, 43, 45,
47, 48, 81
Anna Barbara,
43, 47, 81
Anna Catharina,
43, 46, 47
Anna Catharina
Elisabetha, 83
Anna Elisabeth,
57, 81, 102, 104
Anna Elisabetha,
15, 43(2), 48,
57
Anna Lydia, 42
Anna Maria, 42,
43(2), 44(2),
46, 47(2),
48(2), 90, 149,
150
Anna Regina, 79
Anna Sibylla,
150
Anna Sybilla,
149
Anna Sybillen,
149
Anna Veronica,
43, 47, 48, 81,
89
Antonius, 147
Apollonia, 92
Appollonia, 46
Barbara, 57, 150
Barbara
Elisabeth, 149
Barbara
Elisabetha, 149
Catharina, 46,
49, 148, 149,
150
Catharine, 46
Charles, 150
Christina, 46,
106
Conrad, 15, 16,
43, 47, 48, 57,
81, 83, 89, 90
Elisabeth, 15,
16, 32, 44, 45,
57, 116
Elisabeth
Gertrude, 46
Elisabetha, 15,
16, 43, 48, 78,
147
Elisabetha
Gertrude, 46

Elizabeth, 46
Eva, 149
Eva Maria, 148
Fleny, 47
Frantz, 46(2)
Frederick, 46(2)
Friederich, 81
Friedrich, 47
George, 46
Gertrude, 46
Hans Jacob, 42
Heinrich, 44,
48, 106
Henrich, 15, 43,
47, 48
Henry, 46(2), 49
Joh. Conrad, 15
Joh. Georg, 46
Joh. Görg, 47
Joh. Heinrich,
1, 48
Joh. Henrich,
42, 43, 44, 47,
116
Joh. Jacob, 43
Joh. Melchior,
43(2), 47
Joh. Wilhelm, 45
Johan Caspar, 45
Johan Conrad, 1,
43, 45, 47
Johan Henrich,
45(2)
Johann Henrich,
43, 48, 102, 104

Johann Wilhelm,
45, 102
Johanna Maria,
48
Johannes, 1,
43(3), 44, 45,
47(2), 48, 79,
81, 89, 148,
149, 150
Johannes Jr., 48
Johannes Sr., 48
Johannes, Sr.,
149
John, 46(2), 49,
150
Jörg, 45(2)
Jost, 15, 90
Jost Heinrich,
57
Jost Henrich,
15, 16, 57
Kenneth L., 47
Künigunda, 45
Ludwig, 78

Fischer (continued)
  Magdalena, 43,
    48
  Michael, 46(2)
  Peter, 46(2),
    92(2)
  Philip, 7, 46(2)
  Philipps, 45
  Rosina, 46(2),
    63
  Susanah, 42
  Susanna, 46(2),
    150
  Susanna
    Elisabetha, 43
  Susanna Maria,
    148
  Sybilla, 48, 58,
    150
  Weigel, 45, 47
  Werner, 148
  Weychel, 102
  Weygel, 45
  Wilhelm, 46, 47,
    63
  William, 17, 46
Fishbach,
  Jost, 19
Fisher,
  Anna Mary, 44
  Christian, 44,
    45
  Elizabeth, 44
  Henry, 44, 45
  Jacob, 44, 45
  John, 44, 45
  John Christian,
    44
  Ludwig, 19
  Peter, 42
  Susanna, 44
Fister,
  Jacob, 146
Fitsmeyer,
  John Jost, 41
Fitzmeyer,
  Anna Maria, 41
Fitzmier,
  Philip, 41
Fleischner,
  Catharine, 114
Foust,
  Ann Eliz., 34
  Anna Eliza, 34
  Antony, 32
  Barbara, 37
  George, 34
  Johan Hendrick,
    34
  Johannes, 34

  John, 37
  John Peter, 34
  Matelina, 34
  Micol, 34
  Peter, 38
  Philip, 36
Fox,
  Adam, 54
  Anna Elisabetha,
    54
  Anna Maria, 54
  Elizabeth, 103
  Yost, 54
Franck,
  Anna Elisabeth,
    13
  Jacob, 10
Francke,
  Christoph, 96
Frantz,
  Johann Peter,
    129
Frazer,
  William, 70, 72,
    75
Freiman,
  Georg, 50
  Sawina, 50
Fress,
  Niclaus, 123
Frey,
  Elisabeth, 95
  Henrich, 95
  Maria Catharina,
    95
  Peter, 58
Freÿman,
  Adam, 49
  Ann Sabina, 50
  Anna Catharina,
    50, 141(2)
  Anna Christina,
    49
  Anna Maria,
    49(2)
  Anna Sabina, 49,
    50, 98, 99
  Casper, 142
  Catharine, 23,
    26, 50
  Christina, 50
  Elisabeth, 49,
    100
  Elizabeth, 50
  Ernst, 23, 26,
    49, 50, 51
  Georg, 49, 98,
    99, 101, 141
  George, 50(2)
  Hans, 49

  Heinrich, 142
  Henrich, 141
  Jacob, 24,
    51(2), 116, 141
  Jacob Baltzar,
    49
  Joh. Georg, 98
  Joh. Jacob,
    51(2)
  Johan Ernst, 24,
    50
  Johan Henrich,
    141
  Johan Jacob, 49
  Johann Georg,
    49(2)
  Johann Jörg, 49
  Johann Peter,
    141
  Johannes, 49
  Kunigunda, 51,
    116
  Lenhard, 49, 50,
    67, 141
  Leonhard, 49
  Magdalena
    Elisabetha, 51
  Margaret, 50
  Maria
    Elisabetha, 51,
    141
  Maria Sophia, 51
  Peter, 49, 141
  Sabina, 50
Freÿmann,
  Anna Magdalena
    Elisabetha, 51
  Anna Maria
    Elisabetha, 66
  Anna Rosina, 141
  Anna Sabina, 50
  Anna Sophia
    (Sabina), 101
  Catharina, 99,
    142
  Elisabeth, 50,
    51
  Elisabetha, 66
  Hans, 66, 117
  Henrich, 142
  Jacob, 50
  Joh. Henrich,
    141
  Johann Georg,
    50, 101
  Johann Henrich
    Carl, 51
  Johann Jacob, 51
  Johann Philipps,
    51

Maria Barbara,
141
Maria Magdalena,
141
Freymeurer,
Wilhelm, 139
Frieman,
Henry, 142
Fritz,
Balzer, 110
Frutschy,
Frederich, 99
Frederick, 100
Mrs. Frederick,
99
Fryman,
Georg, 50
Frymeyer,
Jacob, 73
Fuch,
Hans, 30
Magdalena, 30
Fuchs,
Adam, 54, 55
Anna Catharina,
3
Anna Christina,
102
Anna Elisabetha,
52, 53
Anna Margaret,
53
Anna Margretha,
102
Anna Maria, 52,
53, 54, 55, 108
Anna Rosina, 108
Anthon, 51
Anthony, 52, 65
Anton, 52, 77
Antonius, 51,
52, 53
Catharina, 102,
104
Catharine, 53
Christian, 102,
104, 124, 125
Elisabeth, 54,
124, 125
Elisabetha, 52,
53, 54
Elizabeth, 77
Georg, 25, 54,
102
Hans, 93
Joh. Adam, 54,
146
Joh. Conrad, 108
Joh. Michael, 52
Joh. Peter, 52,

53
Johan Conrad,
108
Johan Michael,
53
Johann Adam, 54
Johann Henrich,
76
Johann Michael,
52, 53
Johann Peter,
52(2), 53(3)
Johann Philips,
52, 53
Johannes, 3, 54
John, 53, 55
John Adam, 55
Jörg, 45, 52(2),
54
Jost, 54
Jost Henrich, 54
Juliana, 52, 53
Magdalena, 54
Margaret, 53
Margretha, 93
Michael, 53
Niclas, 54
Niclaus, 102
Peter, 49, 53,
55, 108
Phillipina, 54
Stoffel, 120
Sybilla, 54
Tönges, 25, 52,
53, 99
Wörner, 52, 53

-G-

Gackenbach,
John, 116
Gage,
Christina
Philippina, 12,
13
Johan Philipps,
12, 13
Gans,
John, 152
Gantz,
Gurtrad, 152
John, 152
Gasche,
Anna Catharina,
11
Johan Philipps,
12, 13
Philips, 11
Gaul,
Christian, 27

Hans, 147
Kunigunda, 147
Geerdt,
Wilhelm, 57
Geibel,
Conrad, 116, 118
Joh. Philipps,
116
Philips, 132
Geiger,
Paul, 32
Geisler,
Geo., 110
Gerard,
Hans, 147
Geret,
Wilhelm, 57
Gereth,
Anna Margretha,
55
daughter, 66
Johann Georg, 55
Michael, 66
Gereth?,
Magdalena, 134
Gerets,
Anna Elisabetha,
57
Wilhelm, 57
Gerhard, 78
Anna, 56
Anna Elisabeth,
57(2), 79
Anna Maria, 58
Anna Rosina, 58
Anton, 58
Barbara, 58, 59
Catharina, 56,
58, 123
Conrad, 55, 58,
59
Elisabeth, 58
Elisabetha, 15,
16
Frederick, 59,
150
Friederich, 15,
16, 57
Friedrich, 56,
57, 58(2), 59,
79
Georg, 56
Hans Jörg, 56
Henrich, 56
Jacob, 58
Joh. Henrich, 57
Johann Peter, 57
Johannes, 58
Jörg, 57
Juliana, 79

Gerhard (continued)
Paul, 79, 123
Peter, 57, 58
Wilhelm, 56, 57,
    79
Gerhardt,
Anna, 56
Catharina, 56
Conrad, 111
Friedrich, 151
Georg, 56
Joh. Henrich, 56
Johannes, 56
Johannes Georg,
    56
Paul, 59
Gerhart,
Anna, 56
Anna Elisabeth,
    57
Anna Elisabetha,
    148
Anna Margretha,
    55
Anna Maria, 57
Barbara, 44, 59
Catharina, 56
Catharine, 59
Conrad, 55, 59
Elisabeth, 57,
    59
Frederick,
    59(2), 93
Fredrich, 148
Friderich, 57
Friedrich, 44,
    92
Georg, 56
Jacob, 59(2), 92
Joh. Henrich, 56
Johann Conrad,
    55
Johann Conradt,
    55, 56
Johann Georg, 55
Johann Henrich,
    57
John, 59
Martin, 25
Mary, 59
Michael, 55
Peter, 25, 56,
    59
Rosina, 59
Susanna
    Catharina, 55
Wilhelm, 56,
    57(2), 148
Gerhart?,
Magdalena, 134

Gerigh,
Hans Martin, 36
Gerlach,
Joh. Adam, 2
Gerlitz,
Henrich, 92
German,
Georg, 100
Gerth,
Conrad, 134(2)
Elisabeth, 134
Hans, 111
Johann Conrad,
    134
Magdalena, 134
Giesseman,
Mrs. William, 67
William, 67
Gilbert,
Felix, 69
Glad,
Anna Maria, 44
Elisabeth, 44
Maria, 44
Nicholas, 44,
    150
Nicolaus, 44
Glat,
Anna Maria,
    44(2), 47, 48
Barbara, 44
Elisabeth, 44
Georg, 44
Johann, 44
Nicholas, 47
Niclaus, 58
Nicol, 151
Nicolaus, 44,
    48, 58
Glaude,
Nicholas, 150
Gleber, 89
Anna Elisabetha,
    60
Anna Magdalena,
    60
Anna Rosina, 60
Joh. Henrich, 60
Joh. Michael, 71
Johann Henrich,
    60
Johann Melchior,
    60
Johann Michael,
    60
Johannes, 60
Magdalena, 60
Maria
    Elisabetha, 60
Michael, 60(2)

Michel, 110
Gleim,
Elisabeth, 61
Joh. Michael, 61
John Michael, 62
Susan, 61
Gliem,
Anna Margretha,
    61
Anna Susanna
    Elisabetha, 61
Joh. Michael, 61
Magdalena
    Elisabetha, 61
Michael, 43
Philip, 61
Philips, 61
Goetschy,
Pastor, 95
Goettel,
Anna Christina,
    9
Goettling,
Anna C., 9
Good,
Peter, 121
Gorman,
Georg, 100
Gosche,
Anna Margaretha,
    11
Johan Philipps,
    12, 13
Philip, 11
Goshe,
Johan Philipps,
    12, 13
Gottschalk,
Joh. Nicolaus, 4
Gotz,
Thomas, 64
Grauel,
Ann Eliza, 62
Anna Catharina,
    62, 63
Anna Elisabeth,
    35, 62
Anna Elisabetha,
    62, 118
Conrad, 32, 35,
    62, 102, 104
Elisabeth, 62,
    63
Elisabetha, 118
Helena, 32, 35,
    62, 102, 104
Joh. Conrad, 35
Joh. Michael,
    62, 119
Johan Heinrich,

62
Johan Michael,
62
Johan Peter, 62
Johann Conrad,
63
Maria Elisabeth,
32, 63
Maria Sara, 63
Michael, 33, 35,
46, 62, 63,
118(2)
Peter, 46, 63
Rosina, 46, 63
Sabina, 118
Greber,
Heinrich, 74
Mrs. Heinrich,
74
Green,
David, 50
Grim,
Friedrich, 149
Grimm,
Friedrich, 151
Inspector, 149
Growl,
Michael, 63
Gruber,
John Adam, 61
Grupensch,
Georg, 30
Gutmann,
Catharina, 67

-H-

Haag,
Anna Sybilla,
149
John George, 34
Haak,
Jacob, 42
Haan,
Joh. Thomas, 64
Johannes, 64
Haas,
Abraham, 114
Johannes, 139
John Nicholas,
114
Haas?,
Philip, 115
Haass,
Hans Peter, 74
Hack,
Margretha, 109
Melchior, 109
Hadderich,
Anna Elisabetha,

70
Carl Johan
Henrich, 70
Christian
Ludwig, 70
Conrad, 70
Elisabeth, 70
Joh. Adam, 70
Joh. Caspar, 70
Joh. Jörg, 70
Johan Jörg, 70
Johannes, 70
Maria Catharina,
70
Michael, 70
Haderich,
Anna Maria, 68
Georg Henrich,
74
Johan Adam, 68
Michael, 68
Hadrick,
Adam, 69
Haeffner,
Anton, 1
Catharina, 1
Haffener,
Rosina, 83
Tönges, 83
Haffner,
Maria, 83
Tönges, 83
Hag,
Anna Sibilla,
149
Hager,
Elisabeth, 82
Jonathan, 82
Hahn,
Angelica, 64
Anna Catharina,
64, 66
Anna Maria, 65
Anna Mary, 65
Anna Philippina,
66
Anthony, 52, 65
Augusta Maria,
64
Catharina, 64,
65
Catharine, 65
Conrad, 64, 113
Daniel, 64
Joh. Thomas, 64,
66, 113
Johan Thomas, 64
Johann Adam, 66
Johann Henrich,
64

Johanna
Magdalena, 113
Johannes, 64(2),
65, 66(2), 113
John, 52, 65(2),
152
John Jacob, 65
Justina, 65
Justina Maria,
65
Maria Catharina,
65
Maria Christina,
65, 152
Mary Christina,
65
Michael, 65
Thomas, 64, 65
Hain, 23
A. Maria, 66
Adam, 38
Anna Maria, 54
Benjamin, 29
Elisabeth, 18
Elisabeth
Gertrude, 46
Elizabeth, 23
Georg, 46
Görg, 54
Johann, 66
Johannes, 66
John, 14
Joseph, 29
Magdalena, 14
Maria, 66
Veronica, 46
Hall,
James, 150
Haller,
Henry, 23
Halzen,
George, 19
Hambarger,
Catharina, 67
Michael, 67
Hamberger,
Michael, 67
Hambergher,
Michael, 68
Hamborger,
Johannes, 67
Hamburger, 145
Anna Catharina,
67(2)
Anna Elisabeth,
66, 67
Anna Elisabetha,
52, 53
Anton, 67
Catharina

Hamburger
(continued)
Conrad, 67
Elisabetha, 52,
53, 67
Herman, 66
Joh. Peter, 67
Johan Michael,
67
Johann, 67
Johann Peter,
52, 53, 67
Johannes, 66, 67
Justina Maria,
67
Margretha, 67
Maria, 66
Michael, 66, 68
Michel, 67
Michell, 67
Wörner, 52, 53,
66, 67, 83
Han,
Anna Catharina,
66
Anna Margretha,
64
Anna Philippina,
66
Conrad, 64, 65
Johan Thomas, 64
Johann Adam, 66
Johann Henrich,
64
Johanna
Magdalena, 64
Johannes, 64, 66
Margaretha, 64
Margretha, 65
Harmantrout,
Elizabeth, 69
John, 69
Harmentrout,
Frederick, 70,
72, 75
Harris,
Frederick, 141
Hart,
Conrad, 63
Hartman,
Chas., 101
Endres, 147
J. Crawford, 41
Hartmann,
Johann Philipps,
51
Hatrick,
William, 73
Hause,

Philip, 115
Headrick,
William, 75
Yost, 75
Hean,
George, 110
Magdalena, 110
Hebener,
Johannes, 60
Heck,
Anna Eva, 146
Anna Margretha,
146
Catharina, 86
Johann Jost, 146
John, 88
Jost, 146
Hecker,
Rev. John
Egidius, 99
Heckert,
Anna Maria, 92
Appollonia, 46,
92
Elisabeth
Barbara, 92
Elisabetha
Gertrude, 46
Johannes, 92
John, 42, 46
Michael, 46
Philip, 92
Heckerth,
Johannes, 94
Hedderich,
Adam, 54
Anna Catharina,
68
Anna
Eliesabetha, 140

Anna Elisabetha,
74
Anna Elizabetha,
68
Anna Margreth,
93
Anna Margretha,
68, 73
Anna Maria, 69
Carl, 41, 69,
70, 72(2), 73,
75, 106
Carl Johann
Heinrich, 24
Carl Johann
Henrich, 72, 73
Caspar, 24, 69,
71
Elisabetha, 106

Georg, 69, 71
Joh. Adam, 68,
93, 140
Joh. Caspar, 72
Johannes, 75
Johannes Wirner,
75
Magdalena, 72
Michael, 68, 69,
73
Wilhelm, 74
Hedderig,
Carl, 106
Caspar, 71
Mrs., 71
Heddrich,
Anna Margaretha,
74
Jost, 74
Hederich,
Anna Catharina,
68, 73
Anna Elisabetha,
71
Anna Rosina, 71
Anna Sabina, 71
Carl, 71, 72, 75
Carl Johann
Henrich, 71
Caroll, 74
Catharina
Elisabetha, 73
Charles, 73
Elisabeth, 73,
75
Elisabetha, 68,
72
Georg Henrich,
73
Henrich, 74
Joh. Adam, 68(2)
Joh. George, 71
Johann Adam, 68
Johann Henrich,
71
Johann Wilhelm,
73
Johannes, 75
Johannes Justus,
73
Maria Magdalina,
71
Hederick,
Charles, 73
Elizabeth, 73
Yost, 73
Hedrick,
Casper, 70, 71
Charles, 70, 71
George, 25, 70,

71
Joseph, 25
Jost, 25
Hehn,
Adam, 42
Anna Maria, 19
Fred, 19
George, 144
John, 42
Heibert,
Hanna, 58
Heisser,
G., 58
Heller,
Andreas, 101
Helmud,
Peter, 56
Hempel,
Anna Catharina,
108
Jörg, 108
Hen,
Anna Christina,
38
Johan Henrich,
38
Hen?,
Georg, 110
Henckel,
Anna Catharina,
98
Elisabeth, 98
Henrich, 98
Johan Henrich,
98
Henckhel,
Conradt, 111
Henkel,
Elisabetha, 35
Heinrich, 35
Hep,
Anna Margaret,
110
Georg, 110
Herchenröder,
Anna Margretha,
83
Elisabetha, 54
Johannes, 54
Melchior, 83
Herger,
Henrich, 43, 47
Johannes, 15, 16
Herrmann,
Daniel, 97
Johanna, 96, 97
Maria Catharina
Elisabeth, 97
Salome, 96, 97
Hess,

Johann Conrad,
30
Hetderichin,
Anna Margaretha,
74
Magdalena, 74
Heterich,
Johannes, 75
John, 17
Susanna, 17
Heterick,
John, 76
Susanna, 76
Hetrich,
Adam, 68
Carl, 72
Henrich, 74
Jost, 140
Mrs. William, 74
William, 74
Hetrick,
Adam, 69, 70,
72, 75
Anna Margret, 72
Caspar, 70, 72,
75
Catrina, 72
Coblin, 72
Elizabeth, 69,
72
Johan Henrick,
72
John, 70, 71,
72, 75
John Onst, 72
Magdalene, 74
William, 72, 74
Hetrig,
Joost, 73
Jost, 73
William, 73, 74
Hetterich,
Casper, 34
Catharina,
41(2), 73, 74
Elisabeth, 74
Elisabetha, 74
Henrich, 74
Henry, 41
Johann Peter, 74
Magdalena
Elisabeth, 34
Wilhelm, 74
William, 41, 73
Hetterick,
Henry, 73
Joost, 17
Peter, 38
William, 75
Hettrich, 143

Heussel,
Georg, 136
Heydrig,
John Adam, 68
Heyer,
Adam, 25
Anna Maria, 77
Georg, 77
Heÿliger,
Anna Maria, 76
Johannes, 76
Valentin, 76
Heyll,
John, 110
Hicks,
Conrad, 77
John, 77
Nancy, 77
Hildebrand,
Joh. Hermann,
12, 14
Himmelberger,
John, 75
Hinckel,
Catharina, 111
Conradt, 111
Hinkle,
George, 86
Hix,
Angelica, 17, 18
Anna Catharina,
1, 76, 77
Anna Clara, 77
Anna Elisabetha,
77
Anna Maria, 52,
76, 77, 78
Barbara, 78
Conrad, 17, 52,
76, 77, 78
Daniel, 78
Elisabetha, 78
Elizabeth, 77
Friederich, 1
Georg, 78
George, 77
Heinrich, 77
Henrich, 17, 76,
77, 78, 145
Jacob, 78
Joh. Conrad, 77,
89, 109
Johan Conrad, 76
Johan Henrich,
76(2)
Johan Jörg, 78
Johann Conrad,
18, 76
Johann Henrich,
52, 77

Hix (continued)
  Johann Valentin,
    76, 145
  Johanna
    Magdalena, 109
  Johannes, 76
  Magdalena
    Elisabeth, 76
  Magdalena
    Elisabetha, 17,
    18, 76
  Michael, 77, 78
  Valentin, 17,
    18(2), 76
Hoeffner,
  Anton, 1
Hoffmann,
  Anna Maria, 69
  Henrich, 69
Hoin,
  Friedrich, 78
  Margaretha, 78
Holdeman,
  Mary Eva, 101
Holton,
  Elizabeth, 61
Holtzener,
  Joh. Jacob, 39
  Maria Catharina,
    39
Hornberger,
  Michael, 65
Horr,
  Anna Catharina,
    134
  Georg, 134
House,
  Elizabeth, 26
  George, 26
Höyn,
  Anna Catharina,
    66
  Anna Margretha,
    66
  Anna Maria, 108
  Anna Maria
    Elisabetha, 66
  Anna Philippina,
    66
  Conrad, 64, 66
  Joh. Peter, 8,
    10
  Johann, 108
  Johann Adam, 66
  Johann Ludwig,
    8, 10
  Johannes, 66(2)
Hübener,
  Anna, 142
  Anna Catharina,

  142
  Anna Elisabeth,
    79
  Anna Elisabetha,
    80
  Anna Engel, 3
  Anna Maria, 80
  Anton, 142
  Caspar, 142
  Elisabetha, 122,
    142
  Engel, 3
  Gertraud, 123
  Gertrudis, 122,
    142
  Hans Henrich,
    123
  Henrich, 109,
    142
  Joh. Henrich,
    122, 142
  Johan Henrich,
    66, 122, 142
  Johann, 35
  Johann Henrich,
    142
  Johannes, 109
  Magdalena, 35
  Maria Elisabeth,
    24
  Mrs., 66
  Reinhard, 122,
    142
  Rosina, 3
  Tönges, 3, 32,
    80
Huber,
  Anna Catharina,
    80
  Hans, 80
Huffert,
  Jacob, 27
Hulsinger,
  Joh. Jacob, 51
Hydrick,
  William, 73
Hydrig,
  Jost, 73
Hyx,
  Johan Gorg, 78

-I-

Ichard,
  Mary, 124
Igelbourner,
  Danl, 29
Ihle,
  Georg, 20
Isagar,

  Jonathan, 82
Isler,
  Georg Henrich,
    73
  J. Henrich, 60

-J-

Jacobs,
  Anna Catharina,
    135
  Clos, 135, 136
  Magdalena, 135
Jaegeli,
  Hans Ulrich, 56
  Liesbeth, 56
  Maria, 56
Jeckel,
  Johannes, 130
  Margaretha
    Elisabetha, 130
Joachim,
  Jacob, 109
  Maria Christina,
    109
John,
  David, 81
Johnson,
  Anna Maria, 118
Jones,
  Gabriel, 76, 141
  Hank, 120
  Henry Z, Jr.,
    120, 129, 130,
    131, 132, 133,
    134, 135, 136,
    137, 138
  Hugh, 41
  Thomas, 103
Jost,
  Joh. Jörg, 49
Jung,
  Henrich, 138
Jüngst,
  Pastor, 149

-K-

Kalckgläser,
  Brother Joel,
    143
  Johann Heinrich,
    143
Kalcklöser,
  Christian, 143
  Johann Henrich,
    143
  Maria Magdalena,
    143
Kasler,

Ludwig, 8, 10
William, 8, 10
Kasseler,
  Henrich Wilhelm,
    8, 10
  Johann Ludwig,
    8, 10
  Philip Henrich,
    8, 10
  Wilhelm
    Christian, 8, 10

Kassler, 145
  Ann Elisabeth, 8
  Christina, 8
  Ludwig, 8
  Peter, 8
  Wilhelm, 8(2)
Kayser,
  Joh. Balthasar,
    103
Kearsner,
  Conrad, 86
Keen,
  Susanna, 44
Keisner,
  Martain, 82
Keisser,
  Peter, 91
Keller,
  Anna Margretha,
    73, 116
  Anna Maria, 44
  Johannes, 44, 58
  Johannes Sr., 44
  Nicklas, 116
  Nicolaus, 73
  Samuel, 7
Kelly,
  William, 82
Keoler,
  Johannes, 115
Kerber,
  Valentine, 110
Kerchner,
  Anna Maria, 85
  Conrad, 85
  George, 85
Kerman,
  Georg, 100
Kern,
  Frederick, 7
  Simon, 67
Kerrssoner,
  Connrat, 85
  Connratt, 85
  Conrat, 85
  George, 85
Kerschner,
  Anna Maria, 77,

    86
  Catharine, 86
  Christian, 86
  Conrad, 77, 78,
    86
  Conrad, Sr., 86
  Daniel, 86
  Elisabeth, 86,
    113
  Elizabeth, 114
  George, 88
  John, 86
  John George, 86
  John Peter, 86
  Jonathan, 86
  Magdalena, 86
  Peter, 114
  Sara, 86
Kersener,
  Martin, 89
Kershner,
  Catharine, 86
  Christina, 88
  Conrad, 86, 88,
    107, 144
  Conrad Jr., 42
  Jacob, 88(2), 89
  John, 86, 88(2),
    89
  Marie, 144
  Martin, 88
  Peter, 88, 89
  Peter S., 88
  Philip, 75, 88,
    89
Kersner,
  Catharine, 4
  Conrad, 4, 88
  George, 85
  Martin, 88
Kerssoner,
  John, 85
Kerstner,
  Catharina, 4
  Conrad, 4
Kesler,
  Johannes, 115
Kesler?,
  Johannes, 115
Keÿser, 78
  Anna Catharina,
    64, 78, 80
  Anna Elisabeth,
    57, 79, 83
  Anna Elisabetha,
    80, 83, 148
  Anna Margretha,
    79, 80, 81, 83,
    84, 87
  Anna Maria, 79,

    80, 91
  Anna Maria
    Barbara, 80
  Anna Regina, 79
  Antonius, 80
  Catharina, 79
  Elisabeth, 57
  Elisabetha, 80,
    145
  Giel (Juliana),
    79
  Joh. Conrad, 79,
    80
  Joh. Peter, 79
  Johann Peter,
    79, 80(2), 83
  Johanna Maria,
    80
  Johannes, 57,
    64, 78, 79, 80,
    81, 83, 84, 87,
    91, 145
  Juliana, 79
  Margaretha, 78,
    79
  Rosina, 80
Kieser,
  Adam, 79
Kiltau,
  Eva Maria, 148
  Thomas, 148
Kirchner,
  Anna Catharina,
    144
  Conrad, 144
  Johan, 144
Kirschner, 78,
    143, 145
  An Els (Anna
    Elisabeth), 81,
    84, 87
  Anna, 80, 81,
    85, 137
  Anna Barbara, 81
  Anna Catharina,
    30, 83(2), 85,
    87
  Anna Catharina
    Elisabetha, 83
  Anna Elisabeth,
    81, 83, 87
  Anna Elisabetha,
    24, 80
  Anna Margaretha,
    4
  Anna Margretha,
    81, 83, 84, 86,
    87, 91
  Anna Maria, 78,
    87

Kirschner
  (continued)
  Anna Philippina,
    85
  Anton, 83
  Barbara, 58, 80
  Caspar, 24
  Catharina, 4, 86
  Conrad, 58, 78,
    84, 85, 144
  Conrut, 84
  David, 81
  Elisabeth, 80,
    82
  Elisabetha, 87,
    147
  Georg, 83
  George, 84
  George, Sr., 84
  Gertraud, 32, 84
  Gertrude, 87
  Henrich, 35, 62,
    83
  Joh. Caspar, 81,
    84, 87
  Joh. Conrad, 79,
    85, 86, 87, 91
  Joh. Georg, 43,
    85
  Joh. Jörg, 80,
    81, 85
  Joh. Martin, 81,
    84, 87
  Joh. Peter, 85,
    87
  Johan, 81
  Johan Bernhard,
    83
  Johan Conrad,
    4(2), 83, 86
  Johan Georg, 84,
    122
  Johan George,
    122
  Johan Henrich,
    83
  Johan Jörg, 83,
    84
  Johan Peter, 4,
    86
  Johan Yerek, 84
  Johann, 78, 81,
    83, 84, 87
  Johann Conrad,
    81, 84, 87
  Johann Georg,
    82, 83
  Johann George,
    80
  Johann Henrich,

    83
  Johann Jörg, 48,
    81
  Johanna
    Catharina, 83
  Johannes, 30,
    32, 49, 78, 81,
    83, 84(2), 122,
    149
  John, 87
  Kertroudt, 84
  Margaretha, 79
  Maria, 81, 83
  Martin, 4, 79,
    80, 81, 82, 84,
    86(2), 87(3), 92

  Peter, 81, 84,
    87(2), 137, 147
  Rosina, 83
  Samuel, 78
  see Kerstner, 4
  Wilhelm, 78
  Wörner, 83
Kirshner,
  Conrad, 88
  David, 82
  Elisabeth, 88
  Georg, 83
  George, 82, 84
  George, Sr., 82
  Gertraut, 88
  Jacob, 82
  Johannes, 85
  John, 82
  Madalina, 82
  Margreth, 82
  Margretha, 82
  Martin, 82, 88
  Nicholas, 88
  Peter, 88
  Philip, 88
Kissling,
  Martin, 92
Klapp,
  Anna Catharina,
    151
  Jost, 151
Klawer,
  Michael, 60
Kleber, 89
  Andreas, 60
  Gerdraut, 60
  Johan Henrich,
    60
  Johan Michael,
    60
  Michael, 61
  Michel, 110
Klein,

Adam, 132
Catharina, 123
Christian, 123
Christina
  Magdalena, 123
Michael, 123
Moritz, 123
Kleinhans,
  Maria Catharina,
    51
Kleiss,
  Adam, 94
  Anna Catharina,
    77
  Anna Elisabeth,
    94
  Elisabeth,
    94(2), 95, 96
  Johannes, 77
Kleiz,
  Anna Elisabeth,
    97
Klevering,
  Anne Elizabeth,
    60
Klingenstein,
  Anna Rosina, 146
  Johannes, 146
Kloeber,
  Anna Elisabeth,
    61
  Michael, 61
Klopp,
  Abraham, 88
Klosterman,
  Joh. Wilhelm, 56
Knaus,
  Catharina, 12
  Jacob, 12
Kneskern,
  Johann Peter,
    132
Knies,
  Caspar, 81, 83,
    84, 87
  Johan Bernhard,
    83
  Maria, 81, 84,
    87
Kniess, 143
  Anna Elisabetha,
    2
  Caspar, 2, 121
  Catharina, 144
  Conrad, 145
  Elisabetha, 80,
    145
  Joh. Bernhard,
    145
  Johann Bernhard,

144
Johannes, 80,
144, 145
Magdalena
Elisabeth, 145
Maria, 121
Kniss,
Anna, 33
Anna Barbara, 2
Caspar, 2, 33
Elisabeth, 2
Johannes, 144,
145
Koch, 143
Adolph, 89
Andreas, 89
Anna Catharina,
90
Anna Elisabeth,
90
Anna Elisabetha,
90
Anna Magdalena
Elisabetha, 51
Anna Maria, 43,
47(2), 89, 90
Anna Veronica,
48
Burckhard, 89,
107
Caspar, 43, 47,
89, 90
Catharine, 90,
91
Elisabeth, 89
Henry, 14
Joh. Caspar, 89,
90
Joh. Conrad, 89
Joh. Peter, 11,
79, 89
Johan Jörg, 83
Johan Peter, 107
Johann, 131
Johann Caspar,
90
Johann Georg, 51
Johann Justus,
90
Johann Peter,
89, 90
Johannes, 43,
48, 89, 90
Magdalena, 54,
131
Margaret, 14
Paul, 54
Stoffel, 83
Koellicker,
Anna Maria, 56

Heinrich, 56
Koen,
Samuel, 135
Köhler,
Anna Barbara,
134
Johannes, 134,
135
Kohn,
Brother, 95, 97
Kolb,
Anna Barbara,
145
Antonius, 145
Conrad, 145
Joh. Barthel,
145
Joh. Peter, 145
Johan Conrad,
145
Johan Jost, 145
Köllicker,
Henrich, 55
Komar,
Gail, 63
Krauel,
Catharine, 63
Joh. Michael,
119
Johann Michael,
63
Krebs,
Jacob, 86
Kreigsman,
Johannes, 28
Krick,
Anna Rosina, 146
Francis, 27
Frantz, 46, 146
Joh. Henrich,
146
Peter, 146
Kriegsmann,
Jacob, 28
Krum,
Jost, 137
Kuchler,
Johannes, 123
Maria Magdalena,
123
Kuersner,
Martin, 87
Kuhn, 133
Ann, 134
Anna, 130
Anna Barbara,
134
Anna Catharina,
134, 135
Anna Margretha,

129
Barbara
Elisabetha, 134
Catharina, 134
Elisabetha, 134
Hans, 129, 130,
134, 137
Joh. Jost, 137
Johann Conrad,
134
Johann Herman,
134
Johann Valentin,
134
Marcus, 134
Samuel, 129,
131, 134, 135
Valentin, 135
Valtin, 135
Kun,
Elisabetha, 134
Samuel, 134
Kürschner,
Anna Barbara, 81
Dinnes, 144
Henrich, 142
Joh., 62
Joh. Cunradt, 86
Joh. Jörg, 84,
87
Johan, 84, 87
Johann, 143
Johann Conrad,
84, 87
Johannes, 49,
84, 87
Maria, 84, 87

-L-

Lach,
Hans Conrad, 30
Joh. Jacob, 30
Maria Margretha,
30
Lahmeyer,
Anna Elisabetha,
136
Georg, 135
Gertraud, 135
Johannes, 135,
136(2)
Jörg, 135, 136
Magdalena, 136
Marcus, 136
Laick,
George, 19
Lamb,
Anna Maria, 57,
79

Lamb (continued)
  Catharina, 91,
    111
  John, 93
  Martin, 79, 91
  Peter, 57, 79,
    91, 92, 93, 111
Lambrecht,
  Anthony, 26
Lamm, 78
  Anna Margaret,
    92
  Anna Margaretha,
    92
  Anna Margretha,
    91
  Anna Maria, 91,
    92
  Appollonia, 92
  Elisabeth, 91,
    92
  Joh. Conrad, 80
  Johan Conrad, 91
  Johan Lenhard,
    91
  Johann Peter,
    91, 92
  Johann Philips,
    91
  Johannes, 91, 92
  John, 92, 93
  John Peter, 140
  Martin, 91
  Michael, 91
  Peter, 57, 80,
    91, 92
  Philipp, 92
Lammersdorf,
  Anna Catharina,
    3
Lammersdorff,
  Jörg Fried., 3
Lang,
  Anna, 39
  Conrad, 144
  Görg, 39
  Jacob, 65
Lark,
  Anthony, 101
  Balser, 103
  Casper, 103
  Caterina, 103
  Christopher, 103
  Elizabeth, 103
  Jacob, 103
  Jost, 103
  Margaret, 101,
    103
  Nicholas, 103
  Rachel, 103

William, 103
Lasch,
  Susanna, 114
Laubach,
  Frederick, 101
  Johann Georg, 51
Laucks,
  Anna Barbara, 81
  Peter, 81, 87
Lauer,
  Anna Elisabeth,
    101
  Anna Margaretha,
    99
  Anna Margaretta,
    100
  Anna Margreth,
    101(2)
  Anna Mary, 101
  Catharina, 101
  Conrad, 29
  Henrich, 29
  John George, 101
  John Peter, 101
  Juliana, 28
  Mary Eva, 101
  Michael, 28(2),
    114
  Peter, 101
Laux,
  Margaret, 87
Ledy,
  Jacob, 110
  Maria, 110
Lee,
  Edward, 121
Lehr,
  Conrad, 3
Lehrch,
  Barbara, 93
  Johannes, 93
Leidy,
  Elizabeth, 101
  John, 101
Leimbach,
  Anna Elisabeth,
    93
  Anna Margretha,
    68
  Henrich, 45,
    102, 104
  Joh. Henrich, 68
  Johann Henrich,
    48
  Johanna Maria,
    48
  Johannes, 45
  Michael, 93
Leinbach,
  a son, 93

Abraham, 95
Andreas, 93
Anna, 96, 97
Anna Catharina,
  97
Anna Elisabeth,
  93, 94, 97
Anna Margreth,
  93
Anna Maria, 97,
  98
Barbara, 93, 94,
  97
Benjamin, 95, 96
Catharina, 94,
  95(2), 96
Christian, 97
Christina, 97
Daniel, 96, 97
Elisabeth,
  95(2), 96(2), 97

Elizabeth, 93
Eva, 93
Frederick, 98
Friedrich, 94,
  95, 96, 97
Heinrich, 94, 96
Henrich, 93, 94,
  96, 97
Henry, 98
Jacob, 96
Johan Henrich,
  96
Johann, 97
Johann
  Frederick, 93
Johann Heinrich,
  94
Johann Henrich,
  94
Johanna, 95, 96,
  97
Johanna
  Elisabeth, 94
Johanna Maria,
  94(2)
Johannah Maria,
  94
Johannes, 93(2),
  94(2), 95(2),
  96(2), 97
Johannes, Sr.,
  94, 97
John, 97, 98
Joseph, 95, 96
Ludwig, 95
Magdalena, 96
Maria, 96, 97
Maria Barbara,

94(2), 95, 98
Mrs. Johannes,
97
Rosina, 96
Salome, 97
Samuel, 96
schoolmaster, 93
Leis,
Anna Elisabeth,
66
Bast, 93
Bastian, 66
Johan
Christoffel, 93
Leiss,
Christoffel, 17,
67
Mrs, 17
Wörner, 67
Lemire,
Hance, 136
Lerch,
Abbolona, 99
Andreas, 35, 50,
71, 89, 98, 100,
101, 105
Andrew, 101
Anna, 45, 147
Anna Barbara,
102, 104, 124
Anna
Eliesabetha, 103

Anna Elisabeth,
102, 104
Anna Elisabetha,
43
Anna Eva, 99
Anna Margaret,
99
Anna Margaretha,
99
Anna Margaretta,
100
Anna Margreth,
101
Anna Maria, 55,
99(2), 100(2),
101
Anna Sabina, 50,
98
Anthon, 98, 100
Anthony, 99, 100
Anton, 100
Antonius, 99,
119
Antony, 101
Appolona, 101
Balthasar, 103
Balthaser, 103

Baltzer, 103
Barbara, 93, 94,
103
Caspar, 55, 102,
104
Casper, 103
Catharina, 99,
102, 104
Catharine, 101,
126
Christian, 116,
118
Christopher, 103
Conrad, 98, 147
Conrad, Jr., 118
Cratias, 99
Daniel, 103
Elisabeth, 44,
98, 99, 116, 118

Elisabetha, 35
Elizabeth,
101(2), 114
Eva, 100
Eva Barbara, 100
Frederich, 101
Frederick, 100
Gertraut, 98
Gertrud, 101
Giel, 147
Gratius, 99, 100
Gratus, 101
Helena, 102, 104
Henrich, 118
Henry, 101
Jacob, 55, 101,
105
Joh. Conrad, 89
Johan, 45, 124
Johan Caspar, 45
Johan Henrich,
119
Johann, 43
Johann Henrich,
102, 104
Johann Jost, 104
Johann Peter, 99
Johanna Gertrud,
98, 101
Johannes, 45,
93, 99, 102,
104, 119
Johannes
Balthasar, 103
John, 99,
101(2), 103
John Frederich,
99
John William,
103

Jost, 105
Margaret, 100,
101
Margaretha, 126
Margretha
Elisabetha, 104
Maria, 101
Maria Margaret,
103
Nicholas, 99,
100, 104
Pancratius, 99,
100
Peter, 50, 98,
99, 100, 101,
147
Philip, 101
Rachel, 103
Rosina, 104
Sawina, 50
Stoffel, 98
Susanna, 99,
100, 101
Tobias, 100, 101
Tönges, 98
William, 104
Yost, 104
Lereck,
Anthony, 101
Lerg,
Casper, 103
Lergh,
Gratzius, 100
Lerich,
Anna Maria, 105
Hans Jerich, 105
Johann Georg,
105
Johannes, 105
Lerk,
Caspar, 104
Levering,
Maria Catharina,
95
Leÿss,
Antonius, 52, 53
Maria
Elisabetha, 108
Wörner, 52, 53,
108
Lischy,
Jacob, 149, 151
Loechler,
Jürg Ernst, 32
Lofinck,
Anna Maria, 111
Henrich, 15, 17,
111
Joh. Henrich,
142

Lohefinck,
  Anna Elisabeth,
    93
  Anna Maria, 119
  Peter, 93, 119
Lohfinck,
  Henrich, 138
  Joh. Henrich, 83
  Johann Henrich,
    3
  Peter, 119, 138
Lohmeÿer,
  Anna Barbara,
    135
  Anna Catharina,
    135, 136
  Anna Elisabetha,
    135
  Anna Magdalena,
    136
  Anna Ursula, 135
  Engel, 135, 136
  Georg, 136
  Henrich, 136
  Johann
    Gregorius, 135
  Johann Henrich,
    136
  Johannes,
    135(2), 136
  Jörg, 135
  Magdalena, 135
  Marcus, 135(2),
    136
Lohmyer,
  Anna Elisabetha,
    137
  Marcus, 137
Long,
  Jacob, 65
Loos,
  Jacob, 112
Lörch,
  Andreas, 49
  Anna Christina,
    102
  Anna Margretha,
    102
  Anna Sabina, 49
  Caspar, 102
  Casper, 103
  Heinrich, 136
  Joh. Adam, 49
  Joh. Christoph,
    102
  Johan, 102
  Johann Wilhelm,
    102
  Johannes, 102,
    105

Niclaus, 102
Lörey,
  Oberschultheis,
    117
Lowery,
  Margaret, 103
Luckenbach,
  Catharina, 91
Ludwig,
  Brother, 95
  Daniel, 19, 20,
    21
Lufft,
  Anna, 56
  Johannes, 39
  Magdalena, 39
  Peter, 39
  Thomas, 56

-M-

Machelin,
  Theobald, 99
Mackinet,
  Blasius, 62
McMichael,
  Mr., 10
Man,
  Jacob, 76
Mann,
  Anna Sabina, 50
  Magdalena, 50
  Philip, 50
Martin,
  Maria, 95
Maser,
  Catharina, 8
Mattheus,
  Georg, 138
Maurer,
  Christofel, 38
  Daniel, 38
  Elisabeth, 38
  Frederich, 88
  Philipp, 58
May,
  Johan, 137
  Michael, 137
Mayer,
  Elisabeth, 50,
    51
  Jacob, 50, 51
  John, 150
Mears,
  Frederick, 25
  Mary, 25
Mechlin,
  Anna Elisabeth,
    101
Meelhus,

Peder, 108
Mehl,
  Melchor, 106
Meierly,
  Daniel, 29
Melcher,
  Maria, 100
Mell,
  Anna, 106
  Anna Barbara,
    35, 60, 71
  Anna Catharina,
    90
  Anna Magdalena,
    60
  Anna Maria, 106
  Anna Rosina,
    71(2)
  Carl, 106, 107
  Carl Henrich,
    106
  Carl Johann
    Henrich, 106
  Charles, 107
  Conrad, 60, 66,
    71, 106
  Elisabeth, 106,
    107
  Elisabetha, 106
  Joh. Melchior,
    35
  Joh. Wilhelm,
    107
  Johan Melchior,
    71, 106
  Johann, 107
  Johann Heinrich,
    106
  Johann Melchior,
    106
  Johannes, 90,
    106(2)
  John Melchior,
    106
  Maria, 66
  Melchior, 60,
    71, 106, 107
  Mellchior, 107
  Michael, 107
  Susanna, 106
Mellhausen,
  Anna Catharina,
    108(2)
  Anna Maria, 108
  Anna Rosina, 108
  Anna Ursula, 108
  Caspar, 107, 108
  Catharina, 107
  Christina
    Margretha, 107

Engel, 107
Joh. Jacob, 107
Joh. Peter, 108
Johan Caspar,
    108
Johan Peter,
    107, 108
Johan Wilhelm,
    107, 108
Johann Henrich,
    108
Johannes, 107
Maria
    Elisabetha, 108
Peter, 108
Susanna, 107,
    108
Wilhelm, 108
Meredith,
    Rees, 10
Messerschmidt,
    Cunradt, 86
Meth,
    John, 87
Meurer,
    Philipp, 97
Meyer,
    Anna Catharina,
        86
    Elizabeth, 50
    Jacob, 50
    Johann, 19,
        20(2), 22
    Johannes, 21,
        58(2), 85, 86,
        151
    John, 59
    Margaret, 113
    Margaretha, 58
    Maria Margaret,
        58
    Maria
        Margaretha, 58
Michael,
    Elisabeth, 107
    Joh. Wilhelm,
        107
Michel,
    Gertrud, 101
    Johanna Gertrud,
        101
    Nicholas, 50,
        99, 100, 101
    Paul, 101
Michler, 95, 97
    Johan Wolfgang,
        96
    Maria Barbara,
        96
Miller,

Conrad, 82
Jacob, 59
John, 19, 92
Michael, 19
Yost, 9
Millhouse,
    Casper, 108
    Peter, 108
Mire,
    Anna Margaretha,
        40
    Philip, 40
Moeller,
    Catharine, 90
    Johan Heinrich,
        97
    Joseph, 90
Moers,
    Friedrich, 24
    Maria, 24
Mohn,
    Andilla, 110
    Anna Elisabetha,
        90, 111
    Anna Maria, 79,
        109
    Anna Odilia, 110
    Anna Ottilia,
        111
    Conrad, 52, 53,
        67, 79, 111
    Daniel, 110
    Elisabeth, 110
    Elisabetha, 52,
        53
    Engel, 147
    Hans, 33, 35,
        109
    Henry, 110
    Johann Ludwig,
        109
    Johanna
        Magdalena, 109
    Johannes, 79,
        90, 109(2)
    John, 110(2),
        111
    Juliana, 52, 53
    Künigunda, 33,
        35
    Ludwick, 111
    Ludwig, 61, 110
    Magdalena, 61,
        110(2)
    Margreth, 109
    Margretha, 109
    Maria, 110
    Mrs. Conrad, 67
    Ottilia, 110
    Peter, 109, 110

Susanna, 110
Tonges, 52, 53,
    79, 147
Werner, 110
Wörner, 35, 109
Mohr,
    Augusta Maria,
        64
Moll,
    Henry, 37
Moller, 150
    Werner, 148
Moon,
    Conen Lutwick,
        109
    Johannes, 109
    John, 110
    Lodowick, 110
    Lodwick, 110
    Margaret, 110
    Margret, 109
    Maria, 109
    Matiles, 109
    Vernor, 109
    Werner, 110
    Wörner, 35, 147
Morner,
    Anna Mary, 101
Morris,
    John, 115
    Mr., 10
Moser,
    Elisabeth, 92
    Johannes, 92
Muench,
    Catarina, 34
Mühlhaus,
    Henrich, 109
    Margaret, 109
    Margaretha, 109
    maria Christina,
        109
    Peter, 109
Mull,
    Martin, 93
Müller,
    Anna Maria, 131
    Isaac, 146
    Jacob, 58, 151
    Johan Caspar,
        131
    Johann Henrich,
        140
    Johannes, 97,
        151
    John, 27
    Rosina, 95, 96,
        97
Münch,
    Joh. Georg, 67

Muth,
　Johan Peter, 62
M_____,
　Joh. Jorg, 70

-N-

Nasse,
　Mathias, 12
Naulin,
　Johannes, 101
Neidert,
　(Anna
　　Elisabetha), 77
　Anna Barbara,
　　130
　Anna Maria, 77,
　　87
　Christian, 43,
　　120
　Henrich, 77
　Jacob, 77
　Joh. Henrich, 87
　Joh. Jacob, 43
　Johann Valentin,
　　134
　Samuel, 130, 134
Neisser,
　G., 96
Neubert,
　Hanna, 151
Neukirch,
　Gertraud, 95, 96
　Heinrich, 97
　Henrich, 97
Neukommer,
　Eva Barbara, 100
Neuman,
　Anna Margretha,
　　6
　H. Johann Jacob,
　　6
　Johann
　　Christian, 6
　Maria Margretha,
　　6
Nicholas,
　Jacob, 69
Niedenthal,
　Anna Catharina,
　　69
　John. Jörg, 70
Nirer,
　Anna Barbara, 2
　Georg, 2
Nitchman,
　David, 98
　Maria Barbara,
　　98
Nitschmann,

Barbara, 97
Johan, 95
Nohlen,
　Gertraud, 101
　Johann George,
　　101
　Johannes, 101
Nowlan,
　John, 101
Nowlane,
　Gertrud, 101
　Johannes, 101
Numann,
　Maria, 30

-O-

Oberlin,
　Margaretha, 99
Obermüller,
　Maria Catharina
　　Elisabeth, 97
Ohl,
　Henry, 101

-P-

Parvin,
　William, 4
Parvin Jr.,
　Francis, 4
Paul,
　William, 82
Peck,
　Anthony, 4
　Elisabeth, 4
Pellinger,
　Ffrederick, 129
　Johannes, 129
　Margaret, 129
　Peter, 129
Pence,
　Adam, 69
　George, 69
　Jacob, 69
　Jacob Sr., 69
　Valentine, 69,
　　70, 72, 75
Penn,
　Richard, 74
　Thomas, 74
Peters,
　Maria Gerdraut,
　　27
　Martin, 27
Petry,
　Anna
　　Eliesabetha, 119

　Joh. Georg, 63,

119
Johann Georg,
　118(2), 119
Johann Michael,
　119
Philip, 63
Sabina, 63, 118,
　119
Petz,
　Johannes, 5
　Maria Barbara, 5
Pflasser,
　Charlotta
　　Eleonora, 15, 17
　Georg, 15, 17
Pfundt,
　Joh. Jacob, 39
Phaar,
　Anna Christina,
　　49
　Michael, 49
Pharo,
　Michael, 111
Pielman,
　Anna Maria, 149
　Johann, 149
Plumsted,
　Mr., 10
Pringley,
　Peter, 82
Prinz,
　Elisabeth, 24
　Hannes, 24
Probst,
　Mathias, 116
Putnam,
　Israel, 23
Pyrlaeo,
　Brother, 151
Pyrlaeus,
　Brother, 95

-R-

Räber,
　Anna Catharina,
　　112
　Cath., 114
　Conrad, 112, 113
　Daniel, 111
　Elisabeth, 112
　Johannes, 113,
　　115
　John, 114
　Thomas, 114
Rack,
　Elisabeth, 33
　Hans, 109
　Margretha, 109

Paul, 33
Raeber,
    Abraham, 114
    Anna Maria,
        114(2)
    Catharine, 114
    Elizabeth, 114
    Joh. Michael,
        114
    Joh. Valentin,
        114
    John, 114
    John Nicholas,
        114
    Maria Susanna,
        114
    Peter, 114
    Susanna, 114
    Thomas, 114
    Valentin, 114
Raidel,
    Anna, 39
    Anna Magdalena,
        136
    Caspar, 39
    Jost, 136
Rauch,
    Anna, 151
    Caspar, 107, 108
    Catharina, 107
    Christian, 58,
        95, 96, 151
    Susanna, 107,
        108
Raush,
    Caspar, 30
    Juliana, 30
Rebber,
    Daniel, 115
    Elisabeth, 115
    Johannes, 115
Reber,
    Adam, 112
    Anna, 111
    Anna Elisabetha,
        111
    Anna Magdalena,
        5, 112
    Anna Margaret,
        113
    Anna Maria,
        111(2), 112(2),
        113
    Bernhard, 5,
        111, 112, 113,
        115
    Catharina, 91,
        111
    Catharine, 112,
        114

Conrad, 5, 27,
    70, 111, 112,
    113
Daniel, 91, 111,
    113
Eleonora Amalia,
    112
Elisabeth, 113
Elizabeth, 112,
    114, 115
Hans, 70, 145
Hans Bernhard,
    111
Herman, 111
Jacob, 112
Joh. Bernhard,
    113
Joh. Conrad, 91,
    112
Johan Paul, 111
Johann Bernhard,
    112
Johann Conrad,
    111
Johann Peter,
    111
Johanna
    Magdalena, 113
Johannes, 17,
    64, 111, 113,
    115
John, 112, 113,
    115
Ludwig
    Friederich
    August, 113
Magdalena, 112,
    113, 115(2)
Margaret, 112
Maria, 111
Michael, 91,
    111, 112, 145
Nicholas, 114,
    115
Peter, 112
Susanna, 112,
    114
Thomas, 86, 112,
    113, 114, 115
Valentine,
    112(2)
Rebert,
    Michael, 70
Reedy,
    Peter, 55
Reesar,
    John, 85
Reeser,
    Barbara, 23
    Daniel, 23

John, 4
William, 14, 41
Wm., 88
Rehrig,
    Nichs., 118
Reibert,
    John, 17, 115
Reichard,
    Anna Margretha,
        116
    Catharina,
        116(2)
    Christoffel, 116
    Elisabeth, 116
    Fritz, 116
    Georg, 116
    George, 116
    Henry, 116
    Joh. Philipps,
        116
    Johann Ludwig,
        116
    Künigunda, 116
    Ludwig, 116(2)
    Michael, 116
Reicher,
    Ludwig, 116
Reicherd,
    Catharine, 116
    Catharine
        Elisabeth, 116
    George, 116
    Ludwig, 116
    Margareth, 116
Reichert,
    Andrew, 117
    Catherine, 117
    Elisabetha, 43
    Elizabeth, 117
    Eve Sellomy, 117
    Friedrich, 43
    George, 117(2)
    George William,
        117
    Jacob, 117
    Joh. Henr., 136
    John, 117
    Ludwig, 43, 51,
        116
    Magdalena, 117
    Mary Barbara,
        117
    Michael, 117
    Werner, 133
Reichhart,
    Friederich, 51
    Kunigunda, 51
Reiger,
    Andrew, 115
    Anton, 58

Reiger (continued)
  Barbara, 58
  Judith, 58
Reincke,
  Abr., 8
Reiser,
  William, 25
Reiter,
  Johannes, 30
Rep,
  Anton, 67
  Henrich, 64
Repp,
  Anton, 64
  Johannes, 18, 64
  Magdalena
    Elisabeth, 76
  Magdalena
    Elisabetha, 17
  Margaretha, 64
  Margretha, 65,
    138
  Wörner, 17, 64,
    65, 76, 138
Reus,
  Matthes, 58
Rever,
  Hans, 115
  Johannes, 121
Reyel,
  Johannes, 64
Ricart,
  Ludwig, 117
Richard,
  Ludwig, 116
Richerd,
  Catharina, 116
  Henrich, 116
Richter,
  Joh. Friedrich,
    57
Ridenawer,
  Henry, 82
Riegel,
  John, 53, 68
Rieger,
  Barbara, 58, 59
  Pastor, 58
Riehm,
  Abraham, 97, 98
  Anna Maria, 97,
    98
Riem,
  Catharina, 94,
    95
  Eberhard, 95
  Elisabeth, 95
Rietscher,
  Gabriel, 41
Rigel,

Gertraut, 88
Rigerd,
  Ludwig, 116
Rihel,
  A. Maria, 66
Rihm,
  Eberhard, 98
  Tobias, 98
Ring,
  Peter, 111
Ritinawer,
  Elizabeth, 82
  George, 82
  Margreth, 82
Ritschart,
  Ulrich, 103
Rohn,
  Anna Justina, 67
  Johannes, 67
  John, 65, 67
Röhrich,
  Anna Margretha,
    117
  Anna Maria, 117
  Anna Sabina, 117
  Christina, 117
  Hans Conrad, 117
  .Johan Michael,
    117
  Johann Caspar,
    117
  Johann Jörg, 117
  Johanna Esther,
    117
  Johannes, 117
  Servin, 117
  Servinus, 117
  Severin, 133
Röhrig,
  Anna Maria, 118
  Eva Catharina,
    118
  Georg, 118
  Johan Niclaus,
    117
  Johann Niclaus,
    118
  Juliana, 117
  Michael, 117(2),
    118
  Niclas, 118
  Niclaus, 117
  Nicolaus, 117
  Severin, 117
Roht,
  Anna Maria, 52
  Michael, 52, 53
Ronpel?,
  Conrad, 111
  Maria, 111

Rörig,
  Michael, 117
Rosenzweig,
  Elisabetha, 134
Rosenzweigin, 134,
    135
Rost,
  Pastor, 149
Roth,
  Adam, 139
  Adolff, 98
  Anna Barbara,
    139
  Anna Catharina,
    69
  Anna Elisabetha,
    62, 118
  Anna Maria, 25,
    69
  Anna Sabina, 98,
    118
  Conr., 69
  daughter, 63
  Elisabeth, 70,
    89, 118
  Elisabetha, 118
  Emanuel, 62, 63,
    118
  Emmanuel, 26
  Hans, 43, 47
  Henrich, 118
  Immanuel, 118
  Johann Jacob,
    145
  Johann Peter,
    99, 118
  Johann Valentin,
    145
  Jorg, 25, 69,
    70(2)
  Juliana, 145
  Ludwig Adolff,
    89
  Otto Caspar, 99
  Sabina, 63,
    118(2)
  Valentin, 145
  Wilhelm, 26, 45
Rothermel,
  Johannes, 4
  Sybilla, 4
Ruch,
  Ann Sabina, 50
  Christian, 50
Rudel,
  daughter, 68
  .Johannes, 68, 99
Rüger,
  Cathar., 32
  Hans, 32

Rundt,
  C. Gottfried, 96
Ruppel,
  Anna Maria
    Barbara, 80
  Johannes, 80
Ruppert,
  Anna, 56
  Carl, 56
  Henrich, 56
  Johannes, 56
  Margretha, 27
Rush,
  Charles, 141
  John, 141
Russell,
  George Ely, 39,
    40
Rut,
  (Anna Clara), 77
  Michael, 77
Ruth, 9
  Adam, 42
  Anna Catharina,
    148
  Anna Maria, 18
  Catharine, 42
  Hans, 45
  Henrich, 15, 16
  Jacob, 18
  Johann Peter, 74
  Johannes, 15
  Matthais, 3
  Pastor, 57
  Peter, 46, 74

    -S-

Saeger,
  Nicholas, 121
Schaarman,
  Catharina, 110
Schad,
  Adam, 68, 120,
    124, 125
  Andreas, 141
  Anna Catharina,
    120
  Anna Catharine,
    121
  Anna Catherin,
    121
  Anna Clara, 120,
    121
  Anna Kunigunda,
    120
  Anna Margaretha,
    121, 133
  Anna Maria, 119
  Anna Philippina,

    85
  Antonius, 119,
    120
  Catharina Elis.,
    121
  Conrad, 120(2),
    121, 124
  Gertraud, 135
  Hans, 81, 84,
    87, 93, 121, 123

  Hans Bernhard,
    81, 84, 87, 121,
    122
  Joh. Conrad, 87
  Joh. Henrich, 11
  Joh. Peter, 85
  Johan, 11, 119
  Johan Bernhard,
    122
  Johan Caspar,
    119
  Johan Henrich,
    119
  Johan Peter,
    119, 122
  Johann Caspar,
    133
  Johann Peter,
    122
  Johannes, 55,
    119, 120, 121(2)

  Jörg, 123
  Jost, 120
  Magdalena
    Elisabeth, 121
  Margretha, 93,
    119
  Maria, 81, 84,
    87, 121, 122
  Maria Barbara,
    141
  Maria Clara, 124
  Peter, 17, 78,
    87, 121
  Sabina, 122
  Tönges, 119, 120
Schadt,
  Anna Margretha,
    119
  Anthon, 119
  Anton, 119(2),
    120
  Görg, 49
  Hans, 49
  Hans Caspar, 119
Schäfer,
  H. Lieut., 133
  Ottilia, 133

    Susanna, 29
Schäffer,
  Anna Magdalena,
    112
  Georg, 116
  Johanes, 112
Schaidt,
  Anthony, 120
  Dorothea, 120
Schatten,
  Anna Margarette,
    17
  Peter, 17
Schaub,
  Judith, 58
Schauer,
  Michael, 19
Schehrer,
  Anna Maria, 99
  Peter, 99
Scheid,
  Joh., 148
Scheidt,
  Anthon, 120
Schell,
  Catharina, 101
Scherer,
  Anna Catharina,
    87
  Anna Elisabeth,
    79
  Anna Elisabetha,
    80
  Georg, 60
  Henrich, 79, 80
  Joh. Peter, 87
  Magdalena, 60
  Peter, 91
  Wörner, 52, 53
Scherflex,
  Anna Maria, 13
  Henry, 13
Scherp,
  Anna Catharina,
    141
  Hans Caspar, 141
Scheucher,
  Johannes, 137
Schieser,
  Anna Elisabeth,
    62, 79
  Anna Rosina, 32,
    38
  Christoffel, 32,
    38
  Clos, 62, 79
  Elisabetha, 3,
    52, 53, 67
  Johan Peter, 3
  Nicklas, 67

Schieser
  (continued)
  Tonges, 67
  Wörner, 3, 66
  Wörner Jr., 3
Schiesser,
  Anna Catharina,
    85
  Christoph, 85
  son, 63
  Tönges, 63
Schillinger,
  Elisabeth, 94
Schlaunecker,
  Stephan, 95
Schlemmer,
  Anna Margretha,
    6
  Conrad, 6
  Herman, 6
  Hermann, 6(2)
  Johann Henrich,
    6
  Maria Dorothea,
    6(2)
Schlosser,
  And., 10
  George, 10
Schmid,
  Catharina, 150
Schmidt,
  Jacob, 149, 150
  Pastor, 86
Schmied,
  Bernhard, 129
  Philipps, 129
Schmöhl,
  Michael, 46
Schmöll,
  Elisabetha, 74
Schnauffer,
  George, 109
  Margaret, 109
Schneider,
  Abraham, 86
  Adam, 91
  Andreas, 60, 98
  Anna Elisabetha,
    135, 137
  Balthasar, 137
  Catharina, 91
  Conrad, 104, 123
  Elizabeth, 91
  Jacob, 88
  Johann Jost, 137
  Johannes, 36,
    91, 135, 136,
    137
  John Adam, 91
  Math., 117

Schnell,
  Leonhard, 95, 97
Schott,
  Anna Margreta,
    122
  Peter, 122
Schötte,
  Johann Henrich,
    120
Schröder,
  Adam, 129
Schroff,
  Adam, 73
Schuchard,
  Maria, 151
Schuchardt,
  Anna Catharina,
    151
  Anna Elisabeth,
    151
  Anna Maria,
    151(2)
  Carl, 151
  Catharina, 151
  Heinrich, 150,
    151, 152
  Johann Heinrich,
    151
  Johann Jost, 151
  Johannes, 151
  Maria Catharina,
    151
  Maria Christina,
    151
  Tobias, 151
Schuchart,
  Catharina, 151
  Heinrich, 150,
    151
Schuchert,
  Heinrich, 65
  Johann Henrich,
    150
  Johannes, 150
Schucker,
  Anna Maria, 152
  Heinrich, 151
  Joh. Heinrich,
    151
  Tobias, 65, 151
  Wilhelm Carl,
    151
Schuckert,
  Anna Elisabeth,
    151
  Anna Maria, 150,
    152
  Catharina,
    150(2)
  Catharine, 151

Charles (Carl),
    152
  Henry, 150, 151,
    152
  Joh. Wilhelm,
    150
  Johan, 150
  Johanna Maria,
    152
  John, 152
  John Jost, 151
  Maria
    Elisabetha, 150
  Tobias, 152
Schufert,
  Anna Mar., 123
  Catharina, 123
  Joh. Georg, 123
Schuffard,
  Georg, 122
  Gertrud, 122
  Johannes, 122
Schuffart,
  Gertraud, 84
  Johann, 84
Schuffert,
  Anna Elisabeth,
    87
  Anna Elisabetha,
    123
  Anna Maria, 123
  Anna Veronica,
    43, 47, 89
  Caspar, 43, 47,
    89, 123
  Catharina, 123
  Catreena, 124
  Catrout, 124
  Conrad, 87
  Daniel, 124
  David, 124
  Geooorge, 124
  Georg, 124, 142
  George, 124
  Gertraud, 32,
    87, 123
  Gertrudis, 142
  Henrich, 133
  Jacob, 124
  Joh. Jörg, 123
  Joh. Peter, 87
  Johan Jörg
    Conrad, 123
  Johann Conrad,
    133
  Johanna Maria,
    123
  Johannes, 32,
    87, 123, 124
  John, 124

Maria Clara,
  123, 124
Mary, 124
Mary Clara, 124
Mautlena, 124
Michael, 123(2)
Niclaus, 123
Schumacher,
  Daniel, 77
  John, 78
  Rebecca, 77
Schütz,
  Anna, 137
  Anna Catharina,
    138
  Anna Elisabetha,
    138
  Anna Margretha,
    138
  Anna Maria
    Margretha, 138
  Conrad, 137,
    138(2)
  Henrich, 138
  Hermann, 137
  Johann Michael,
    137
Schwab,
  Elisabeth, 95
Schwartz,
  Johannes, 93
Schwartzhaupt,
  Anna Margaret,
    53
  Anna Margaretta,
    53
  John, 53
Sean,
  Peter, 117
Seefried,
  Joseph, Jr., 116
Seely,
  Jonas, 54
Seisinger,
  Anna Maria, 41
  Nicolas, 41
Seitzinger,
  Alexander, 41
  Margaretha, 41
  Maria Magdalena,
    41
  Michael, 41
  Nicholas, 41(2)
Sell,
  Maria, 27
Seman,
  Elizabeth, 77
Seysinger,
  Nicholas, 125
Shad,

Peter, 122
Shade, 122
Shaffer,
  Jacob, 42
  Margaret, 42
Shearer,
  Christopher, 25
Sheetz,
  Conrad, 138
Sheyed,
  Anthon, 119
Shnebely,
  Henry, 82
Shodt,
  Conrad, 120
Shoemaker,
  Benjamin, 60, 61
Shofart,
  Nichlas, 123
Shoot,
  Conrad, 120
Shott,
  Anna Catrina,
    120
  Anna Clara, 120
  Conhenas, 120
  Conrad, 120, 121
  Johannes, 120
Shrove,
  Adam, 73
Shuckert,
  Anna Elisabeth,
    152
  Henry, 65
  Maria Christina,
    65, 152
Shuford,
  Daniel, 124
  David, 124
  Georg, 123
  George, 124
  John, 124
  Rodey, 124
Shultz,
  George, 82
Shumacher,
  Hannes, 78
Shymer,
  Anna Maria, 101
  John, 101
Siegendahler,
  Mary, 25
  Peter, 25
Siegenthal,
  Peter, 24
  Rosina, 24
Sinn,
  Anna Elisabeth,
    61
  Dietrich, 61

Smith,
  Jacob, 55
  John, 92
  Mathis, 55
  Samuel, 44
Sneyder,
  Johan Joest, 137
Soelle,
  Brother, 96, 97
Sohl,
  Anna Maria, 28
  Dietrich, 28
  Johannes, 29
  Rosina, 29
Spatz,
  William, 93
Spayd,
  John, 112
Spindler,
  Christoffel, 60
  Gerdraut, 60
  Johan Henrich,
    125, 146
  Michael, 11, 60,
    117, 125, 146
Sprenger,
  Anna Maria, 150
Stam,
  Adam, 126
  Anna Margretha,
    40
  Barbara, 125
  David, 124, 125
  Elisabeth, 124,
    125, 126
  Hans Adam, 125
  Johan Adam, 125
  Johan Jost, 126
  Verner, 41
  Werner, 125, 126
Stamm,
  Adam, 33
  Anna Barbara,
    40(2), 124(2),
    125
  Anna Cath., 125
  Anna Margretha,
    40, 79, 80, 83,
    124
  Anna Maria, 124,
    126
  Catharina, 126
  Catharine, 126
  Christina, 125
  David, 40,
    124(2), 125(2)
  Elisabeth, 33,
    124, 125
  Fred, 126
  Frederick, 126

Stamm (continued)
    Gertraut, 126
    Hans, 124, 125
    Hans Jörg, 80
    Joh., 125
    Joh. Adam, 40,
        66, 124, 125
    Joh. Jost, 33
    Johan Henrich,
        125
    Johann Adam,
        124, 125
    Johann Jost, 126
    Johannes, 126
    John, 33
    John Yost, 33
    Margaretha, 126
    Maria Catharina,
        28
    Nicholas, 125,
        126
    Nickolas, 126
    Philip, 125
    Rachael, 40
    Rachel, 124, 125
    Werner, 125, 126
    Winer, 125
    Wörner, 124, 125
    Yost, 125
Starr,
    John, 4
Staudt,
    John George, 104
Staut,
    Johannes, 104
    John, 103
Steger,
    Johannes, 30
Stehely,
    Jacob, 19
Stein,
    Friedrich, 92
    Johann Peter, 5
Steuel,
    Johan Friedrich,
        133
    Johan Peter, 133
Stichel,
    Johann Gorg, 55
Stoer,
    Barbara, 58
Stoever,
    Rev., 118
    Rev. Johann
        Caspar, 122
    Rev. John
        Caspar, 2
Stoffel,
    Johannes Justus,
        73

Stöhr,
    Barbara, 58
    Henrich, 150,
        151
Stör,
    Henrich, 58
Stouch,
    Anna Elisabeth,
        24
Stout,
    John, 50
Stöver,
    Caspar, 149, 151
Straub,
    Elisabetha, 122,
        142
    J. Henrich, 142
    J.Henrich, 122
    Johan, 122, 142
Strauss,
    Anna
        Eliesabetha, 144
    Joh. Philipp,
        144
Ströder,
    Anna Margretha,
        102
    Joh. Christoph,
        102
    Joh. Henrich,
        102
Stromb,
    Georg, 131
Strud,
    Stoffel, 123
Sulzbach,
    Joh. Philip, 13
Summey,
    Jacob, 124
Swank,
    Scott T., 144
Swartz,
    Frederick, 54
    George, 4

            -T-

Tag,
    Anna Margretha,
        61
    Joh. Georg, 61
Tannenberg,
    David, 9
    Rosina, 9
Tenig,
    Barbara, 12
    Henry, 12
Theel,
    Christen, 38

    Magdalena, 38
Thompson,
    Grace, 37
Tippel,
    Maria Magdalena,
        14
    Peter, 14
Traill,
    Robert, 101
Traut,
    John, 106
Trechsler,
    Johannes, 91
    Melchior, 91
Trechssler,
    A daughter, 16
    a daughter, 15
    Elisabeth, 15,
        16
    Henrich, 15, 16
    Johannes, 15, 16
    Melchior, 15, 16
    Susanna
        Elisabetha, 15,
        16
Treser,
    Peter, 25
Tresler,
    Peter, 17, 70,
        72, 75, 76
Tresser,
    Peter, 70, 72,
        75
Tressler,
    Melchior, 43, 47
    Peter, 17, 25,
        115
Treud,
    Johann Conrad,
        5, 6
    Philips, 5, 6
Troid,
    Catharina, 116
    Joh. Peter, 118
    Tönges, 116
Troutman,
    Christina, 19
    George, 19
Troÿd,
    David, 116
    Ludwig, 116

            -U-

Umberger,
    Johann, 30
Uthley,
    Brother, 95, 96,
        97

-V-

Van Aken,
  Henry, 60
van Ried,
  John, 38
vanReed,
  Henry, 112
von Eysenberg,
  Herr, 64
  Herrn, 8, 10
von Horn,
  Herr Hauptmann,
    8, 10
von
  Isenburg-Buedin
  gen,
  Ernst Casimir,
    61
von Neida,
  John, 19
Votring,
  Elisabeth, 44
  Johannes, 44

-W-

Wacker,
  Anna Elisabetha,
    36
  Anna Maria, 2,
    146
  Anton, 36, 62
  Bartel, 2, 13
  Catharina, 28
  Elisabeth, 62
  Joh. Henrich, 30
  Johann Peter, 13
  Johannes, 146
  Niclaus, 18, 64,
    102
Wagenhörst,
  Daniel, 24
Wagner,
  Adam, 78
  Anton, 58, 149,
    150
  Antony, 58
  Christopher, 51
  Elisabeth, 58
  Philips, 1
Wagoner,
  Mathias, 55
Weber,
  Anna Catharina,
    98
  Anna Susanna
    Elisabetha, 61
  Friederich, 61
  Jost Henrich,

    43, 47, 98
Wegenschmit,
  John, 36
Wehage,
  Henrich, 81
Wehrheim,
  Filip, 41
Weidner,
  Catharina, 143
  Trivena, 143
Weimer,
  Magdalena, 38
  Nicolaus, 38
Weiser,
  Conrad, 36, 44,
    85
  Samuel, 110, 152
Weiss,
  Anna, 33
  Elisabetha
    Catharina, 34
  John George, 19
  Martin, 2, 33
Weitzel,
  Frederick, 46
  Wirner, 75
Weizel,
  Werner, 110
Werner,
  Henry, 113
  Magdalena, 113
  Margaret, 113
  William, 113
Werth,
  Conrad, 112
Wetzel,
  Hans, 1, 116
  Kunigunda, 116
  Magdalena
    Elisabeth, 1
Weys,
  Elisabetha
    Catharina, 33
  Martin, 33
Wilkins,
  Samuel, 123
Winck,
  Anna Clara
    Elisabetha, 28
  Elisabetha, 27
  Georg, 28
  Joh. Conrad, 28
  Johan Georg, 27
  Johann Georg, 28
  Johannes, 16,
    27, 28
  Judith, 16
  Maria Judith, 28
Windecker,
  Hartmann, 131

Winterstein,
  Bastian, 28
  Sebastian, 28
Wirheim,
  Conrad, 41
Wistar,
  Casper, 121
Witman,
  John, 112
Wohl,
  Caspar, 147
Wolf,
  Johann Heinrich,
    146
  Juliana Maria,
    146
Wolff,
  Anna Margretha,
    5, 6, 66
  Anna Maria, 108,
    146
  Engel, 5, 120,
    146
  Hans, 5, 6, 120,
    146
  Isaac, 146
  Johan Henrich,
    146
  Johann Henrich,
    146
  Johanna
    Catharina, 120
  Johannes, 7, 108
  Jost Caspar, 5,
    66
Wood,
  William, 19
Wörner,
  Elisabeth, 15,
    16
  Johann, 15, 16,
    148
Wunder,
  George, 110

-Z-

Zacharias,
  Catharine, 89
  Daniel, 63, 89
  Elizabeth, 89
  George, 89
  Peter, 89
Zegenfuse,
  Andrew, 117
  Magdalena, 117
Zerbe,
  Johannes, 58
Zieg,
  Clos, 134

Zieg (continued)
  Elisab., 134
Ziegen,
  Barbara, 130
  Niklas, 130
Ziegler,
  Anna Catharina,
    90
  J. Fred., 90
Zimmerman,
  Catharina, 30
Zimmermann,
  Anna, 131
  Anna Margretha,
    138
  Emmanuel, 44
  Hans Jörg, 131
  Jacob, 138
Zimmermannin, 138
Zöller,
  Peter, 74
Zuber,
  Elisabetha, 132
  Henrich, 132
Zwealler,
  Martin X, 36